A PRACTICAL GUIDE TO SNMPV3 AND NETWORK MANAGEMENT

David Zeltserman

ISBN 0-13-021453-1

9 780130 214539

90000

Prentice Hall Series in
Computer Networking and Distributed Systems
Radia Perlman, editor

Kaufman, Perlman & Speciner	*Network Security: Private Communication in a Public World*
Dayem	*PCS and Digital CellularTechnologies: Accessing Your Options*
Dayem	*Mobile Data and Wireless LAN Technologies*
Kadambi, Kalkunte & Crayford	*Gigabit Ethernet: Migrating to High Bandwidth LANS*
Kercheval	*TC/IP Over ATM: A No-Nonsense Internetworking Guide*
Kercheval	*DHCP: A Guide to Dynamic TCP12P Network Configuration*
Solomon	*Mobile IP: The Internet Unplugged*
Zeltserman & Puoplo	*Building Network Management Tools with Tcl/Tk*
Zeltserman	*A Practical Guide to SNMPv3 and Network Management*

A PRACTICAL GUIDE TO SNMPv3 AND NETWORK MANAGMENT

David Zeltserman

Prentice Hall PTR
Upper Saddle River, NJ 07458
www.phptr.com

Library of Congress Cataloging-in-Publication Data

Zeltserman, Dave.
　　A practical guide to SNMPv3 and network management / David Zeltserman.
　　　　p.　cm. -- (Prentice Hall series on computer networking and
distributed systems)
　　Includes bibliographical references and index.
　　ISBN 0-13-021453-1
　　1. Simple Network Management Protocol (Computer network protocol)
2. Computer networks--Management. I. Title. II. Series.
I. Title. II. Series.
TK5105.583.Z45　1999
004.6'2--dc21　　　　　　　　　　　　　　　　　　99-24579
　　　　　　　　　　　　　　　　　　　　　　　　　　　　CIP

Editorial/production supervision: *Nicholas Radhuber*
Manufacturing manager: *Alexis Heydt*
Acquisitions editor: *Mary Franz*
Marketing manager: *Dan Rush*
Cover design: *Talar Agasyon*
Cover design director: *Jerry Votta*

Prentice Hall books are widely used by corporations and government agencies for training, marketing, and resale.　The publisher offers discounts on this book when ordered in bulk quantities. For more information, contact:
　　　　Phone: 800-382-3419, Fax: 201-236-7141
　　　　E-mail: corpsales@prenhall.com
　　　　or write:
　　　　Corporate Sales Department
　　　　Prentice Hall PTR
　　　　1 Lake Street
　　　　Upper Saddle River, NJ 07458

Printed in the United States of America
10 9 8 7 6 5 4 3 2 1

ISBN 0-13-021453-1

Prentice-Hall International (UK) Limited, *London*
Prentice-Hall of Australia Pty. Limited, *Sydney*
Prentice-Hall Canada Inc., *Toronto*
Prentice-Hall Hispanoamericana, S.A., *Mexico*
Prentice-Hall of India Private Limited, *New Delhi*
Prentice-Hall of Japan, Inc., *Tokyo*
Prentice-Hall (Singapore) Pte. Ltd., *Singapore*
Editora Prentice-Hall do Brasil, Ltda., *Rio de Janeiro*

Contents

Preface

Wile I was working on this book, I would tell people the title, *A Practical Guide to SNMPv3 and Network Management*, and the most common response I would get would be, "Isn't that an oxymoron?" It's a good line but it's not really true. SNMPv3 is conceptually simple. While its use within a network will add complexity, it addresses a major weakness of SNMP which is the lack of strong security. You can't add sophisticated features like authentication, encryption, and access control without adding some complexity to how these features are configured. Still, I have talked with several engineers I know who develop network management software, and they have dismissed SNMPv3 without even attempting to understand it. I feel this is a mistake. I have this image in my mind of SNMPv3 as a series of dark clouds that are rolling in over the horizon. Like it or not the storm is coming and you'd better be prepared for it.

One of the goals for this book is to prepare you for SNMPv3. This means making it understandable at both a conceptual and practical level. For me, understanding it at a practical level means understanding how to work with it. This book will show how to configure SNMPv3 for generating notifications, proxy forwarding, authentication, security, and access control. It is not a goal for this book is to describe the logical subsystems that make up an SNMPv3 architecture, or any of the abstract service interfaces that are used between these subsystems. While this information might be useful to people implementing SNMPv3 engines, this book is intended for network managers who need to use SNMPv3 and for software developers who need to build network management applications using SNMPv3. Besides, the INTERNET-DRAFT documents do a fine job of defining these various subsystems and their abstract service interfaces, probably a better job than I could do.

Another goal for this book is to make RMON2 understandable. RMON2 is one of the more important advancements that have been made to the network management space. One of the keys to managing a network is understanding it. RMON2 lets you understand both the network-layer and application-layer traffic going across your network. You can further understand the network-layer and application-layer conversations occurring on your network. By understanding the protocol usage and conversations occurring on a network (and by tracking this over time) a network manager can better plan for network growth and optimize client-server communications.

Over the past year I have talked with several customers who have expressed confusion over how to configure and use RMON2. While the RMON2 MIB is rather imposing, it is fairly consistent in its configuration and in how its data tables are accessed. The RMON2 chapter in this book shows how to configure RMON2 and how to access its data tables. It also suggests several RMON2 applications that can be built.

The major goal for this book, however, is to provide practical insights into building SNMP-based applications. I have spent the past sixteen years building both network devices and network management products. As such my focus is more on the practical nature of getting things built then on the theoretical or academic nature. This book is really for network managers and developers who need to focus on getting things built.

NOTATION

Pseudocode is used throughout the book to describe the logic in configuring and accessing SNMPv3 and RMON2 MIB tables. The format of the psuedocode is a loose combination of C and Tcl, with a little Java thrown in where it makes sense. All pseudocode is shown in a courier font.

The pseudo code is meant to be descriptive and obvious. The command line, x <- 100, assigns x the value 100. A foreach command loops through a collection. For example, the psuedocode

```
foreach x in Col
{
    ProcessObject(x)
}
```

will call the procedure ProcessObject for each object in the collection Col.

The following pseudocode will perform an SNMP Get operation, collecting sysDescr.0 and sysUpTime.0, and will assign the response pdu to the variable responsePDU.

```
pdu <- {sysDescr.0, sysUpTime.0}
responsePDU <- SnmpGet(pdu)
```

The following pseudocode will perform an SNMP Set operation, setting the operational status of interfaces 2 and 3 to down.

```
pdu <- { ifAdminStatus.2 <- 'down',
         ifAdminStatus.3 <- 'down' }
responsePDU <- SnmpSet(pdu)
```

There are several places in the book where I show how an SNMP entity determines something, such as what target addresses to send notifications to. In these examples I use a foreach statement to cycle through all the rows in a MIB table. I also access the MIB objects directly. The following pseudocode will cycle through each row in the ifTable, printing the ifSpeed value:

```
foreach inst in ifTable
{
    print ifSpeed.inst
}
```

BOOK ORGANIZATION

The chapters of this book are divided into three parts. In the first part we describe SNMPv1 and SNMPv2. Chapter 2, SNMP Basics, shows the basic data types that are used to represent management information and then shows textual conventions that are used to represent abstract data types. The chapter then proceeds to show the rules for naming and defining managed objects. It then describes the operations that were defined for SNMPv1, and extensions that were defined for SNMPv2. Chapter 3 focuses on the management information represented by MIB-II, specifically how this management information can be utilized by a network manager.

Part II focuses on SNMPv3. Chapter 4 describes the framework defined for SNMPv3. It also shows new textual conventions that have been defined for SNMPv3, along with a new SNMPv3 message format. Chapter 5 spends a little time discussing the SNMPv3 applications that can run within an SNMP entity. The focus in the chapter, however, is on configuring notifications and proxy forwarding using MIBs that have been defined for SNMPv3. Chapter 6 discusses the security features that are provided by SNMPv3. Again, the focus on this chapter is both understanding how the security features work and how they are configured using new SNMPv3 MIBs. Chapter 7 shows how the view-based access control model works, and how it can be configured using new SNMPv3 MIBs. Chapter 8 examines coexistence issues between the different SNMP versions.

Part III takes a look at several practical network management issues. Chapter 9 describes RMON2, and shows how RMON2 can be utilized to understand the network-layer and application-layer traffic running on a network. Chapter 10 examines several Cisco Private MIBs, and shows how they can be used to do useful stuff.

BOOK THANKS

I would first like to thank my wife, Judy, for her patience, support, and understanding. This is the third book she has had to go through in a year, and she deserves a medal for it.

I would like to thank all my reviewers, but especially David Levi and Juergen Schoenwarlder. David is one of the co-authors of the SNMP Applications document and has had his hands in most of the other SNMPv3 documents. Juergen is also very well known and highly respected in the SNMP community. Their help in getting this book accurate was invaluable. I would also like to thank a couple of industry friends of mine who acted as informal reviewers, Andy Levin and Marat Vaysman.

Thanks to the editors and staff at Prentice Hall, especially to Mary Franz.

CHAPTER 1

Introduction

$\mathbf{I}$s it simple? That's probably the most important question people have about SNMPv3. Well, the answer is yes and no. Conceptually SNMPv3 is simple; implementing it and using it in a large network may not be so simple. This chapter will provide an introduction to version 3 of the Simple Network Management Protocol and touch on some of the complexities in using it. Following chapters will describe both SNMP and SNMPv3 in detail. After that, you can decide for yourself whether it's still a simple network management protocol.

So what is SNMPv3? Here's the part that's simple. Conceptually SNMPv3 is nothing more than a framework for extending SNMP. The two major extensions it addresses are for security and administration. The framework also allows for the continued evolution of SNMP.

If you are developing network management applications, the fact that you are using SNMPv3 should for the most part be transparent to you. SNMPv3 uses the same protocol operations that were defined for SNMPv1 and SNMPv2, namely Get, GetNext, GetBulk, Set, Inform and SNMPv2 Traps. While it uses Reports (which were defined for SNMPv2 but never used), Reports provide engine to engine communication and will be transparent to any network management applications that you build. You will continue to be able to access the same management information or MIBs that you were able to access before. The message format that is used by SNMPv3 will be different, but this is the type of detail which should be hidden in an SNMP library routine. A network management application written using SNMPv2c should port almost directly to SNMPv3. And since the SNMPv3 framework provides support for SNMPv1 and SNMPv2c, current applications should be able to continue to access management information from SNMPv3 supported devices.

SNMPv3 defines new MIBs for configuring security, notifications, proxy forwarding, and view-based access control. This is a double-edged sword. For the first time we have a standard

1

way for a network administrator to remotely configure these features. On the other hand, configuring security and view-based access control adds complexity. As I will show in later chapters this could add quite a bit of complexity to configuring a medium to large network. Without good bulk configuration and configuration consistency checking tools, trying to utilize these MIBs could easily create more network management problems than they address. For someone like me who makes a living building network management applications this is great news!

SNMPv3 defines new terminology. A quick overview of this terminology is as follows:

- What used to be called SNMP Agents and SNMP Managers are now called SNMP entities.

- Each SNMP entity contains one SNMP engine. Putting it in the simplest terms, an SNMP engine performs the processing of SNMP messages, along with security and access control.

- For SNMPv3, when we refer to applications, we are referring to applications within an SNMP entity as opposed to what you might normally think of, such as a network management application to do trending or configuration. Currently there are five types of applications defined:

  1. command generators — generate SNMP commands to collect or set management data.

  2. command responders — provide access to management data.

  3. notification originators — initiate Trap or Inform messages.

  4. notification receivers — receive and process Trap or Inform messages.

  5. proxy forwarders — forward messages between SNMP entities.

From this list, you can see that command generators and notification receivers are what we used to think of as part of an SNMP Manager, while command responders and notification originators are what we used to think of as part of an SNMP Agent.

Probably the most important feature of SNMPv3 is security. With SNMPv1 data is protected by nothing more than a password. Over the years people have coped with this in several ways, including the use of firewalls and vendors implementing proprietary access control methods. Some vendors simply don't allow their devices to be configured through SNMP. However, as more sensitive information is being made accessible through SNMP, such as billing information, the need for security has become more critical.

SNMPv3 addresses this by offering both strong authentication and data encryption for privacy. Currently, SNMPv3 defines the use of HMAC-MD5-96 and HMAC-SHA-96 as the authentication protocols and CBC-DES as the privacy protocol. The SNMPv3 framework allows for other authentication and privacy protocols to be used. Both the MD5 and SHA authentication protocols require private keys. A network manager must initially configure at least one private key value through some method other than SNMP. The size of a private key for MD5 is 16 octets; the size of a private key for SHA is 20 octets. This makes it clear that stronger authentication is provided by the SHA protocol and it should be used if possible over the MD5 protocol. Once private keys have been initially configured, they can be modified remotely using SNMP.

So what does authentication buy you? Really two things:

1. That only authenticated parties can communicate to each other. This ensures that a management station can collect data from a device or configure a device only if the device allows that management station to be able to do so.

2. That messages are received in a timely fashion. This prevents messages from somehow being saved and replayed later in order to cause malicious damage. For example, if an SNMP Set message is saved and replayed later, you could conceivably change the desired configuration of a device. As far as the SNMP entity that is responding to the message is concerned, the message would have been properly authenticated.

As already mentioned the CBC-DES is used by SNMPv3 for privacy, but other encryption protocols can be used in the future. DES requires a private key to be initially configured through some means other than SNMP. This key can later be modified remotely through SNMP. Privacy can only be used if authentication is also used, so your security choices are no authentication and no privacy, authentication only, authentication and privacy.

To wrap up this introduction to SNMPv3, we will briefly mention that there are two parts to SNMPv3 adminstration. One is configuring SNMPv3 Applications, specifically notification originators and proxy forwarders. What this means in plain English is

    a. setting up to whom to send trap or inform messages to
    b. setting up proxy forwarding

The second part is defining MIB views that can be accessed by different users. Using this you can control which MIB variables different users can have access to. Notifications, proxy forwarding, and MIB access control can all be configured remotely through a set of fairly complex MIB tables that we will be looking at later on.

Well, there you have it — an introduction to SNMPv3 in roughly three pages. Conceptually, it seems simple. But as we'll be seeing, the devil is in the details.

CHAPTER 2

SNMP Basics

T he Simple Network Management Protocol (SNMP) allows both for management data to be collected remotely from devices and for devices to be configured remotely. It has been around since 1990 and since that time its use has exploded. It is now supported by most network devices and is also being used to help manage high-end printers, large applications (like Oracle), and workstations. With Sun's Java Dynamic Management Kit, SNMP management support can be built into virtually any Java application.

The reason for SNMP's popularity and massive growth is its simplicity. In fact it only has four operations — two to retrieve data, one to set data, and for a device to send an asynchronous notification. The complexity is really in the management data that SNMP accesses. Network devices, for example, can maintain a huge amount of management data. Among other things, this data can help provide insight as to how the network interfaces are performing, what type of network protocol usage is being seen on a segment, and networkwide problems being seen. This data can also be used to understand how a device is configured, and of course, to change the configuration of the device. Not all the data maintained by a device is useful (we'll get more into this later!). Part of what makes building useful network management applications difficult is understanding which management data to look at and how to analyze it.

There are really three parts to understanding SNMP:

1. The SNMP protocol. This includes understanding the SNMP operations, the format of the SNMP messages, and how messages are exchanged between an application and a device.
2. Structure of Management Information (SMI). This is the set of rules for specifying the management information that a device maintains. To be more precise, the management information is actually a collection of managed objects, and these rules are used to both name and define these managed objects.

3. Management Information Base (MIB). This is a structured collection of all the managed objects maintained by a device. The managed objects are structured in the form of a hierarchal tree.

This chapter will first show an example of how SNMP can be used. It will then show the basic data types that are used to specify management information and then show abstract types (which have been defined as textual conventions) that make the use of the management information both more obvious and standardized. After that we will show how managed objects are defined with SMI rules, and how these managed objects are represented in a hierarchal tree and how they can be accessed. We will then show the SNMP protocol operations and how they can be used to access managed objects.

Around 1994 standards for something called SNMP version 2 were started to address several weaknesses within SNMP, specifically security weaknesses. For various reasons SNMPv2 didn't succeed (which is why we now have SNMPv3!) but what survived out of this is something called SNMPv2c. SNMPv2c doesn't address any of the security issues that SNMPv2 addressed, and in fact uses the same password scheme that SNMP uses. It does, though, extend SNMP in a few ways, including adding a couple of new operations, new data types, new abstract data types (textual conventions), and a modified SMI (SMIv2).

Since SNMPv2c really adds only a few extensions to SNMP, instead of discussing these extensions in a separate chapter, the extensions will be shown in this chapter within the appropriate sections. Hopefully, this will make things clearer.

2.1 How It All Works

Before we start digging into the specifics of SNMP, lets take a look at a practical example of how SNMP can be used. Let's say we want to write a trending application that periodically monitors a group of Ethernet switches to calculate how heavily utilized (or underutilized) each individual Ethernet segment is. There are a wide variety of SNMP packages that can be used on Windows and UNIX platforms for a variety of languages (C++, Java, Tcl, Perl). These packages allow you to deal with SNMP at a high level, hiding most of the details of the protocol operations, and letting you for the most part only be concerned with what management information to collect or modify. Of course, some packages are better at hiding the details of SNMP than others.

Each Ethernet switch that we want to monitor must have something called an SNMP agent running (for SNMPv3, this will be called an SNMP entity). An SNMP agent is a software process (or a number of processes) that will listen on UDP port 161 for SNMP messages. Each SNMP message sent to the agent will contain a list of management objects to either retrieve or modify. It will also contain a password (called a community name). If the community name doesn't match what the SNMP agent is expecting, the message will be discarded and a notification may be sent out to a network management station to indicate that someone tried to falsely access this agent. If the community name is known by the agent, the agent will attempt to process the request.

Getting back to our trending application, if an Ethernet switch supports MIB-II (which all SNMP-enabled devices should!), then that device will maintain management information about each of its interfaces. This information will include things like the type of interface (Ethernet, FDDI, ATM, etc.), the transmission rate, a running count of how many octets have been received on the interface, a running count of how many octets have been sent from the interface, whether the interface is operational, and how long it has been in its current state. This particular set of information will be stored in a table where each row of the table is indexed by the interface number. Our trending application can access this table for specific interfaces or can walk the table and collect information about all interfaces.

Ethernet utilization will be calculated by figuring out how many bits have been received and transmitted over an interface during a specific time interval. Dividing that by the time interval gives us a rate of how busy the interface is. Dividing that by the linespeed of the interface and multiplying this result by 100 gives us a percentage of how utilized the interface is.

So what our simple trending application is going to do is periodically ask a device for its interface information. It does this by sending out an SNMP Request within a UDP packet to the IP address of an Ethernet switch. The UDP packet is sent to port 161. The SNMP Request will contain a list of managed objects that we want to retrieve values for. These managed objects will represent the operational status of an interface, its count of received octets, its count of transmitted octets, its linespeed, when the interface last changed state, and how long the SNMP agent has been running.

Since UDP is unreliable, the SNMP Request that was sent may or may not make it to the Ethernet switch (and similarly, its response may or may not make it to the workstation that is running this trending application). To handle this unreliability and to give the application a reasonable chance of getting a response to its request, an SNMP timeout and retry count will be defined. Typically timeout values of between 2 and 5 seconds and 2 retries are sufficient. If the trending application sends a request and doesn't get back a response, it could be for several reasons: the UDP packets are getting lost, the device that the request is being sent to is either unreachable or down or too busy to process SNMP requests, or the community name being used in the request is wrong.

If a response is received, it could either indicate an error or contain the values of the managed objects that had been requested. Assuming the requested objects were collected, the trending application would require two collections before it could calculate utilization. This is because the count of received octets and transmitted octets are meaningless by themselves. Once a second sample has been collected, then the difference between the two received octet counts and the transmitted octet counts can be used to calculate how fast bits are being received and sent over the interface. Of course, the interface could have reset between the two collections, or the device could have rebooted. By collecting information about how long the SNMP agent has been running and how long the interface has been in its current state,we can determine if either of those conditions had occurred. Finally, based on the Ethernet switch the Ethernet interface could be configured for the more standard half-duplex Ethernet or full-duplex mode. In order to correctly calculate utilization we would have to know which mode the interface has been configured for.

So now that we have given a bigger picture of how SNMP can work, let's get down to the details.

2.2 Data Types

Four primitive data types are defined for SNMP for representing management information. Several more abstract types have been built on these primitives. Both these primitve and abstract data types make up the core SMI (Structure of Management Information) data types. The four primitive data types are:

- INTEGER: this is a 32-bit value in two's complement representation. The range of values are between -2147483648 and 2147483647. INTEGERs are typically used to represent an enumeration. For example, the managed object representing the operational status of an interface is defined as an INTEGER, with value 1 representing an operational state of up, 2 representing an operational state of down, and 3 representing an operational state of testing.

- OCTET STRING: this is zero or more octets. Each octet in the string has a value between 0 and 255. This is typically used to represent a text string. For example, the managed object representing the system description of a device is defined as an OCTET STRING.

- OBJECT IDENTIFIER: this is a sequence of integers which traverses a hierarchal MIB tree. Every managed object is defined by an OBJECT IDENTIFIER. We will be looking at this in more detail later.

- NULL

Several more abstract types have been defined on top of these primitive types. These are called application-wide types. SNMPv1 defined the following application-wide types:

- NetworkAddress: this abstract type represents a choice from one of possibly several protocol families. Only one protocol family, the Internet family, was ever presented in this choice. This type isn't being used anymore in SMIv2.

- IpAddress: this represents an IP address. It is defined as a 4-byte OCTET STRING.

- Counter: this is a 32-bit non-negative integer. Its value ranges between 0 and 4294967295 (2^{32} - 1). When it reaches its maximum value, it will wrap around and start increasing again from 0. Counters are typically used to represents things like the number of errors seen, or the number of bytes transmitted on an interface, etc. A counter value is meaningless unless you have a point of reference. An application that monitors counter values will need to collect at least two samples at different points in time in order to do something useful with it. *Note*: When an SNMP agent resets, the counter values are unknown. Some devices will initialize all counter values to zero, some won't. This is why special care needs to be taken to determine whether an SNMP agent has reset (typically caused by a device rebooting) between collections.

- Gauge: this is a 32-bit non-negative integer. Its value ranges between 0 and 4294967295 (2^{32} - 1). The value of a gauge may increase or decrease but cannot increase past a maximum value or decrease below a minimum value. A gauge is typically used to represent something that is being measured, like a packet rate or the number of errors detected within a certain time interval.

- TimeTicks: this counts the time in hundredths of a second since some epoch. It is represented by a 32-bit non-negative integer and its value can range between 0 and 4294967295 (2^{32} - 1). For example, the managed object representing the amount of time that an SNMP agent has been up and running is defined as an application type TimeTicks. *Note*: A Time-Ticks value will wrap its value back to 0 every 42949672.95 seconds, which is roughly every 497 days. That means if a network device has been up and running for 497 days without its SNMP agent resetting, and you try to collect the managed object representing how long that agent has been up and running, you may get back a value indicating that the SNMP agent has been reset recently.

- Opaque: an opaque type allows arbitrary data to be encoded as an OCTET STRING. In reality, the opaque type is rarely (if ever) used.

SNMPv2 further defines some additional types:

- Integer32: this is the same as an INTEGER.
- Counter32: this is the same as a Counter.
- Gauge32: this is the same as a Gauge.
- Unsigned32: this is indistinguishable from Gauge32.

• Counter64: this is a 64-bit counter, with values ranging from 0 to 18446744073709551615. Counter64 was defined so it could be used in place of a Counter32 if a Counter32 could wrap in less than one hour.

From this you can see that SNMPv2 formalized the naming of these types and introduced one new type — a 64-bit counter. As interface data rates have gotten faster the amount of time it takes for certain counters to wrap, such as the counters representing the number of octets received and transmitted on an interface, has gotten shorter. The following table demonstrates this.

Table 2-1   Possible Counter Wraparound Times

Interface Speed	32-bit Counter Wraparound Times
10 MBits	57.26 minutes
100 MBits	5.73 minutes
155 MBits	3.69 minutes
1 Gigabit	0.57 minutes

Again, two collections of a counter value are needed to do anything meaningful. With 32-bit counters, if we're trying to calculate Ethernet utilization for a gigabit interface, we would have to poll that interface faster than 0.57 minutes in order to trust its values. If we poll slower than 0.57 minutes, the value could have wrapped. For example, the first poll could give us a counter value of 100, the second poll could give us a counter value of 200. We wouldn't know if the difference between the two polls was 100 or 4294967395. And of course this situation gets worse if a 10 gigabit interface exists — which might happen by the time this book comes out!

There are ways to get around this problem without 64-bit counters. One way is to define two counters for management information that wraps quickly. The first counter represents the high-order 32 bits, the second counter represents the low-order 32 bits. Every time the low-order 32-bit counter wraps, the high-order 32-bit counter is incremented. This is for the most part identical to a 64-bit counter, the only difference being you need to specify and collect two managed objects instead of one.

Another way to get around this is if managed objects exist to represent things like the utilization of an interface over the past 5 minutes, or the bit rate of an interface over the past 15 minutes. Then, instead of dealing with counters, you can simply collect the managed objects representing these things. Quite a few vendors have built non-standard managed objects like this into their devices.

2.3 Structure of Management Information (SMI)

2.3.1 SMI

The Structure of Management Information (SMI) specifies a set of rules for naming and defining managed objects. Let's first look at how a managed object is named.

All managed objects are arranged in a hierarchical tree structure. An object's location in this tree structure very neatly identifies how to access this object. Let's look at the top of the MIB tree defined by RFC 1155 (SMI):

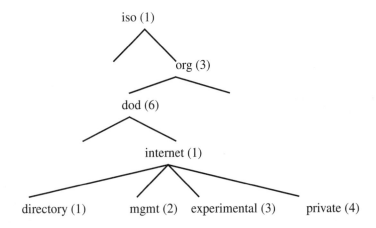

From this tree, the dod object can be identified by

{iso org (3) dod (6)}

which can be expressed in shorthand as: 1.3.6

Similarly the mgmt object can be identified as

{iso org (3) dod (6) internet (1) mgmt (2)}, or as: 1.3.6.1.2

This identification is called an OBJECT IDENTIFIER and is used to authoritatively name an object. It further identifies how to access the object within the MIB.

As shown from this picture four subtrees have been defined under the internet node:

- directory: is reserved for future use with the OSI directory.
- mgmt: is used to identify objects which are defined in IAB-approved documents. For example, the MIB-II subtree is defined under this subtree.
- experimental: is used to identify objects used in Internet experiments.
- private: is used to identify objects defined unilaterally. One child, enterprises (1), has so far been defined under private. Vendors can build subtrees under enterprises by using their assigned enterprise numbers. For example, Cisco has been assigned an enterprise number of nine and has defined their own private MIB tree under {iso org (3) dod (6) internet (1) private (4) enterprises (1) Cisco (9)} or 1.3.6.1.4.1.9.

Let's now look at the mgmt subtree:

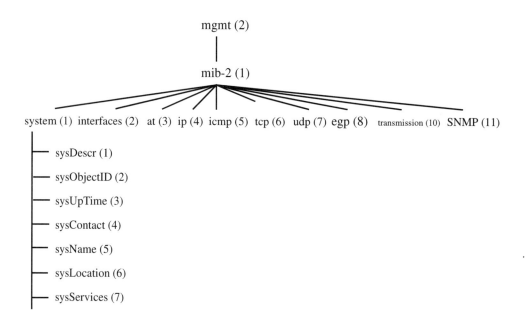

This diagram shows the subtrees or groups under the MIB-II subtree and also shows the managed objects under the system group. We'll be going over MIB-II in detail in the next chapter.

As another example, the sysDescr object is referenced by the OBJECT IDENTIFIER:

{iso org (3) dod (6) internet (1) mgmt (2) mib-2 (1) system (1) sysDescr (1)} or
1.3.6.1.2.1.1.1

Similarly, sysName is referenced by the OBJECT IDENTIFIER 1.3.6.1.2.1.1.4.

When collecting or modifying data within an SNMP operation, you can only reference leaf objects (such as sysDescr) as opposed to subtree objects (such as system).

The definition of a managed object consist of five fields:

1. OBJECT, a textual name, termed the object descriptor, along with its corresponding OBJECT IDENTIFIER.
2. SYNTAX, the abstract syntax for the object type. This must resolve to a primitive data type (INTEGER, OCTET STRING, OBJECT IDENTIFIER, or NULL).
3. Definition, textual description of the object type.
4. Access, how the object may be accessed. Values can be read-only, read-write, write-only, or not-accessible.
5. Status, which defines whether the object needs to be implemented in order to claim that a MIB group is fully supported. Values can be mandatory, optional, or obsolete.
For example, the definition of the sysDescr object is

```
sysDescr OBJECT-TYPE
        SYNTAX  DisplayString (SIZE (0..255))
        ACCESS  read-only
        STATUS  mandatory
        DESCRIPTION
            "A textual description of the entity.  This value
            should include the full name and version
            identification of the system's hardware type,
            software operating-system, and networking
            software.  It is mandatory that this only contain
            printable ASCII characters."
::= { system 1 }
```

An optional default value clause may be specified. If specified, the value will be used when a new object instance is created.

The OBJECT-TYPE macro shown above is defined within RFC 1212.

The managed object, sysDescr, is an example of a scalar object. A scalar object is an object that has only one instance within a MIB (as opposed to a tabular object, which could have one instance for each row in the table). Each device will have only one system description (sys-

Descr). In order to distinguish between an object type and an object instance, a 0 must be appended to a scalar object to form its instance identifier. So in this example sysDescr.0 would be used to access the system description information for a device.

A table is defined as a sequence of rows. Each row in a table is then defined as a sequence of managed objects. Finally, each managed object within this sequence is then defined.

```
ipAddrTable OBJECT-TYPE
    SYNTAX   SEQUENCE OF IpAddrEntry
    ACCESS   not-accessible
    STATUS   mandatory
    DESCRIPTION
        "The table of addressing information relevant to
        this entity's IP addresses."
    ::= { ip 20 }
```

You can see from this definition of ipAddrTable that a table object by itself is not accessible and that it is made up of a sequence of IpAddrEntry objects. Each IpAddrEntry object will be a row in the table. ipAddrEntry is defined as follows:

```
ipAddrEntry OBJECT-TYPE
    SYNTAX   IpAddrEntry
    ACCESS   not-accessible
    STATUS   mandatory
    DESCRIPTION
        "The addressing information for one of this
        entity's IP addresses."
    INDEX    { ipAdEntAddr }
    ::= { ipAddrTable 1 }
```

Again, from this definition you can see that a row by itself is not accessible. If you want to retrieve a row from a table, then each managed object within the row must be collected. This definition also tells you how a row within a table is indexed. In this example, it is indexed by a managed object, ipAdEntAddr. *Note*: An index can be specified as the value of one or more managed objects.

A definition of IpAddrEntry gives us the sequence of managed objects that make up a row in the ipAddrTable:

```
IpAddrEntry ::=
    SEQUENCE {
```

```
        ipAdEntAddr
            IpAddress,
        ipAdEntIfIndex
            INTEGER,
        ipAdEntNetMask
            IpAddress,
        ipAdEntBcastAddr
            INTEGER,
        ipAdEntReasmMaxSize
            INTEGER (0..65535)
    }
```

From this you can see that each row within the ipAddrTable is made up of up to five managed objects. *Note*: Objects within a row can be missing. When collecting objects from a row, an application needs to take into account the case where holes (missing objects) exist.

We can see from these examples that each row within a table is indexed by a specified value. For the example given for ipAddrTable, a row would be accessed by an IP address. To specify which objects within a table to retrieve or modify, you must specify the instances of that object. For example, the OBJECT IDENTIFIER

ipAdEntNetMask.158.101.121.6

would specify the network mask object indexed by the IP address 158.101.121.6 (if that row actually exists within the table).

A quick note about enumerated values: a managed object of type INTEGER can be defined to have a list of enumerated values. This allows a more obvious text value to be thought of instead of the actual numeric value. For example, when defining the possible operational values for an interface, 1 would translate to up, 2 to down, and 3 to testing. This would allow a MIB Browser to show a value of "up" as opposed to a less obvious value of 1.

While it is recommended that enumerated values start at 1, any valid INTEGER value can be used, including 0. Also, their values don't need to be contiguous.

2.3.2   SNMPv2 Extensions to SMI (SMIv2)

RFC 1902 extended SMI for SNMPv2. These extensions/changes include

- additional primitive data types. We have already shown these when we talked about data types that were introduced for SNMPv2.
- MAX-ACCESS clause replacing the ACCESS clause.

- modification of the STATUS clause.
- NOTIFICATION-TYPE for defining SNMPv2-Traps.
- BITS construct.
- AUGMENTS clause. This clause is used to add additional columns to an already existing table. An example of this is the ifXTable (from RFC 2233) augmenting the ifTable.
- UnitsPart clause. This is an optional clause, which contains a textual definition of the units associated with an object. For example, for an object representing a measurement of time, this value might be "milliseconds."

2.3.2.1   MAX-ACCESS clause

Managed objects can be defined with a MAX-ACCESS value of

- not-accessible, an object cannot be retrieved or modified.

- accessible-for-notify, an object is accessible only via a notification.

- read-only, an object can be retrieved.

- read-write, an object can be retrieved or modified, but not created.

- read-create, an object can be retrieved, modified, or created.

2.3.2.2   STATUS clause

The STATUS clause has been modified to have the following values:

- current, an object is valid for the current standard.

- obsolete, an object should not be implemented.

- deprecated, an object is obsolete but should still be implemented to foster interoperability with older implementations.

2.3.2.3 NOTIFICATION-TYPE

SNMPv2 Traps are defined by a NOTIFICATION-TYPE macro. An example of this is the linkDown trap, taken from the Interfaces MIB (RFC 1573):

```
linkDown NOTIFICATION-TYPE
     OBJECTS { ifIndex, ifAdminStatus, ifOperStatus }
     STATUS  current
     DESCRIPTION
        "A linkDown trap signifies that the SNMPv2 entity,
        acting in an agent role, has detected that the
        ifOperStatus object for one of its communication links
        is about to enter the down state from some other state
        (but not from the notPresent state).  This other state
        is indicated by the included value of ifOperStatus."
::= { snmpTraps 3 }
```

In the above example, the OBJECTS clause specifies three additional objects to include in the traps variable bindings. It also defines the OBJECT IDENTIFIER for the linkDown trap as snmpTraps.3.

2.3.2.4 BITS construct

The BITS construct represents an enumeration of named bits. This collection is assigned non-negative, contiguous values, starting at zero. Only the bits enumerated may be present in a value.

While there is no limit on the number of enumerations (and therefore on the length of the value), it is recommended that no more than 128 bits be used. Labels for the bits used must consist of one or more letters or digits and up to a maximum of 64 characters. The first character in a label must be a lower-case letter.

2.4 Textual Conventions

SMIv2 introduces textual conventions which allow managed objects to be defined in a more standardized and abstract way. You can think of textual conventions as refinements of basic types — and if fact textual conventions resolve to primitive data types. In this section we hit the chicken and the egg problem. In order to make several of the textual conventions understandable, I need to show examples of how they're used but we haven't yet gotten to the SNMP operations available. In any case, we'll take that leap for now.

2.4.1   DisplayString

A DisplayString represents NVT ASCII text. It resolves to an OCTET STRING. A Dis-playString can be at most 255 characters long.

Any management information that represents text is typically defined as a DisplayString. Examples of this include the managed objects that represent the device description, the device contact, the device name, and the device location.

The following ASCII characters have special meanings

Table 2-2   DisplayString — ASCII Characters with Special Meanings

Character	Code	Description
NULL (NUL)	0	No operation.
Line feed (LF)	10	Move to the next line keeping the same horizontal position.
Carriage Return (CF)	13	Move to the left margin of the current line. The sequence CR LF means newline. The sequence CR NUL means carriage return.
BELL (BEL)	7	Produces an audible or visible signal.
Back space (BS)	8	Move one character position towards the left margin.
Horizontal Tab (HT)	9	Move to the next horizontal tab stop.
Vertical Tab (VT)	11	Move to the next vertical tab stop.
Form Feed (FF)	12	Move to the top of the next page.

2.4.2   PhysAddress

A PhysAddress represents a media- or physical-level address. It resolves to an OCTET STRING. As we mentioned earlier if a device supports MIB-II, it will maintain information about each of its interfaces. One of the managed objects maintained about an interface is the interface's address at the protocol layer immediately "below" the network layer in the protocol stack. This managed object (ifPhysAddress) is defined as a PhysAddress.

2.4.3   MacAddress

A MacAddress represents an 802 MAC address in "canonical" order (as if it were transmitted least significant bit first). It resolves to a 6-byte OCTET STRING.

2.4.4   TruthValue

A TruthValue represents a boolean value of either true (1) or false (2). It resolves to an INTEGER.

2.4.5   TestAndIncr

TestAndIncr is used to prevent two management stations from trying to modify the same management information at the same time. Let's say you have management information that is represented by a table (call this table x) and you want to prevent two management stations from trying to modify rows in this table at the same time. What you would do is create a managed object of type TestAndIncr (let's name this new managed object xSpinLock). Before trying to modify a row in x you would retrieve the current value of xSpinLock. When you later send an SNMP Request to modify a row in x, you would also specify in that request to set xSpinLock to the value that was earlier retrieved. If you try setting xSpinLock to something other than what it is currently set to, the SNMP Request will fail — which will cause the row not to be modified. If the SNMP Request succeeds, not only will the row in x be modified but xSpinLock will be incremented by one. Note. if xSpinLock is currently set to the maximum INTEGER value (2147483647), incrementing it will cause it to wrap back to zero.

Let's run through a quick example of how this works:

Current value of xSpinLock: 34

Management station 1 retrieves the value of xSpinLock (34)

Management station 2 retrieves the value of xSpinLock (34)

Management station 1 issues a request to modify a row in x and set xSpinLock to 34
Management station 2 issues a request to modify a row in x and set xSpinLock to 34

The remote SNMP Agent receives the request from management station 2. The value of xSpinLock matches the requested new value and the request completes successfully. The row in x is modified and xSpinLock is incremented. The value of xSpinLock is now 35.

The remote SNMP Agent now receives the request from management station 1. The value of xSpinLock (35) no longer matches the requested value (34) and the request fails. Management station 1 will receive an error indication of `inconsistentValue`. Management Station 1 will most likely wait some random amount of time and then try again to modify x.

2.4.6   AutonomousType

An AutonomousType represents some sort of identification value. It resolves to an OBJECT IDENTIFIER. It is usually used to define a MIB subtree or a particular type of hardware or protocol.

2.4.7   VariablePointer

A VariablePointer is used to point to a specific object instance. For example, lets say we have sixteen interfaces on a device. The managed object that references an interface's line speed is called ifSpeed. A VariablePointer that references interface 4's line speed would be ifSpeed.4. This resolves to an OBJECT IDENTIFIER.

2.4.8   RowPointer

A RowPointer represents a pointer to a conceptual row. The value is the name of the instance of the first accessible object in the conceptual row. A RowPointer resolves to an OBJECT IDENTFIER.

An example of this interface information is represented in a table called ifTable. The first accessible managed object in a row of this table is the interface number, which is named ifIndex. ifIndex.6 would point to the sixth row in the ifTable.

2.4.9 RowStatus

RowStatus provides a standard way to add and delete rows from a table. Several of the RowStatus values are used to indicate a row's state, other values are used as commands to create, destroy or make a row active. The following values can be either written or read from a RowStatus object:

- `active` (1)
- `notInService` (2)
- `notReady` (3)
- `createAndGo` (4)
- `createAndWait` (5)
- `destroy` (6)

The values `active`, `notInService`, and `notReady` can be read from a RowStatus object. The values `active`, `notInService`, `createAndGo`, `createAndWait`, and `destroy` can be written to a RowStatus object.

To create a new row in a table is fairly straightforward. The first thing you do is select an instance-identifier for the table that is currently not in use. This instance-identifier will be used to reference a row in the table. There are several ways to pick an unused instance-identifier. One method would be to pick a pseudorandom number. Then you could try to retrieve the RowStatus object indexed by that pseudorandom number. If the object exists, then that instance-identifier is already in use and you need to pick another pseudorandom number and try again. Eventually you'll find an instance-identifier that's not in use. We'll call that value n.

Now that we have found an unused instance-identifier n, we can create a new row in one of two ways:

1. The new row is made up of several managed objects. Certain objects need their values to be set in order to create this new row (some of the managed objects can use default values). If all the necessary managed objects are provided in the set operation, then the RowStatus.n object can be set to `createAndGo`. If this is successful, the RowStatus.n object will transition to the value active and the new row has been created.
2. Set the RowStatus.n object to `createAndWait`. Then set the required objects for that row and set the RowStatus.n object to `active`. If this is successful, the new row has been created; otherwise the RowStatus.n object will have the value `notReady`.

Once a row is active, it may be necessary to make the row inactive before changing any of the values of the managed objects for that row. That is done by setting the RowStatus.n object to `notInService`. A row can be deleted by setting the RowStatus.n object to `destroy`.

Let's demonstrate this by looking at an RMONv2 table, addressMapControlTable. This table is defined in the RMONv2 MIB and allows you to control mapping network layer addresses to physical addresses for specific interfaces.

Table 2-3   addressMapControlTable, Indexed by addressMapControlIndex

Object	Type	Access
addressMapControlIndex	Integer32	non-accessible
addressMapControlDataSource	DataSource	read-create
addressMapControlDroppedFrames	Counter32	read-only
addressMapControlOwner	OwnerString	read-create
addressMapControlStatus	RowStatus	read-create

Each row in the table has five objects. Two new textual conventions have been introduced: OwnerString which resolves to an OCTET STRING, and DataSource which resolves to an OBJECT IDENTIFIER. The object addressMapControlIndex is used to index the table and can not actually be read from the table. A row is added to this table to specify an interface to perform network layer to physical layer address mapping on. The actual interface is specified by the addressMapControlDataSource object (more about this later). Let's now look at an example of adding a new row to the addressMapControlTable:

```
flag <- true
while {flag = true} {
    n <- random()
    code <- SnmpSet(addressMapControlStatus.n <- createAndWait)
    if {code == noError} {
            flag <- false
    }
}

code <- SnmpSet(addressMapControlDataSource.n <- datasource,
                addressMapControlOwner.n <- ownerstring,
                addressMapControlStatus.n <- active)
```

The above pseudocode first searches for an unused instance-identifier. It does this by setting *n* to a random number and then setting the addressMapControlStatus object that is indexed by *n* to `createAndWait`. If the object already existed, the set operation would fail and we would get back an error code of either `badValue` or `inconsistentValue` (depending on the SNMP version). If the set operation succeeded, then a new has been created for the address-MapControlTable, and this row will be indexed by *n*. If we were to retrieve the value of address-MapControlStatus.*n*, the value would be `notReady`. If all the information necessary for the row had been set (for example, if all the other objects take default values), then the value would be `notInService`.

Now that a new row has been created, we simply set the data source and owner objects to the desired values and set the RowStatus object to `active`. If we were to retrieve addressMap-ControlStatus.*n*, it would have a value of `active`. If we later set addressMapControlStatus.*n* to `destroy`, row *n* would be removed from the addressMapControlTable and network layer to physical layer address mapping for the interface specified in that row would stop.

2.4.10 TimeStamp

The value of a TimeStamp object is the value of how long the SNMP agent has been running (sysUpTime) when a specific occurrence happened. TimeStamp resolves to a TimeTicks.

2.4.11 TimeInterval

TimeInterval represents a period of time, measured in hundredths (0.01) seconds. This resolves to an INTEGER and has a maximum value of 21474836.47 seconds (roughly 248 days).

2.4.12 DateAndTime

DateAndTime resolves to either an 8- or 11-byte OCTET STRING. It is used to represent a date-time specification. The way the OCTET STRING is decoded is as follows:

Table 2-4   DateAndTime

Octets	Description	Range
1-2	Year	0 - 65536
3	Month	1 - 12
4	Day	1 - 31
5	Hour	0 - 23
6	Minutes	0 - 59
7	Seconds	0 - 60 (60 is used for a leap second)
8	Deci-seconds	0 - 9
9	Direction from UTC	'+' (43) or '-' (45)
10	Hours from UTC	0 - 11
11	Minutes from UTC	0 - 59

A value of type DateAndTime should be displayed using the following format:

"2d-1d-1d,1d:1d:1d.1d,1a1d:1d"

For example, Friday January 15, 1999 at 1:30:15 PM EDT would be displayed as:

1999-1-15,13:30:15.0,-4:0

The actual OCTET STRING would be

07 cf 01 0f 0d 1e 0f 00 2d 04 00

The year would be obtained by (0x7 * 256) + 0xcf. The rest is straightforward.

If only local time is known, then time zone information (bytes 9 - 11) would not be present and the OCTET STRING would be 8 bytes.

2.4.13 StorageType

StorageType is used as a standard way to specify how a row should be stored in memory. This resolves to an INTEGER with the possible values:

- `other` (1).
- `volatile` (2). Setting a StorageType object to this value means its corresponding row is to be stored in volatile memory and will be lost if the device is rebooted. A StorageType object with a value of `volatile` cannot later be modified to `permanent` or `readOnly`.
- `nonVolatile` (3). Setting a StorageType object to this value means its corresponding row is to be stored in nonvolatile memory (e.g., NVRAM). If the device is rebooted, the row will be restored. A StorageType object with a value of `nonVolatile` cannot later be modified to `permanent` or `readOnly`.
- `permanent` (4). A row which is permanent is stored in nonvolatile memory (e.g., ROM). The row can be changed but not deleted. A RowStatus object with value `permanent` cannot be changed.
- `readOnly` (5). A row which is `readOnly` is stored in nonvolatile memory (e.g., ROM) and can not be either changed or deleted. A RowStatus object with value `readOnly` cannot be changed.

2.4.14 TDomain

TDomain resolves to an OBJECT IDENTIFIER and is used to denote a kind of transport service. RFC 1906, which specifies transport mappings for SNMPv2, defines five possible transport services. Additional transport services can be defined in the future. The five transport services defined by RFC 1906 are

- SNMP over UDP
- SNMP over CLNS
- SNMP over CONS
- SNMP over DDP
- SNMP over IPX

2.4.15 TAddress

TAddress resolves to an OCTET STRING and is used to represent a transport address. The encoding of a TAddress value depends on the transport domain that the address is associated with.

For a UDP domain, TAddress is a 6-byte OCTET STRING. The first four bytes contain the IP address in network-byte order and the last 2 bytes contain the UDP port in network-byte order.

For both CLNS and CONS domains, TAddress represents an OSI address. The first byte (*n*) specifies the length of the NSAP portion of the OSI address. The next *n* bytes are the NSAP portion; the remaining bytes are the TSEL portion of the address.

For a DDP domain, TAddress represents a NBP name. The first byte (*n1*) specifies the length of the object portion. The next *n1* bytes are the object portion. The next byte (*n2*) specifies the length of the type portion. The next *n2* bytes are the type portion. The next byte (*n3*) specifies the length of the zone portion. The next *n3* bytes are the zone portion.

For an IPX domain, TAddress represents an IPX address. The first 4 bytes represent the network number, the next 6 bytes represent the physical address, and the last 2 bytes represent the socket number. All of these are in network-byte order.

2.5 SNMPv1 Operations

SNMPv1 supports four operations:

- get, which is used to retrieve specific objects.
- get-next, which is used to retrieve objects by traversing the MIB tree.
- set, which is used to modify or create objects.
- trap, which is used by an agent to send an unsolicited notification to one or more preconfigured management stations.

All SNMPv1 operations are embedded within an SNMP message. The format of an SNMP message is

version	community	SNMP PDU

where

- version specifies the SNMP version number (for SNMPv1 this is 0).

- community is an OCTET STRING which serves as a password for either retrieving or modifying management data.

- SNMP PDU specifies whether the message is an SNMP operation (get, get-next, or set), a response to an SNMP operation, or a trap.

For a get, get-next, or set operation the format for SNMP PDU is:

type	reqid	0	0	variable bindings

where

- type is hex 0xA0 for a get, 0xA1 for get-next, 0xA3 for set

- reqid (request identifier) is a unique integer used to identify the request. When an agent responds to this request with a GetResponse PDU, it will use this same request identifier value. This allows a management station to send out multiple requests at a time and correlate the responses when they arrive.

- variable bindings is a list of management information to either retrieve or modify.

We will describe the SNMP PDUs for responses and traps later.

2.5.1   Community Names

SNMP supports trivial authentication by using what amounts to a password — called a community name. The simplest explanation is you use the read community name to retrieve objects (using get or get-next operations) and the write community name to modify objects (using a set operation).

A more precise explanation is you use a community name to access objects within that community. Getting back to the simple explanation, there are typically two communities defined by an agent: one for all the managed objects that can be read (objects with read-only or read-write access), the other for objects that can be modified (objects with read-write access). However, a community can be any collection of objects within a device's MIB with an access mode of read-only or read-write applied to the whole community. The number of communities an agent supports is up to its implementation.

Again, getting back to the simple explanation, most devices (if not all) that you find will support two communities — a read community and a write community.

2.5.2   Variable Bindings

The variable bindings specify the managed objects to either collect or modify. To be more precise the variable bindings are a list of OBJECT IDENTIFIER — value pairs. For a get or get-next request, the value part is ignored.

The managed objects specified for a get or set operation must be leaf objects — that is fully instanced objects. Table and row objects cannot be specified. If you want to collect all the objects in a table, you must collect each leaf object individually.

Since a get-next operation does a MIB tree traveral with the managed objects provided in the variable bindings, any objects in the MIB tree can be specified.

2.5.3   When an Agent receives an SNMP message

Whan an agent receives an SNMP message, it performs the following actions to determine whether the message should be processed:

1. Checks the encoding to see if the message can be parsed. If it can't, the message is discarded

2. Checks to see if the SNMP Version number is one the agent recognizes. If it isn't, the message is discarded.

3. It passes the community name, the PDU portion of the message, and the source and destination transport addresses to an authentication service. If authentication fails, the message is discarded.

4. It checks to see if the PDU can be parsed. If it can't, the message is discarded.

2.5.4 Responses

When an agent receives a get, get-next, or set request, it will try to retrieve or modify the objects specified in the variable bindings and will send a response back to the originator of the request. The format of this response is

0xA2	reqid	es	ei	variable bindings

where

- the value of the first field, hex A2, indicates that the SNMP PDU is a GetResponse.

- reqid (request identifier) is the same value used in the original request.

- es (error-status) indicates whether the agent was able to successfully process the request. The values for this are

• noError (0), request was successfully processed.

• tooBig (1), the agent could not fit the results of the request into a single SNMP message. There are several reasons why this might happen which we'll discuss later. The simplest case, where the original request contained too many managed objects, can be handled by breaking up the request into two or more requests.

• noSuchName (2), an object was specified which the agent, based on the community specified, didn't know about. For example, if you try to modify with a set operation a variable defined with read-only access, that variable won't be known under the write community and the operation will generate a noSuchName error. The most common (and obvious) cause of this error is trying to read objects that don't exist.

• badValue (3), a set operation tried to modify an object to an invalid or inconsistent value.

• readOnly (4), this was defined to indicate that a set operation tried to modify a variable that, according to the community profile, may not be written to. In reality this isn't used. If you try to set a read-only variable you'll get back a `noSuchName` error-status.

• `genErr` (5), any other error.

- ei (error-index), if this is non-zero it indicates the position of the first variable in the request that was in error. This value will be non-zero only for `noSuchName`, `bad-Value`, `readOnly`, and `genErr` errors. The first variable starts at position 1.

- variable bindings, a list of variables, each containing an object identifier and a value.

An agent will use the following logic to process a get request:

1. If an object is not available under the specified community for a get, then issue a GetResponse with an error-status of `noSuchName` and an error-index of that object's position within the variable bindings.
2. If the generated PDU is too big, then issue a GetResponse with an error-status of `tooBig`.
3. If a value cannot be retrieved for any other reason, then issue a GetResponse with an error-status of `genErr`,an error-index of that object's position within the variable bindings..
4. Issue a GetResponse with the generated PDU.

An agent will use the following logic to process a get-next request:

1. If no next object exists, then issue a GetResponse with an error-status of `noSuchName` and an error-index of that object's position within the variable bindings.
2. If the generated PDU is too big, then issue a GetResponse with an error-status of `tooBig`.
3. If a value can not be retrieved for any other reason, then issue a GetResponse with an error-status of `genErr` and an error-index of that object's position within the variable bindings.
4. Issue a GetResponse with the generated PDU.

An agent will use the following logic to process a set request:

1. If an object is not available under the specified community for a set, then issue a GetResponse with an error-status of `noSuchName` and an error-index of that object's position within the variable bindings.
2. If the value specified for the object is inconsistent, then issue a GetResponse with an error-status of `badValue` and an error-index of that object's possition within the variable bindings.
3. If the generated PDU is too big, then issue a GetResponse with an error-status of `tooBig`.

4. If an object cannot be set for any other reason, then issue a GetResponse with an error-status of `genErr` and an error-index of that object's position within the variable bindings.

5. Issue a GetResponse with the generated PDU.

How big can an SNMP response be? Well, an agent must be able to support SNMP message sizes at least as large as 484 bytes — the maximum size, though, is what can fit in a UDP packet. Most agent implementations will typically set the maximum size to what can fit within an Ethernet frame (1500 bytes).

So given a message size of 484 bytes, how many variables can that contain? That depends on the length of the object identifiers and the type of data being collected or set. If you're collecting integer or counter values, you can probably fit 20 variables in a request.

2.5.5   Get

A get request is used to retrieve specific objects. Given the following MIB table:

Table 2-5   Example Data

Instance	ifIndex	ifDescr	ifType
1	1	ethernet	6
2	2	ethernet	6
3	3	serial	22
4	4	ppp	23
5	5	ethernet	6
6	6	ethernet	6

The first column in Table 2-5 shows the instance to use to access different rows in the MIB table. What's shown in this example is actually a subset of the ifTable, which will be shown in detail in the next chapter. For the purpose of this example, let's assume the table has only six rows.

A get-request specifying objects {sysUpTime.0, ifIndex.1, ifDescr.2, ifType.4} will return in a response the variable bindings:

sysUpTime.0   287231

ifIndex.1	1
ifDescr.2	ethernet
ifType.4	23

As you can see from this example, a get-request can specify objects from different rows (as well as scalar objects and objects from different tables) within the same request.

A get-request specifying objects {ifIndex.1, ifDesc.2, ifType.7} will return a response with an error-status of noSuchName and an error-index of 3.

Remember, only specific objects (leaf objects) can be retrieved. A get-request specifying object {ifTable} will return a response with an error-status of noSuchName and an error-index of 1.

2.5.6   Get-Next

While get is useful for collecting specific objects, get-next allows you to traverse the MIB tree and figure out what objects exist. This allows you to figure out what rows exist in a table.

So how does get-next work? For each object identifier specified in the variable bindings, a MIB tree traversal is done to retrieve the next leaf object in lexicographic order. Given the following subset of ifTable:

Table 2-6   Get-Next Example

Instance	ifInOctets	ifInUcastPkts	ifInNUcastPkts
1	200123	5601	912
2	4587213	8876	1790
3	755943	8761	
4	8837722	110211	4390
5	3987653211	301392199	56421
6	983101	65211	3451

A get-next specifying objects {ifInOctets, ifInUcastPkts, ifInNUcastPkts} will return in a response the variable bindings:

ifInOctets.1	200123
ifInUcastPkts.1	5601
ifInNUcastPkts.1	912

A get-next specifying the objects {ifInOctets.1, ifInUcastPkts.1, ifInNUcastPkts.1} will return in a response the variable bindings:

ifInOctets.2	4587213
ifInUcastPkts.2	8876
ifInNUcastPkts.2	1790

A get-next specifying the objects {ifInOctets.2, ifInUcastPkts.2, ifInNUcastPkts.2} will return in a response the variable bindings:

ifInOctets.3	755943
ifInUcastPkts.3	8761
ifInNUcastPkts.4	4390

As this example shows, tables can have holes in them. The row indexed by instance 3 has no object for ifInNUcastPkts. As a result, traversing the MIB tree from ifInNUcastPkts.2 will find as the next leaf object, ifInNUcastPkts.4.

If you're writing an application which uses get-next to collect rows in a table, you need to be aware of the possibility of holes and check the returned object identifiers to make sure you're getting back both the expected objects and the expected instances.

Also, as a minor point, if you're using get-next to collect columns that have counter values, when you reach the end of the table, you could end up collecting large octet strings — causing a `tooBig` error. Not a very important point, just something to be aware of so that your code can handle this case.

2.5.7   Set

A set request is used to modify or create managed objects. The variable bindings provided in the request define the variables to be set and the values to set them to. The set operation is atomic — either all the variables get set or none of them do. So if one of the variables can't be set or a bad value was given, none of the variables will be set and a response will be sent back to the originator specifying the error status and error index.

If the set was successful, the response message will contain the same variable bindings that were provided in the request.

How do you add or delete rows from a table? It depends how the objects for the table are defined. If a RowStatus object is being used, then a row can be added or deleted in a standard way. However, you will find tables that have been defined (mostly in private MIBs) that add or remove rows in proprietary ways.

2.5.8   Traps

An agent can look for certain events and on detecting them, send a trap message to preconfigured management stations. Unlike SNMP Request and Response messages, a trap message gets sent to UDP port 162.

The format of a Trap PDU is

0xA4	ent.	addr	gen.	spec.	ts	variable bindings

where

- the value of the first field, hex 0xA4, indicates that the SNMP PDU is a trap.

- enterprise identifies the device which generated the trap. This value is the sysObjectID (from the System group of MIB-II).

- agent address is the IP address of the device that generated the trap.

- generic-trap.

- specific-trap.

- timestamp is the value of sysUpTime (from the System group of MIB-II) when the trap was generated.

- variable bindings allow different traps to provide additional information.

Six generic traps have been defined. If the generic-trap number is between zero and five, then the trap is one of the following:

- `coldStart` (0) indicates that the agent has reset. This most likely indicates the device has rebooted.
- `warmStart` (1) indicates the agent is reinitializing itself, but the managed objects in its view have not been altered.
- `linkDown` (2) indicates an interface has gone from the up to the down state. The first variable in the variable bindings identifies the interface.
- `linkUp` (3) indicates an interface has changed to the up state. The first variable in the variable bindings identifies the interface.
- `authenticationFailure` (4) indicates an SNMP message has been received which failed authentication (e.g., a bad community name).
- `egpNeighborLoss` (5) indicates that an EGP neighbor has transitioned to the down state. The first variable in the variable bindings identifies the IP address of the EGP neighbor.

If the generic-trap number is 6, then the trap is defined to be enterprise specific and the specific-trap number defines the trap. An obvious problem with this scheme is that different vendors are going to pick the same specific-trap numbers to represent their device-specific traps. That means that in order to decode an enterprise-specific trap, you first have to figure who the vendor is from the enterprise value, and from that figure out the meaning of the specific-trap number. As we will be seeing soon, SNMPv2 defines a new Trap PDU which solves this problem.

Vendors tend to define enterprise-specific traps to signal events like a high temperature being discovered on a board or a fan failing or some other potentially catastrophic event. Since trap messages are sent over UDP, which is unreliable, it is possible that a discovered catastrophic event will go unreported. As we will also be seeing soon, SNMPv2 defines a new message, Inform, which attempts to solve this problem.

An aside:

Like everything else, not all the traps defined by vendors are equal. Some vendors (or at least some of their devices) do a good job of announcing real events, others can produce a lot of noise with little useful information. With some devices simply catching the traps that they send and displaying them is not very useful. What would be far more useful would be filtering out traps that are really noise, correlating the others, and performing some sort of analysis to understand what device or network events are really occurring.

2.5.9   SNMPv2 Extensions

SNMPv2 extends the protocol operations by defining an SNMPv2-Trap PDU, an Inform message which is basically a trap that gets acknowledged, and a Get-Bulk Request message which is really a souped-up extension to get-next. It also defines additional error statuses and changes the way responses to get and get-next requests are handled if one of the objects speci-fied in the variable bindings cannot be retrieved.

The SNMP message format is unchanged from SNMPv1. An SNMP version number of 1 indicates the message is an SNMPv2 message. Get, get-next, set, and response PDUs are unchanged from SNMPv1.

SNMPv2 also defines other transport protocols that SNMPv2 may run over.

2.5.9.1   SNMPv2 Traps

The format for an SNMPv2-Trap PDU is

0xA7	reqid	0	0	variable bindings

Note: The PDU format is identical to that of a get, get-next,or set PDU, with a type value of hex 0xA7 indicating that the PDU is an SNMPv2 Trap. Also, the role played by an SNMPv2 Trap is identical to that of an SNMP Trap.

The information about the trap is embedded in the variable bindings. The first variable provides the agent's value of sysUpTime when the trap was generated. The next variable is snmpTrapOID.0, which identifies what type of trap it is. Additional variables are added based on the trap type.

The generic traps defined for SNMPv1 have had trap object identifier values defined for SNMPv2. For example, a linkDown trap has a trap object identifier value of snmpTraps.3. So the variable bindings for a linkDown trap would be something like this:

sysUpTime.0	32216671
sysTrapOID.0	snmpTraps.3
ifIndex.4	4
ifAdminStatus.4	up
ifOperStatus.4	down

The variables ifIndex, ifAdminStatus, and ifOperStatus are defined by linkDown notification definition.

By defining unique trap object identifiers for each trap, you no longer have the problem with SNMPv1 traps where vendors used the same enterprise-specific trap numbers. This meant that for a management station to figure out the meaning of an enterprise-specific SNMPv1 Trap it had to correlate the device's enterprise object identifier with the enterprise-specific trap number.

2.5.9.2   Informs

As we saw with SNMP Traps, they can be used to signal potentially catastrophic events (such as a high temperature measured within a device). The problem, though, is they're sent over an unreliable transport mechanism (UDP). Inform messages address this problem.

An inform message is really nothing more than an SNMPv2 Trap that gets responded to. This way an agent implementation can take it upon itself what to do if it doesn't receive a response back. For example, it could try resending the inform message some number of times until it either gets a response back or it exhausts its retry count.

The format for an InformRequest-PDU is

0xA6	reqid	0	0	variable bindings

A type value of hex 0xA6 indicates the PDU is an InformRequest-PDU. Other than that, the PDU format is identical to the SNMPv2-Trap PDU.

When an SNMP entity, such as an SNMP manager, receives an inform message, it tries to send back a response message with the same request identifier and variable bindings. If the size of the response message is too big for this entity to send, it will instead send a response message with the same request identifier, an error status of `tooBig`, an error index of zero, and an empty variable bindings field.

Note: While informs were introduced to help alleviate the problem of traps being lost, it obviously can't completely solve the problem since the problem is really fundamental to the unreliable nature of a network. Also, there's a price to be paid for using informs — namely, additional load on the network and more resources consumed by the device that sends the Inform. And if traps are being lost due to congestion, resending them is only going to add to the congestion problem.

2.5.9.3   Get-Bulk

The idea behind the get-bulk operation is to allow you to retrieve portions of a table. This is similar in concept to writing logic which walks a table through repeated get-next commands. With a get-bulk request you specify a variable binding list and also two additional values: a non-repeaters value and a max-repetitions value.

A non-repeaters value of *n* means treat the first *n* variables in the variable bindings list as a simple get-next operation. For the remaining variables, try to perform up to *m* (the max-repetitions value) iterations of get-next operations.

As an example,

```
GetBulkRequest( non-repeaters = 1, max-repetitions = 3,
                varbindlist = {sysUpTime, ifInOctets, ifInErrors} )
```

will return in a response the variable bindings:

sysUpTime.0	1233413
ifInOctets.1	345322
ifInErrors.1	76
ifInOctets.2	9981
ifInErrors.2	5
ifInOctets.3	228809
ifInErrors.3	0

Note: The order of the variables in the response are the non-repeater variable(s) first, followed by the get-next results of each of the remaining variables in turn.

A nice feature of the get-bulk operation is if the response is too big to fit in a message, it will be trimmed down so that the largest message possible will be sent. If for any of the non-repeaters, or for any of the variables that are being iterated, there is no lexicographic successor, a value of `endOfMibView` will be used. If the agent decides that the processing of a get-bulk operation is taking too long, a partial variable bindings may be returned.

In any case, a get-bulk operation will either return the complete collection that was requested, or the largest possible collection it either had time for or that could fit in a response. A get-bulk operation could possibly return a response with an error-status of `genErr` if processing of a variable name fails for any reason other than `endOfMibView`, but unless a variable name is improperly formed I don't see how this could happen.

The format of a GetBulkRequest PDU is

0xA5	reqid	n	m	variable bindings

where

  - the value of the first field, hex 0xA5, indicates that the SNMP PDU is a GetBulkRequest.

  - reqid is the request identifier (which will also be used in the response).

  - *n* is the non-repeaters value. If *n* is less than 0, it will be treated as 0.

  - *m* is the max-repetitions value. If *m* is less than 0, it will be treated as 0.

  - variable bindings specifies the variables to collect. The first *n* variables will be treated as a get-next operation. The rest of the variables will go through as many as *m* get-next interations.

2.5.9.4   Additional Error Statuses

SNMPv2 defines the following additional error statuses:

  - noAccess (6), if you try to set a variable that is not accessible.

  - wrongType (7), if you try to set a variable to a value whose type is inconsistent with what the variable requires.

  - wrongLength (8), if you try to set a variable to a value whose length is inconsistent with what the variable requires.

  - wrongEncoding (9), if you try to set a variable to a value whose ASN.1 encoding is inconsistent with the field's ASN.1 tag.

  - wrongValue (10), if you try to set a variable to an incorrect value. An example of this is if you try to set a RowStatus object (which resolves to an INTEGER) to a value of 10 (which is outside the enumerated values for RowStatus).

  - noCreation (11), if you try to modify or create a variable that does not exist and could never be created.

- inconsistentValue (12), if you try to set a variable to a value that under other circumstances could be valid but is presently inconsistent. An example of this is trying to set a RowStatus object that currently has a value of active to createAndWait.

- resourceUnavailable (13), if you try to set a variable to a value which requires allocation of a resource which is presently unavailable.

- commitFailed (14), if a set operation fails (even with the previous validations).

- undoFailed (15), if a set operation fails and not all the assignments could be undone.

- authorizationError (16), if a get, get-next, get-bulk, set, or inform request cannot be properly authorized.

- notWritable (17), if you try to set a variable that exists but cannot be modified regardless of what value is specified.

- inconsistentName (18), if you try to set a variable that doesn't exist and cannot be created under the present circumstances.

2.5.9.5   Difference with Get and Get-Next requests

The only difference between an SNMPv1 get-request and an SNMPv2 get-request is in the way the responses are handled if one of the variables specified cannot be retrieved. With SNMPv1, either all the values are retrieved or none of them are. With SNMPv2, the variables that can be retrieved will be, and the ones that can't will have a value of either noSuchObject or noSuchInstance in the returned variable bindings.

As an example, let's assume we send an SNMPv2 get-request specifying objects {ifIndex.5, ifDescr.20, protocolDistStatsPkts.1} to a device that doesn't have an interface with an index of 20 or support RMONv2 (which protocolDistStatsPkts is an object of). We would get back a response with the following variable bindings

ifIndex.5	5
ifDescr.20	noSuchInstance
protocolDistStatsPkts.1	noSuchObject

Similarly, an SNMPv2 get-next request will retrieve all the variables it can. If one of the variables in the request is past the end of the MIB tree, a value of endOfMibView will be returned in the variable bindings for that variable. Previously, with SNMPv1 you would get back a response with an error-status of `noSuchName` with none of the other values retrieved.

2.5.9.6 SNMPv2 Transport Protocols

RFC 1906 defines several transport protocols other than UDP that SNMPv2 may run over. These include

- OSI ConnectionLess-Mode Network Service (CLNS)
- OSI Connection-Oriented Network Service (CONS)
- Novell Internetwork Packet Exchange (IPX)
- Appletalk

2.6 Some Additional Thoughts

Network management applications should have at most an insignificant effect on the network. Applications that are monitoring devices for trending and performance information should not adversely effect either the devices or the network performance. This is obvious — but unless an application developer is careful, damage can easily be done.

The fact is not all agent implementations are equal. Some vendors architect their agents at the beginning of the product development cycle, designing upfront how many SNMP messages a second the agent will be able to handle. Other vendors treat network management (both on the agent and application side) as an afterthought, adding the agent at the tail end of the development. Still others have complex devices with complex distributed agent architectures — and as with any complex system oversights can easily be made. And then sometimes you have conceptual mistakes made in the design process. One of the devices I had built applications for had been designed so that the SNMP agent process had the highest priority on the system. If I loaded the device with enough SNMP messages (which were not that many), the SNMP processing would freeze out the spanning tree and other processes, causing these other processes to crash.

When building network management applications, you need to understand the devices you'll be accessing. Specifically, you need to understand the limitations and quirks of these devices. For example,

- What type of load (how many SNMP messages per second) can the device handle?
- Are there situations where the agent performs poorly?
- Are there bugs in the device which can cause a valid (or invalid) SNMP message to crash the system?

Part of the difficulty (and challenge) in building network management applications is learning the limitations devices have and figuring out how to work around them. If you're building a real-time status monitoring application that needs to poll interface data at a high rate (such as every 30 seconds), based on the number of interfaces on the device and the amount of data you need to collect for each interface — you could end up generating a fairly high constant stream of SNMP messages. By first understanding how many SNMP messages a second the device can handle, you can build the logic to throttle the messages so you don't overwhelm the device.

Over the years I've seen quite a few quirks in different devices. One extremely complicated device that I worked with had a virtual circuit table distributed over its different boards. Performing a GetNext Request on that table would cause thousands of internal messages to be generated as it tried to locate both the next port and board that had circuits allocated to it. The less populated the circuit table was, the more internal messages that would be generated. What I thought was a harmless GetNext Request ended up adversely affecting the performance of the device. Eventually, this problem was solved by caching this virtual circuit table within the main agent.

Once you understand the agent limitations and make sure your application isn't overwhelming an agent, you need to make sure your application recognizes when an agent gets busy. An agent will typically queue the SNMP messages it receives and process them when it has time. When the queue fills up, new messages will be discarded. As an example of this, let's say an agent can queue forty messages. If the system gets busy doing things like processing routing table updates and can't allocate the SNMP agent any processing time, the queue could fill up quickly. Now assuming the queue has filled up and the system is too busy to process the received messages, the management stations will start to time out their SNMP Requests and resend the original messages. Any space that had been freed up in the queue will now be filled up by duplicate messages. With a retry count of three, we could conceivably flood the agent with 120 duplicate messages. If the applications keep pumping more SNMP messages at the agent, it will just make the situation worse.

What's needed if you see a timeout (or maybe several timeouts) from an agent, you should back off and give the agent a chance to catch up. Maybe wait a minute before sending that agent any more SNMP messages. And maybe when you do start sending the agent messages again, lower the throttle rate so you're sending messages less frequently.

Overwhelming an agent is one issue you need to be concerned with. Adding traffic to the network is another. If our application is sending out a constant four SNMP messages a second, with each message being about 200 bytes, then we're consuming about 800 bytes per second of bandwidth (6400 bits per second). On an Ethernet network, this is fairly insignificant. If our traffic is going over a 56-Kbit line, then we're consuming over 11 percent of the bandwidth. How much traffic your applications can generate depends on the networks they'll be running on.

Understanding how much SNMP traffic you can send to a device, when to back off sending it more traffic, and what (if any) requests can cause the device to act poorly requires experience, time, and a lot of experimentation. However, all this is necessary if you're going to build applications that won't, under any circustance, impact the network that they're trying to monitor.

MIB-II

T his chapter looks at the management information that was historically defined in MIB-II (RFC 1213). MIB-II was made up of nine groups: system, interfaces, at, ip, icmp, tcp, udp, egp, and snmp. Nearly all of the definitions have been moved into separate documents. There were several reasons for doing this, one of them being so that the groups could be defined under SMIv2 and that they could be changed without needing to write a MIB-III. The address translation group (at) has been deprecated for many years now and will go away once RFC 1213 gets retired. The EGP group is also not used anymore and will not be described in this chapter. MIB-II also defined a transmission group, but this was really more of a place holder. Other MIB documents define management objects for X25, Ethernet, FDDI, Token Ring, etc. which are placed under the transmission group.

This chapter will look at the managed objects from MIB-II and show examples of how they can be used to effectively manage both devices and networks. Changes that were made to the MIB-II groups when they were moved to other documents are shown at the end of this chapter. Okay, now lets get to some fun stuff.

3.1 System Group

The system group is made up of the following objects:

Table 3-1   System Group

Object	Type	Access
sysDescr	DisplayString	read-only
sysObjectID	OBJECT IDENTIFIER	read-only
sysUpTime	TimeTicks	read-only
sysContact	DisplayString	read-write
sysName	DisplayString	read-write
sysLocation	DisplayString	read-write
sysServices	INTEGER	read-only

sysDescr: provides a description of a device. How useful this is really depends on the vendor. Some vendors provide the type of device and the revision of the software being used. Other vendors provide much less.

sysObjectID: identifies the agent software. A value of sysObjectID will have the following format:

1.3.6.1.4.1.*ve.vs.vs*....

where *ve* would be the vendor enterprise number, and *vs* would be vendor-specific information. The vendor enterprise number for Cisco, for example is 9, so collecting sysObjectID from a Cisco 2509 Router would return a value of

1.3.6.1.4.1.9.1.25

where the seventh number in the OBJECT IDENTIFIER (9) indicates that the vendor is Cisco. The next two numbers, 1 and 25, are vendor specific, and in this case Cisco has defined the 1 to indicate that the sysObjectID is for a product, and the 25 to indicate that the product is a Cisco 2509 Router. *Note*: Vendors can put whatever they want in the vendor-specific portion. Some vendors encode the hardware and software revisions; other vendors keep it simple and simply encode the product family. *Note*: 1.3.6.1.4.1 is the OBJECT IDENTIFIER for the enterprise's subtree.

sysUpTime: gives a count in one hundredths of a second how long the SNMP agent has been running. This is typically how long the device has been up and running, but it is possible for some devices to stop and restart the SNMP agent. For example, a value of 251957 would be 2519.57 seconds, which would be roughly 42 minutes. It is useful to monitor the sysUpTime value for key devices to understand how often they're rebooting. If you're collecting counter information for trending purposes, you should collect sysUpTime with each collection so you can determine whether previous counter information is valid. When a device reboots, counters are left in an unknown state (although most devices simply reset the counters).

sysContact: name and possibly phone number for the person responsible for managing this device. This object, along with sysName and sysLocation, needs to be set by the user. Life is made a lot easier if these objects are set.

sysName: name of the device. Again, this should be configured by the user.

sysLocation: the physical location of the device. Again, this should be configured by the user.

sysServices: shows the services that a device potentially offers. Bits 0 through 6 of this value correspond to ISO layers 1 through 7.

Table 3-2 sysServices

Layer	Functionality
1	physical (e.g., RMON probes)
2	data-link (e.g., bridges)
3	internet (e.g., IP)
4	end-to-end (e.g., TCP)
5	session
6	presentation
7	application (e.g., TFTP)

Personally, I find this at best marginally useful but to be complete let's run through an example. A sysServices value of 0x03 would correspond to $2^0 + 2^1$, which would indicate the device supports layers 1 and 2 (physical and data-link layers). A value of 0x78 would correspond to $2^6 + 2^5 + 2^4 + 2^3$, which indicates the device supports layers 7, 6, 5, and 4 (end-to-end, session, presentation, and application).

3.2 Interfaces Group

The interfaces group is made up of two top-level objects, ifNumber which indicates the number of interfaces present on the device, and ifTable which contains information about each interface. *Note*: ifTable can provide information for both physical and virtual interfaces. A WAN interface could have hundreds of frame relay circuits layered on top of it and each of those circuits could be seen in the ifTable as a virtual interface. Of course, I've seen vendors who are supposed to provide detailed information about each frame relay circuit in the ifTable, and instead end up duplicating the information for the physical interface underneath. And of course this isn't what either the customer or I were hoping for. So when it comes to virtual circuits, what actually ends up in the ifTable (and how useful the information is) is completely up to the vendor's implementation.

Table 3-3   ifTable, Indexed by ifIndex

Object	Type	Access
ifIndex	INTEGER	read-only
ifDescr	DisplayString	read-only
ifType	INTEGER	read-only
ifMtu	INTEGER	read-only
ifSpeed	Gauge	read-only
ifPhysAddress	PhysAddress	read-only
ifAdminStatus	INTEGER	read-write
ifOperStatus	INTEGER	read-only
ifLastChange	TimeTicks	read-only
ifInOctets	Counter	read-only
ifInUcastPkts	Counter	read-only
ifInNUcastPkts	Counter	read-only
ifInDiscards	Counter	read-only
ifInErrors	Counter	read-only
ifInUnknownProtos	Counter	read-only
ifOutOctets	Counter	read-only
ifOutUcastPkts	Counter	read-only
ifOutNUcastPkts	Counter	read-only
ifOutDiscards	Counter	read-only
ifOutQlen	Gauge	read-only
ifSpecific	OBJECT IDENTIFIER	read-only

ifIndex: each interface is identified by a unique value, with the values ranging from 1 to the value of ifNumber. For a simple device the ifIndex value for an interface usually matches the physical port number, but there is no guarantee of this. For a more complex device, such as a chassis device with multiple boards, the ifIndex values probably aren't even close to the port numbers.

So given an interface's ifIndex value, how do you map that into a slot and port number? That's a good question and the answer is not very satisfying. If it can be done at all it will be in a proprietary way. To make matters worse the same vendor may provide this mapping differently for each of their devices. So understanding how a vendor provides this mapping for one device won't necessarily help you understand how their other devices work. One way some vendors provide this mapping is to encode the slot-port numbers in the ifDescr textual string. Another way is to implement a private MIB table that you need to read to discover this mapping. Other devices might have this mapping tied to their hardware implementation and the only way to understand it is if it is documented.

Another potential problem with chassis devices is accessing the ifTable. With some chassis devices if you walk the ifTable, you will only access a subset of the interfaces for that device. Usually to access interfaces for the different boards requires you to use some sort of proprietary method. And again, each device is going to use its own scheme. What it usually comes down to, though, is figuring out what community string to use to access a specific slot. Some devices will provide a private MIB table that gives you the community string to use for each slot. Others use a simple algorithm for determining the community string (for example, simply appending the slot number to the chassis community string). And still others provide complex schemes of assigning different ports on different cards to virtual bridges, and then providing a scheme to map a virtual bridge number to a community string. Why do vendors do this? Most chassis devices use a distributed SNMP agent implementation where the information is spread out between the chassis and the different boards — in effect a subagent on each board maintains the ifTable information for the ports on that board.

Given all these difficulties in mapping interface numbers to slot-port numbers and in even accessing ifTable information for chassis devices, is the ifTable worth dealing with? Definitely! The ifTable provides critical information for understanding how your interfaces and devices are operating. All this means is when building an application to deal with a complex chassis device, you have to work harder. The first thing you need to do is understand how the device works and how you need to access the interface information for each slot. And remember, most devices in your network are going to be single board devices and you most likely won't run into these types of problems.

ifDescr: provides a description of the interface. The information provided in this description is completely up to the vendor. Some vendors will provide information such as the media type and the slot-port numbers; others are not quite as kind.

ifType: identifies the type of interface. The mapping of enumerated value to interface type is maintained in the IANAifType-MIB. This MIB is updated periodically, and one source for it is

ftp://ftp.iana.org/mib/ianaiftype.mib

The following table provides the ifType values as of April 1998.

Table 3-4   ifType Values

Code	Type	Code	Type	Code	Type
1	other	40	x25ple	79	rsrb
2	regular1822	41	iso88022llc	80	atmLogical
3	hdh1822	42	localTalk	81	ds0
4	ddnX25	43	smdsDxi	82	ds0Bundle
5	rfc877x25	44	frameRelayService	83	bsc
6	ethernetCsmacd	45	v35	84	async
7	iso88023Csmacd	46	hssi	85	cnr
8	iso88024TokenBus	47	hippi	86	802.5r
9	iso88025TokenRing	48	modem	87	eplrs
10	iso88026Man	49	aal5	88	arap
11	starLan	50	sonetPath	89	propCnls
12	proteon10Mbit	51	sonetVT	90	hostPad
13	proteon80Mbit	52	smdsIcip	91	termPad

Table 3-4   ifType Values (Continued)

Code	Type	Code	Type	Code	Type
14	hyperchannel	53	propVirtual	92	frameRelayMPI
15	fddi	54	propMultiplexor	93	x213
16	lapb	55	100BaseVG	94	adsl
17	sdlc	56	FibreChannel	95	radsl
18	ds1	57	hippiInterface	96	sdsl
19	e1	58	frameRelayInterconnect	97	vdsl
20	basicISDN	59	atm802.3	98	802.5CRFPInt
21	primaryISDN	60	atm802.5	99	myrinet
22	propPointToPointSerial	61	atmcctEmul	100	voiceEM
23	ppp	62	100BaseT	101	voiceFXO
24	softwareLoopback	63	isdn	102	voiceFXS
25	eon	64	V.11	103	voiceEncap
26	ethernet3Mbit	65	V.36	104	voiceOverIp
27	nsip	66	g703at64k	105	atmDxi
28	slip	67	g703at2mb	106	atmFuni
29	ultra	68	qllc	107	atmIma
30	ds3	69	100BaseFX	108	pppMultilinkBundle
31	sip	70	channel	109	ipOverCdlc
32	frameRelay	71	ieee80211	110	ipOverClaw
33	rs232	72	ibm370parChan	111	stackToStack
34	para	73	escon	112	virtualIpAddress
35	arcnet	74	dlsw	113	mpc
36	arcnetPlus	75	isdns	114	ipOverAtm
37	atm	76	isdnu	115	802.5j
38	miox25	77	lapd	116	tdlc
39	sonet	78	ipSwitch	117	gigabitEthernet

ifMtu: the size of the largest packet which can be either sent or received over this interface. The value is specified in octets. Small or mismatched MTU sizes can cause packets to be fragmented which can cause your device and network to behave less efficiently. A useful application might be something which checks the MTU sizes of all the interfaces in your network.

ifSpeed: the transmission rate in bits/second.

ifPhysAddress: the interface's media-specific address. If an interface doesn't have a physical address (such as a serial line), this value will be an OCTET STRING of zero length.

A network manager sometimes finds that a device is sending packets that are disrupting the network (for example the same IP address may have inadvertantly been assigned to two MAC addresses). In this case the network manager may be capturing packets with an RMON probe or packet analyzer and know the MAC address of the interface that is sending these disruptive packets. In order to restore order to the network, the beleaguered network manager needs to know what device the MAC address is associated with and hopefully what Ethernet segment or switch port the device is attached to. Building a MAC address to IP address mapping can help (RMONv2, as will be shown later, can be used to address this problem).

ifAdminStatus: used to configure the state of the interface. The state can be set to one of three values:

- up (1)
- down (2)
- testing (3)

Setting ifAdminStatus to up does not automatically mean the operational state of the interface will be up. For example, if nothing is connected to an Ethernet interface the operational state will stay down. Setting ifAdminStatus to testing means that no operational packets can be passed through the interface.

ifOperStatus: provides the current operational state of an interface. The operational state can have one of three values:

- up (1)
- down (2)
- testing (3)

If the operational state is down and the administrative state has been configured to be up, there is a potential problem.

ifLastChange: the value of sysUpTime at the time the interface entered its current operational state. This value will be zero if the current state was entered before the SNMP agent was last reset. Using this, you can determine how often an interface is resetting.

Note: If an interface resets, the counter values maintained for that interface are left in an unknown state. If you are periodically collecting interface counters (e.g., ifInOctets, ifInErrors, etc.) for trending or diagnostic purposes, you need to know whether the interface has reset between the current collection and the previous collection. If a reset has occurred, you need to flush the previous collected counter values.

ifInOctets: the total number of octets received on the interface.

ifInUcastPkts: the total number of unicast packets delivered to a higher-layer protocol.

ifInNUcastPkts: the total number of broadcast/multicast packets delivered to a higher-layer protocol. In a broadcast storm within a switched environment, the typical symptoms seen on an Ethernet switch will be a large number of broadcast packets being received on one interface and a large number of broadcast packets being transmitted on the rest of the interfaces. By monitoring for this condition, you have a reasonable chance of detecting a broadcast storm and shutting it down before it causes too much damage. Unfortunately, ifInNUcastPkts counts both broadcast and multicast packets, and it could be normal for an interface to be receiving a constant high rate of multicast packets.

RFC 1573 defines an extension to the ifTable, called ifXTable (which we'll be looking at later). This extension defines separate counters for both broadcast and multicast packets. This table, though, was defined using some Counter64 objects. Most network devices in use today have implemented SNMPv1 agents (as opposed to SNMPv2), and don't support the ifXTable extension. This is unfortunate, because in building trending and diagnostic products it is extremely useful to understand how much of the non-unicast packets are broadcast or multicast packets.

ifInDiscards: number of packets discarded due to resource limitations. A high percentage of discarded packets for an interface is a good indication of a congestion problem.

ifInErrors: number of inbound packets that were discarded due to errors. A high percentage of errors can indicate a receiver problem or a bad line.

ifUnknownProtos: the number of inbound packets that were discarded because of an unknown or unsupported protocol.

ifOutOctets: the total number of octets transmitted from this interface.

ifOutUcastPkts: the total number of packets that were requested to be transmitted to a subnet-unicast address. This includes both packets that were sent and discarded.

ifOutNUcastPkts: the total number of broadcast/multicast packets that were requested to be sent. This includes packets that were both sent and discarded.

ifOutDiscards: the total number of outbound packets that were discarded due to resource limitations. A high discard rate is a good indication that more buffer space needs to be allocated for an interface.

ifOutErrors: the total number of outbound packets that were discarded due to errors. A high error rate is a strong indication of a hardware problem.

ifOutQlen: the number of packets in the output packet queue.

ifSpecific: this was supposed to provide a reference to MIB definitions specific to the particular media being used to realize the interface. In reality, it was never used and has been deprecated in the Interfaces MIB (RFC 1573). Reading this value will return an OBJECT IDENTIFIER with value {0 0}.

The key to managing your network is understanding it. On a large switched network understanding which ports are under or heavily utilized can help you balance the traffic on your segments better. Understanding which ports are seeing congestion or high error rates can be critical. Even something as simple as understanding which ports are operationally up — and what percentage of time they're operationally up in a given 24 hour period — can be an eye opener to a network manager.

In the rest of this section I will provide some expressions that use ifTable objects to calculate things like utilization. In these expressions, the function delta means the difference between two counter values at different time intervals. Again, for a counter value to be useful you need at least two samples — one to provide a point reference, the other so you can calculate how much the value has changed. In calculating delta(seconds), sysUpTime will need to be collected.

$$\text{rx. utilization} = \frac{\text{delta(ifInOctets)} \times 8}{\text{ifSpeed} \times \text{delta(seconds)}} \times 100 \tag{3.1}$$

The above expression is used to calculate the receive utilization of an interface. This is independent of the media type, and for a full duplex line this tells you how much of the bandwidth is typically being used. On a serial line, if you're approaching 90% utilization, you may want to consider upgrading the line to avoid potential congestion problems.

As we had shown earlier, how often you need to collect samples depends on the speed of the line. For a Fast Ethernet interface, the ifInOctets counter could conceivably wrap in less than six minutes so you would want to collect your samples faster than that — probably at a rate of around five minutes. Also, you need to make sure that neither the SNMP agent nor the interface has reset between collections. And also, if you're calculating this expression (or any of the others in this section), make sure the operational status of the interface (ifOperStatus) is up.

The expression to calculate the transmit utilization of an interface is similar:

$$\text{tx. utilization} = \frac{\text{delta(ifOutOctets)} \times 8}{\text{ifSpeed} \times \text{delta(seconds)}} \times 100 \tag{3.2}$$

For a normal half-duplex Ethernet segment, the utilization for the segment would simply be the sum of the transmit and receive utilization parts. To be precise, you would have to take into account the gap that is placed between each frame, but that portion is so neglible it is not worth worrying about.

$$\text{Ethernet Utilization} = \text{rx. utilization} + \text{tx.utilization} \tag{3.3}$$

What utilization value is okay really depends on how many hosts you have hanging off a segment. If you have an Ethernet switch where you have one host per port, then there is no reason you can't approach one hundred percent utilization. If you have a hub attached to the switch port with several hosts attached to the hub, then you have to worry about collisions — and 40 percent is probably what you want to target as a maximum utilization.

Over the years I have built a number of status monitoring/diagnostic products with each product being a stepping stone to the next. Initially I looked at error and congestion problems by determining the percent of traffic with errors and the percent of traffic being discarded. Over time, with exposure to quite a few customers' networks, I've learned this is not necessarily what you want to do. Simply seeing a discard rate at a certain level, regardless of the amount of traffic, is enough to know you have a congestion problem. If packets are being fragmented, discarding fragmented pieces will be enough to cause quite a bit of traffic to be resent. Similarly, seeing interface errors is symptomatic of either hardware, cable, or line problems regardless of what percent of traffic the errors are.

$$\text{receive discard rate} = \frac{\text{delta(ifInDiscards)}}{\text{delta(seconds)}} \tag{3.4}$$

$$\text{transmit discard rate} = \frac{\text{delta(ifOutDiscards)}}{\text{delta(seconds)}} \tag{3.5}$$

$$\text{receive error rate} = \frac{\text{delta(ifInErrors)}}{\text{delta(seconds)}} \tag{3.6}$$

$$\text{transmit error rate} = \frac{\text{delta(ifOutErrors)}}{\text{delta(seconds)}} \tag{3.7}$$

Similarly, what's important in identifying broadcast storms within a switched network is not seeing a high percentage of overall packets being broadcast packets, but seeing a high broadcast packet rate. Actually, for lightly utilized interfaces, the majority of traffic is going to be spanning tree and routing table updates — which are broadcast packets. Since ifInNUcastPkts and ifOutNUcastPkts counts both broadcast and multicast packets, if you have multicast traffic running in your network, these rates could be high without indicating a problem. Monitoring these rates, though, can at least give you an indication that a broadcast storm has arrived.

$$\text{receive broadcast/multicast packet rate} = \frac{\text{delta(ifInNUcastPkts)}}{\text{delta(seconds)}} \quad (3.8)$$

$$\text{transmit broadcast/multicast packet rate} = \frac{\text{delta(ifOutNUcastPkts)}}{\text{delta(seconds)}} \quad (3.9)$$

3.3 IP Group

The IP Group is made up of both scalar objects, an address table, a routing table, and a network address to media table. You can use this group to help troubleshoot routing problems and to help discover network topologies.

Note: Some devices implement several routing modules and maintain IP Group objects for each module. You typically access the different IP Groups through either proxy community strings or through different IP addresses.

The scalar objects making up the IP Group are

Table 3-5 IP Group Scalar Objects

Object	Type	Access
ipForwarding	INTEGER	read-write
ipDefaultTTL	INTEGER	read-write
ipInReceives	Counter	read-only
ipInHdrErrors	Counter	read-only
ipInAddrErrors	Counter	read-only
ipForwDatagrams	Counter	read-only
ipInUnknownProtos	Counter	read-only
ipInDiscards	Counter	read-only
ipInDelivers	Counter	read-only
ipOutRequests	Counter	read-only
ipOutDiscards	Counter	read-only
ipOutNoRoutes	Counter	read-only
ipReasmTimeout	INTEGER	read-only

Table 3-5   IP Group Scalar Objects (Continued)

Object	Type	Access
ipReasmReqds	Counter	read-only
ipReasmOKs	Counter	read-only
ipReasmFails	Counter	read-only
ipFragOKs	Counter	read-only
ipFragFails	Counter	read-only
ipFragCreates	Counter	read-only
ipRoutingDiscards	Counter	read-only

ipForwarding: can be either forwarding (1) or not-forwarding (2). When IP forwarding is enabled, the device acts as a normal router and will forward IP packets from one subnet to another when required. When IP forwarding is disabled, the device discards IP packets not addressed to one of its locally defined interfaces. It will also increment the ipInAddrErrors counter for each packet that it discards.

ipDefaultTTL: default TTL (Time-To-Live).

ipInReceives: total number of input datagrams received from all interfaces, including those with errors.

ipInHdrErrors: number of input datagrams discarded due to errors in their IP headers. This includes bad checksums, version number mismatch, other format errors, time-to-live exceeded, and errors discovered in processing their IP options.

ipInAddrErrors: number of input datagrams discarded because the destination IP Address is not valid. This includes invalid addresses (such as 0.0.0.0), addresses of unsupported classes and for packets that cannot be forwarded because IP forwarding has been turned off [ipForwarding set to not-forwarding (2)]. The first thing to check if you're receiving a large amount of address errors is the value of ipForwarding.

ipForwDatagrams: number of datagrams forwarded.

ipInUnknownProtos: number of datagrams received successfully but discarded because of either an unknown or unsupported protocol.

ipInDiscards: number of input datagrams discarded due to resource limitations, such as lack of buffer space.

ipInDelivers: number of datagrams delivered to the local IP user-protocols.

ipOutRequests: number of IP datagrams requested for transmission. This counter does not include any datagrams counted in ipForwDatagrams.

ipOutDiscards: number of output datagrams discarded due to resource limitations.

ipOutNoRoutes: number of output datagrams discarded because no route could be found to the destination address.

ipReasmTimeout: timeout value in seconds for which received IP fragments are held while they are awaiting reassembly.

ipReasmReqds: number of IP fragments received which needed to be reassembled.

ipReasmOKs: number of IP datagrams successfully reassembled.

ipReasmFails: number of reassembly failures.

ipFragOKs: number of IP datagrams successfully fragmented.

ipFragFails: number of IP datagrams needing fragmentation but which had to be discarded because they had the IP flag "Don't Fragment" set.

ipFragCreates: number of IP fragments created.

ipRoutingDiscards: number of routing table entries that were discarded due to resource limitations.

Monitoring these objects can both help you isolate routing problems and understand how your routers are operating. These objects can specifically help you identify

- resource limitiations
- large number of packets are being fragmented. This could be caused by MTU mismatches. Reducing the amount of fragmentation will most likely improve your network performance.
- a large number of packets are being reassembled. Again, this is most likely caused by MTU mismatches.
- a high percentage of no routes. This could indicate that a device isn't properly receiving routing updates or that a routing table has been misconfigured and doesn't contain valid routes.
- a high percent of failed reassembles. This could indicate either that fragments are being corrupted or IP fragments are being discarded due to resource limitations.
- a high percent of failed fragmentations. This probably indicates that devices have been configured to set the "Don't Fragment" flag.

While knowing that you are detecting a large number of packets with header or address errors can be useful, troubleshooting the specific problem is not so easy. It would be nice if additional header or address error information were stored in MIB objects, but they're not. In order to determine the specific problem you're going to have to put a packet analyzer on the wire and capture the offending packets. Since routers (or switches with routing capability) can have a large number of interfaces, finding the right interface to attach an analyzer to could take quite a while. Hopefully, vendors in the future will try to add more troubleshooting information in their private MIB extensions.

The following expressions can be useful in detecting routing problems. These expressions introduce a function *rate*, which is simply the *delta* value divided by the number of seconds between the two collections, e.g., $\text{rate(ipInDiscards)} = \frac{\text{delta(ipInDiscards)}}{\text{delta(seconds)}}$.

$$\% \text{ of IP input packets discarded } = \frac{\text{rate(ipInDiscards)}}{\text{rate(ipInReceives)}} \times 100 \qquad (3.10)$$

$$\% \text{ IP output packets discarded } = \frac{\text{rate(ipOutDiscards)}}{\text{rate(ipForwDatagrams)} + \text{rate(ipOutRequests)}} \times 100 \quad (3.11)$$

$$\% \text{ fragmented } = \frac{\text{rate(ipFragOKs)} + \text{rate(ipFragFails)}}{\text{rate(ipForwDatagrams)} + \text{rate(ipOutRequests)}} \times 100 \qquad (3.12)$$

$$\% \text{ needing reassembly } = \frac{\text{rate(ipReasmReqds)}}{\text{rate(ipInReceives)}} \times 100 \qquad (3.13)$$

$$\% \text{ no routes } = \frac{\text{rate(ipOutNoRoutes)}}{\text{rate(ipForwDatagrams)} + \text{rate(ipOutRequests)}} \times 100 \qquad (3.14)$$

$$\% \text{ failed reassemblies } = \frac{\text{rate(ipReasmFails)}}{\text{rate(ipReasmReqds)}} \times 100 \qquad (3.15)$$

$$\% \text{ failed fragmentations } = \frac{\text{rate(ipFragFails)}}{\text{rate(ipForwDatagrams)} + \text{rate(ipOutRequests)}} \times 100 \qquad (3.16)$$

The IP Group has a table object ipAddrTable, which keeps track of the IP addresses associated with the device.

Table 3-6   ipAddrTable, Indexed by ipAdEntAddr

Object	Type	Access
ipAdEntAddr	IpAddress	read-only
ipAdEntIfIndex	INTEGER	read-only
ipAdEntNetMask	IpAddress	read-only
ipAdEntBcastAddr	INTEGER	read-only
ipAdEntReasmMaxSize	INTEGER	read-only

ipAdEntAddr: IP address.

ipAdEntIfIndex: interface IP address has been assigned to.

ipAdEntNetMask: subnet mask.

ipAdEntBcastAddr: value of the least-significant bit in the IP broadcast address. For example, if a broadcast address of all ones is being used, the value of this will be 1.

ipAdEntReasmMaxSize: the largest IP datagram that can be reassembled. This can have a maxium value of 65535.

Walking a device's ipAddrTable produce's results like this:

Table 3-7   ipAddrTable dump

ipAdEntAddr	ipAdEntIfIndex	ipAdEntNetMask	ipAdEntBcastAddr	ipAdEntReasmMaxSize
10.23.15.251	2	255.255.255.0	1	18024
134.240.6.18	4	255.255.255.240	1	18024
134.240.231.42	9	255.255.255.252	1	18024

The IP Group has a table object ipRouteTable, which maintains a device's IP routing table. By searching through the IP routing table you can trace IP paths, check routing updates, and build network discovery algorithms.

An Aside:

Network discovery algorithms will typically use a seed router to find all routers one hop away. Then it will keep expanding its search until it hits some predefined limits. Given this information, the discovery algorithm can then draw a map of these routers and how they're connected. It also knows all the subnetworks attached to each router. It can then go through each subnet address range pinging each address to find the devices. If these devices support SNMP, then system and IP address information can be further collected.

Building the logical IP map is fairly easy. If spanning tree is running, you can build the spanning tree and somewhat understand the physical topology. However, there is no standard way of understanding what hubs or repeaters are hanging off of what switch ports. The only way to get this type of information is through proprietary means.

Table 3-8   IpRouteTable, Indexed by ipRouteDest

Object	Type	Access
ipRouteDest	IpAddress	read-write
ipRouteIfIndex	INTEGER	read-write
ipRouteMetric1	INTEGER	read-write
ipRouteMetric2	INTEGER	read-write
ipRouteMetric3	INTEGER	read-write
ipRouteMetric4	INTEGER	read-write
ipRouteNextHop	IpAddress	read-write
ipRouteType	INTEGER	read-write
ipRouteProto	INTEGER	read-only
ipRouteAge	INTEGER	read-write
ipRouteMask	IpAddress	read-write
ipRouteMetric5	INTEGER	read-write
ipRouteInfo	OBJECT IDENTIFIER	read-only

ipRouteDest: destination IP address.

ipRouteIfIndex: this identifies the interface by which the next hop is reached.

ipRouteMetric1: primary routing metric for this route. The meaning of this metric is determined by the routing protocol specified by ipRouteProto.

ipRouteMetric2: an alternative routing metric.

ipRouteMetric3: an alternative routing metric.

ipRouteMetric4: an alternative routing metric.

ipRouteNextHop: next hop IP address.

ipRouteType: type of route. It can have one of four values:

• other (1)

• invalid (2), setting a route entry to invalid has the effect of invalidating that entry. It is up to the agent implementation as to whether an invalidated entry is removed from the ipRouteTable.

• direct (3), route to directly connected subnetwork.

• indirect (4), route to a nonlocal host, network, or subnetwork.

ipRouteProto: mechanism used to learn the route. It can have one of the following values:

• other (1)
• local (2), manually configured.
• netmgmt (3), set through a network management protocol.
• icmp (4), learned through an ICMP redirect message.
• egp (5)
• ggp (6)
• hello (7)
• rip (8)
• is-is (9)
• es-is (10)
• ciscoIgrp (11)
• bbnSpfIgp (12)
• ospf (13)
• bgp (14)

ipRouteAge: number of seconds since route was last updated.

ipRouteMask: subnet-mask for route. In order to determine that this route entry should be used, the destination address should be logically ANDed with the subnet-mask and the value should be compared to ipRouteDest.

ipRouteMetric5: an alternative routing metric.

ipRouteInfo: this is supposed to reference to MIB definitions specific to the particular routing protocol which learned this route. In reality, I've never seen this used and its value is typically {0 0} which indicates the information is not present.

Given a local router, R, and a destination address, D, the following pseudocode will search through R's routing table to find the next hop to get to D.

```
create SNMP session to R
inst <- D
while {inst != finished} {
    code <- SnmpGet( ipRouteDest.inst,
                 ipRouteNextHop.inst,
                 ipRouteMask.inst,
                 ipRouteType.inst,
                 ipRouteIfIndex.inst)
    if {code == noError} {
        dest <- value collected for ipRouteDest.inst
        nexthop <- value collected for ipRouteNextHop.inst
        mask <- value collected for ipRouteMask.inst
        type <- value collected for ipRouteType.inst
        ifIndex <- value collected for ipRouteIfIndex.inst

        if {(type != invalid) && ((D AND mask) == dest)} {
                // next hop found
                inst <- finished
                nexthopfound <- true
        }
    }

    if {inst == 0.0.0.0} {
        inst <- finished
        error('Can't trace Next Hop.')
    }

    if {inst != finished} {
        inst <- SetLeastSignificantBitToZero(inst)
    }
}
```

This algorithm does a stealth search through a device's routing table. Initially, inst is set to the destination address. If a matching entry is not found, the least significant bit of inst will be set to zero. This will continue until either a match is found, or a search for the default route

0.0.0.0 fails. By setting the least significant bit of inst to zero, we are in effect trying each possible subnet mask. This limits the number of searches through the routing table to 31. Otherwise, if we tried walking the complete routing table to find possible matches, we could be searching for hours (routing tables can get very large).

To make things a little clearer, let's walk through an example of searching for a destination address of 158.101.121.6. We will in turn search for each of the following entries in the routing table until a match is found (or the Next Hop search fails):

```
First pass: 158.101.121.6
next:       158.101.121.4
next:       158.101.121.0
next:       158.101.120.0
next:       158.101.112.0
next:       158.101.96.0
next:       158.101.64.0
next:       158.101.0.0
next:       158.100.0.0
next:       158.96.0.0
next:       158.64.0.0
next:       158.0.0.0
next:       156.0.0.0
next:       152.0.0.0
next:       144.0.0.0
next:       128.0.0.0
next:       0.0.0.0
```

Finally, the IP Group has a table object, ipNetToMediaTable. This is the IP address translation table, added in MIB-II to supercede the atTable. Like the atTable, it provides a mapping between IP and media-specific addresses.

Table 3-9 ipNetToMediaTable, Indexed by ipNetToMediaIfIndex.ipNetToMediaNetAddress

Object	Type	Access
ipNetToMediaIfIndex	INTEGER	read-write
ipNetToMediaPhysAddress	PhysAddress	read-write
ipNetToMediaNetAddress	IpAddress	read-write
ipNetToMediaType	INTEGER	read-write

ipNetToMediaIfIndex: interface number.

ipNextToMediaPhysAddress: media-dependent "physical" address.

ipNetToMediaNetAddress: IP address.

ipNetToMediaType: how the IP to physcial address mapping was determined. This can have one of four values:

- other (1)
- invalid (2), setting this value to invalid will invalidate the entry. Whether an agent removes an invalidated entry from the ipNetToMediaTable is completely up to the implementation of the agent.
- dynamic (3)
- static (4)

3.4 ICMP Group

The ICMP Group provides counts for each ICMP message type both received and sent by the device. It also keeps track of the total number of ICMP messages received, sent, received in error, or not sent due to resource limitations. The ICMP group can be useful in identifying potential routing problems.

Table 3-10   ICMP Group

Object	Type	Access
icmpInMsgs	counter	read-only
icmpInErrors	counter	read-only
icmpInDestUnreachs icmpOutDestUnreachs	counter	read-only
icmpInTimeExcds icmpOutTimeExcds	counter	read-only
icmpInParmProbs icmpOutParmProbs	counter	read-only
icmpInSrcQuenchs icmpOutSrcQuenchs	counter	read-only

Table 3-10   ICMP Group (Continued)

Object	Type	Access
icmpInRedirects icmpOutRedirects	counter	read-only
icmpInEchos icmpOutEchos	counter	read-only
icmpInEchoReps icmpOutEchoReps	counter	read-only
icmpInTimestamps icmpOutTimestamps	counter	read-only
icmpInTimestampReps icmpOutTimestampReps	counter	read-only
icmpInAddrMasks icmpOutAddrMasks	counter	read-only
icmpInAddrMaskReps icmpOutAddrMaskReps	counter	read-only
icmpOutMsgs	counter	read-only
icmpOutErrors	counter	read-only

icmpInMsgs: number of ICMP messages received.

icmpInErrors: number of ICMP messages received with errors (such as bad checksums, bad length, etc.).

icmpInDestUnreachs: number of ICMP Destination Unreachable messages that the device has received. Receiving these messages indicates that the device is sending IP packets that could not be forwarded to a destination address. This could be for several reasons: the destination device is down, the destination address doesn't exist, or a route doesn't exist to the destination network.

What do you do next if you see a high number of ICMP Destination Unreachable messages being received by a device? It would be helpful if more MIB information were made available — such as the destination address and the source of the ICMP Destination Unreachable message. Unfortunately, it's not — so unless you've got a device that has been built by a vendor that had the foresight to make your life easier (by storing this information in a private MIB), you've got to use a protocol analyzer to capture the ICMP Destination Unreachable packets. And since the device could have quite a few interfaces, putting the analyzer on the right one and capturing the packets could be a challenge!

icmpInTimeExcds: number of ICMP Time Exceeded messages that the device has received. Receiving these messages means that the device is sending out IP packets whose time-to-live field expires before they reach their destination.

What do you do next? First you can check the configuration of the IP time-to-live parameter on this device. Next, if you can determine the intended destination address you can try to determine whether there's a routing loop between the device and the destination address.

Again, as with most of these counters, if additional information about the ICMP packets were made available through MIB objects, troubleshooting these problems would be a lot easier. And since this information is available in the ICMP messages being received (and sent), vendors should take it upon themselves to extend the MIB support in their devices so that they can more easily identify these types of routing problems.

icmpInParmProbs: count of ICMP Parameter Problem messages that the device has received. Receiving these messages indicates the device is sending out IP packets that have problems in the IP options portion of their IP headers. The first thing to do is check the IP configuration of this device; the next thing to do is get out the protocol analyzer.

icmpInSrcQuenchs: count of ICMP Source Quench messages that the device has received. Receiving these messages indicates that IP packets originated at this device are being processed by a router with resource problems. The first thing you need to do is identify the source of the ICMP Source Quench messages — and either expand the capacity of that router or figure out how to divert traffic away from that router.

icmpInRedirects: count of ICMP Redirect messages that the device has received. Receiving an ICMP Redirect message indicates the device is sending an IP packet to a router which then forwards it to another router on the same network. The easiest way to resolve this problem is to find the destination address of the packets that are causing the ICMP Redirect messages, and then examine the routing tables of this device as well as of the routers.

icmpInEchos: count of ICMP Echo Request messages received.

icmpInEchoReps: count of ICMP Echo Reply messages received.

icmpInTimestamps: count of ICMP Timestamp messages received.

icmpInTimestampReps: count of ICMP Timestamp Reply messages received.

icmpInAddrMasks: count of ICMP Address Mask Request messages received.

icmpInAddrMaskReps: count of ICMP Address Mask Reply messages received.

icmpOutMsgs: count of ICMP messages this device attempted to send.

icmpOutErrors: count of ICMP messages that this device did not send due to resource limitations.

icmpOutDestUnreachs: count of ICMP Destination unreachable messages sent by this device. This means the device is being asked to forward IP packets to a destination that it can't reach (for example, the distance to the destination network is infinity). Without belaboring the point too much, you need to obtain more information (for example, the destination address and the original source address) to troubleshoot this problem.

icmpOutTimeExcds: count of ICMP Time Exceeded messages sent by this device. This means the device is being asked to forward or process IP packets with a time-to-live value of zero.

icmpOutParmProb: count of ICMP Parameter Problem messages sent by this device. The potential sources of this problem are an option that is not implemented or an invalid option value. Again, to troubleshoot this problem you need to find the originator of these packets.

icmpOutSrcQuenchs: count of ICMP Source Quench messages sent by this device. This indicates IP packets are being (or in the danger of being) discarded due to resource limitations. The next step to resolving this problem is to check the device's memory capacity, buffer space allocation, CPU capacity, etc.

icmpOutRedirects: count of ICMP Redirect messages sent by this device. This indicates IP packets forwarded by this device could have taken a more direct route and bypassed this device altogether.

icmpOutEchos: count of ICMP Echo messages sent by this device.

icmpOutEchoReps: count of ICMP Echo Reply messages sent by this device.

icmpOutTimestamps: count of ICMP Timestamp messages sent by this device.

icmpOutTimestampReps: count of ICMP Timestamp Reply messages sent by this device.

icmpOutAddrMasks: count of ICMP Address Mask messages sent by this device.

icmpOutAddrMaskReps: count of ICMP Address Mask Reply messages sent by this device.

Receiving or sending out an occasional ICMP message is not necessarily indicative of a routing problem. However, if you're seeing

- a large number of ICMP error messages being received by a device compared to the number of IP packets that device is sending or forwarding,

- a large number of ICMP error messages being generated by a device compared to the number of IP packets that the device is receiving,

then you probably have a problem that you need to look into. The following expressions can be useful in helping to identify routing problems:

$$\frac{\text{rate(icmpInDestUnreachs)}}{\text{rate(ipOutRequests)}} \times 100 \qquad (3.17)$$

Expression (3.17) will give you an idea of what percent of IP packets a device is sending out to devices that can't be reached.

$$\frac{\text{rate(icmpInParmProbs)}}{\text{rate(ipOutRequests)}} \times 100 \tag{3.18}$$

Expression (3.18) will give you an idea of what percent of IP packets a device is sending out that have parameter problems.

$$\frac{\text{rate(icmpInTimeExcds)}}{\text{rate(ipOutRequests)}} \times 100 \tag{3.19}$$

Expression (3.19) will give you an idea of what percent of IP packets a device is sending out that never reach their destination because of the time-to-live field reaching zero.

$$\frac{\text{rate(icmpOutDestUnreachs)}}{\text{rate(ipInReceives)}} \times 100 \tag{3.20}$$

Expression (3.20) will give you an idea of what percent of IP packets a device receives that cannot be forwarded because the destination address can not be reached.

$$\frac{\text{rate(icmpOutParmProbs)}}{\text{rate(ipInReceives)}} \times 100 \tag{3.21}$$

Expression (3.21) will give you an idea of what percent of IP packets a device receives which have problems in the IP options portion of the IP header.

$$\frac{\text{rate(icmpOutTimeExcds)}}{\text{rate(ipInReceives)}} \times 100 \tag{3.22}$$

Expression (3.22) will give you an idea of what percent of IP packets a device receives which have their time-to-live field value set to zero.

ICMP Source Quench messages (both received and sent by a device) are a strong indication of resource limitations. With this, simply looking at the delta change in counter values is probably sufficient.

3.5 TCP Group

The TCP Group is made up of both scalar objects and a table of the TCP connections for a device.

Table 3-11 TCP Group Scalar Objects

Object	Type	Access
tcpRtoAlgorithm	INTEGER	read-only
tcpRtoMin	INTEGER	read-only
tcpRtoMax	INTEGER	read-only
tcpMaxConn	INTEGER	read-only
tcpActiveOpens	Counter	read-only
tcpPassiveOpens	Counter	read-only
tcpAttemptFails	Counter	read-only
tcpEstabResets	Counter	read-only
tcpCurrEstab	Gauge	read-only
tcpInSegs	Counter	read-only
tcpOutSegs	Counter	read-only
tcpRetransSegs	Counter	read-only
tcpInErrs	Counter	read-only
tcpOutRsts	Counter	read-only

tcpRtoAlgorithm: algorithm used to determine the timeout value for retransmissions. Values are

- other (1)
- constant (2)
- rsre (3), MIL-STD-1778
- vanj (4), Van Jacobson's algorithm

tcpRtoMin: minimum retransmission timeout in milliseconds.

tcpRtoMax: maximum retransmission timeout in milliseconds.

tcpMaxConn: maximum number of TCP connections allowed. A value of -1 indicates the maximum number of TCP connections is dynamic.

tcpActiveOpens: count of times TCP connections have transitioned from the CLOSED state to the SYN-SENT state.

tcpPassiveOpens: count of times TCP connections have transitioned from the LISTEN state to the SYN-RCVD state.

tcpAttemptFails: count of failed connection attempts.

tcpEstabResets: count of times connections have reset.

tcpCurrEstab: number of current connections.

tcpInSegs: count of segments received.

tcpOutSegs: count of segments sent.

tcpRetransSegs: count of segments retransmitted.

tcpInErrs: number of received segments discarded due to errors (such as bad TCP checksums).

tcpOutRsts: number of segments sent with the RST (reset) flag.

The TCP Connection Table (tcpConnTable) maintains information about a device's existing TCP connection information.

Table 3-12 tcpConnTable, Indexed by
tcpConnLocalAddress.tcpConnLocalPort.tcpConnRemAddress.tcpConnRem.Port

Object	Type	Access
tcpConnState	INTEGER	read-write
tcpConnLocalAddress	IpAddress	read-only
tcpConnLocalPort	INTEGER	read-only
tcpConnRemAddress	IpAddress	read-only
tcpConnRemPort	INTEGER	read-only

tcpConnState: connection state. This can have one of the following values:

- `closed` (1)
- `listen` (2)
- `synSent` (3)
- `synReceived` (4)
- `established` (5)
- `finWait1` (6)
- `finWait2` (7)
- `closeWait` (8)
- `lastAck` (9)
- `closing` (10)
- `timeWait` (11)
- `deleteTCB` (12), this is the only value that can be set by a management station. Setting this will result in the immediate termination of the associated TCP connection.

tcpConnLocalAddress: local IP address.

tcpConnLocalPort: local TCP port.

tcpConnRemAddress: remote IP address.

tcpConnRemPort: remote TCP port.

Dumping a TCP connection table produces results like this:

Table 3-13   portion of a tcpConnTable dump

State	Local Address	Local Port	Remote Address	Remote Port
established (5)	207.180.134.9	80	196.27.12.75	2191
established (5)	207.180.134.9	80	196.27.12.75	2453
timeWait (11)	207.180.134.9	80	196.27.12.75	16433
timeWait (11)	205.181.132.10	80	142.177.186.1	3518
timeWait (11)	205.181.132.10	80	142.177.186.1	3519

From this dump you can see five Web connections (TCP port 80). Two of the connections are active, three of the connections are in the Time-Wait state (waiting to terminate the connection).

There are quite a few applications today that try to determine network delay by periodically sending ICMP Echo messages from a network management station to server machines and and measuring the roundtrip delay. By doing this every fifteen minutes or so and saving the roundtrip information to a database, the applications try to understand what the average network delay to a server is, and what the typical delay is at different times of the day. Of course, what they're really measuring is not the network delay clients are seeing, but the delay from the network management workstation to the server.

What would be interesting is to have an application running on a server which periodically reads the TCP Connection Table and performs ICMP Echo tests to the server's active clients. This would provide the actual network delay clients are seeing, as opposed to trying to extrapolate this delay from the workstation-server measurements.

Note: You could run this mythical application on a workstation on the same LAN segment as the server and get roughly the same measurements.

3.6 UDP Group

The UDP Group contains four scalar objects and a UDP Listener Table (udpTable).

Table 3-14   UDP Scalar Objects

Object	Type	Access
udpInDatagrams	Counter	read-only
udpNoPorts	Counter	read-only
udpInErrors	Counter	read-only
udpOutDatagrams	Counter	read-only

udpInDatagrams: UDP datagrams delivered to UDP users

udpNoPorts: received UDP datagrams for which there was no application at the destination port.

udpInErrors:UDP datagrams discarded due to format errors.

udpOutDatagrams: count of UDP packets sent from this device.

The UDP listener table maintains information about UDP ports for which local applications are accepting datagrams.

Table 3-15   udpTable, Indexed by udpLocalAddress.udpLocalPort

Object	Type	Access
udpLocalAddress	IpAddress	read-only
udpLocalPort	INTEGER	read-only

udpLocalAddress: local IP address.

udpLocalPort: local UDP port.

An application which periodically reads this table from different server machines can help check that required UDP applications are indeed running on those machines.

3.7 Transmission Group

The transmission group is really a place-holder for media-specific MIBs. The following are examples of some of the MIBs that have been defined under the transmission group:

- RFC 1650 — Ethernet-Like MIB
- RFC 1315 — Frame Relay MIB
- RFC 1512 — FDDI MIB
- RFC 2127 — ISDN MIB
- RFC 1382 — X.25 MIB
- RFC 1660 — Parallel Printer-like MIB
- RFC 1659 — RS232 MIB
- RFC 1381 — LAPB MIB
- RFC 1406 — DS1 MIB
- RFC 1407 — DS3 MIB
- RFC 1471 — PPP/LCP MIB
- RFC 1595 — SONET MIB
- RFC 1748 — Token Ring MIB

3.8 SNMP Group

The SNMP group contains scalar objects for understanding how busy a device's SNMP agent is, what type of errors the agent is seeing, and how much SNMP traffic a network management station is creating.

Table 3-16   SNMP Group

Object	Type	Access
snmpInPkts	Counter	read-only
snmpOutPkts	Counter	read-only
snmpInBadVersions	Counter	read-only
snmpInBadCommunityNames	Counter	read-only
snmpInBadCommunityUses	Counter	read-only
snmpInASNParseErrs	Counter	read-only

Table 3-16   SNMP Group

Object	Type	Access
snmpInTooBigs	Counter	read-only
snmpInNoSuchNames	Counter	read-only
snmpInBadValues	Counter	read-only
snmpInReadOnlys	Counter	read-only
snmpInGenErrs	Counter	read-only
snmpInTotalReqVars	Counter	read-only
snmpInTotalSetVars	Counter	read-only
snmpInGetRequests	Counter	read-only
snmpInGetNexts	Counter	read-only
snmpInSetRequests	Counter	read-only
snmpInGetResponses	Counter	read-only
snmpInTraps	Counter	read-only
snmpOutTooBigs	Counter	read-only
snmpOutNoSuchNames	Counter	read-only
snmpOutBadValues	Counter	read-only
snmpOutGenErrs	Counter	read-only
snmpOutGetRequests	Counter	read-only
snmpOutGetNexts	Counter	read-only
snmpOutSetRequests	Counter	read-only
snmpOutGetResponses	Counter	read-only
snmpOutTraps	Counter	read-only
snmpEnableAuthenTraps	INTEGER	read-write

Ocassionally collecting some of these objects from network devices can give you some idea of how much work your network management applications are adding to these devices. Similarly, collecting some of these objects from the workstations running the network management applications (assuming these workstations have SNMP agents running on them) can give you some idea of how much SNMP traffic the network management applications are generating.

Some of these objects are more meaningful if collected from network devices than a network management workstation. These objects will be marked by an (N). The objects that are more meaningful if collected from a workstation will be marked by a (W). The objects that make sense for either will be marked by a (B).

snmpInPkts: count of SNMP messages received. (B)

snmpOutPkts: count of SNMP messages sent. (B)

snmpInBadVersions: count of SNMP messages received for SNMP versions that the agent doesn't support. (N)

snmpInBadCommunityNames: count of SNMP messages received with community names that were unknown. (N)

snmpInBadCommunityUses: count of SNMP messages received that were for operations not allowed given the supplied community name. For example, a Set operation where the read community name was provided. (N)

snmpInASNParseErrs: count of SNMP messages received with ASN.1 or BER errors. (N)

snmpInTooBigs: count of PDUs received with error-status of `tooBig`. (W)

snmpInNoSuchNames: count of PDUs received with error-status `noSuchName`. (W)

snmpInBadValues: count of PDUs received with error-status `badValue`. (W)

snmpInReadOnlys: count of PDUs received with error-status `readOnly`. (W)

snmpInGenErrs: count of PDUs received with error-status `genErr`. (W)

snmpInTotalReqVars: count of MIB objects that have been retrieved through SNMP Get-Request and Get-Next PDUs. (N)

snmpInTotalSetVars: count of MIB objects that have been modified through SNMP Set-Request PDUs. (N)

snmpInGetRequests: count of SNMP Get-Request PDUs that have been accepted and processed by the device. (N)

snmpInGetNexts: count of SNMP Get-Next PDUs that have been accepted and processed by the device. (N)

snmpInSetRequests: count of SNMP Set-Request PDUs that have been accepted and processed by the device. (N)

snmpInGetResponses: count of SNMP Get-Response PDUs that have been accepted and processed by the device. (W)

snmpInTraps: count of SNMP Trap PDUs that have been accepted and processed by the device. (W)

snmpOutTooBigs: count of PDUs sent with error-status of `tooBig`. (N)

snmpOutNoSuchNames: count of PDUs sent with error-status of `noSuchName`. (N)

snmpOutBadValues: count of PDUs sent with error-status of `badValue`. (N)

snmpOutGenErrs: count of PDUs sent with error-status of `genErr`. (N)

snmpOutGetRequests: count of SNMP Get-Request PDUs sent. (W)

snmpOutGetNexts: count of SNMP Get-Next PDUs sent. (W)

snmpOutSetRequests: count of SNMP Set-Request PDUs sent. (W)

snmpOutGetResponses: count of SNMP Get-Response PDUs sent. (N)

snmpOutTraps: count of SNMP Traps that have been sent. (N)

snmpEnableAuthenTraps: is used to configure whether the SNMP agent should generate authenticationFailure traps. Possible values that can be written are `enabled` (1) or `disabled` (2). *Note*: SNMPv3 provides a standard way to configure the addresses to send notifications to. Prior to SNMPv3, specifying which network management stations to send traps to needed to be done in a proprietary way.

3.9 Extensions to MIB-II

As we stated at the beginning of this chapter, nearly all the MIB-II groups have been moved into other documents. The following table shows the MIB-II groups and the documents that they have been moved into.

Table 3-17   MIB-II Groups and the Documents They Have Been Moved To

Group	Document
system	RFC 1907
interfaces	RFC 2233
ip	RFC 2021
IP Routing Table	IP Forwarding MIB (RFC 2096)
icmp	RFC 2011
udp	RFC 2012
snmp	RFC 1907

Part of the SNMPv2 defintion, RFC 1907, added objects to the following MIB-II groups:

• System Group — an object resource table was added to describe the SNMPv2 entity's (statically and dynamically configurable) support of various MIB modules.

• SNMP group — two additional Scalar objects were added, along with obsoleting previous SNMP group objects.

3.9.1   System Group Changes

A new scalar object, sysORLastChange, and table object, sysORTable, were added to the System group.

> **sysORLastChange**: is defined with syntax TimeStamp and has read-only access. This is the value of sysUpTime when sysORTable was last changed.

The sysORTable describes an SNMPv2 entity's (statically and dynamically configurable) support of various MIB modules.

Table 3-18   sysORTable, Indexed by sysORIndex

Object	Type	Access
sysORIndex	INTEGER	not-accessible
sysORID	OBJECT IDENTIFIER	read-only
sysORDescr	DisplayString	read-only
sysORUpTime	TimeStamp	read-only

sysORIndex: unique integer used to identify rows in sysORTable.

sysORID: object ID of this entry. You can think of this as being analogous to the sysObjectID object.

sysORDescr: textual description of the object resource.

sysORUpTime: value of sysUpTime when this row was last instantiated.

3.9.2   Redefinition of the SNMP Group

RFC 1907 redefines the SNMP Group as follows:

Table 3-19   SNMPv2 Redefinition of the SNMP Group

Object	Type	Access
snmpInPkts	Counter32	read-only
snmpInBadVersions	Counter32	read-only
snmpInBadCommunityNames	Counter32	read-only
snmpInBadCommunityUses	Counter32	read-only
snmpInASNParseErrs	Counter32	read-only
snmpEnableAuthenTraps	INTEGER	read-write
snmpSilentDrops	Counter32	read-only
snmpProxyDrops	Counter32	read-only

The two new scalar objects defined are

> **snmpSilentDrops**: total number of GetRequest-PDUs, GetNextRequest-PDUs, GetBulkRequest-PDUs, SetRequest-PDUs, and InformRequest-PDUs delivered to the SNMP entity which were silently dropped because the size of a reply containing an alternate Response-PDU with an empty variable-bindings field was greater than (a) a local constraint or (b) the maximum message size that the originator of the request can handle.

> **snmpProxyDrops**: total number of GetRequest-PDUs, GetNextRequest-PDUs, GetBulkRequest-PDUs, SetRequest-PDUs, and InformRequest-PDUs delivered to the SNMP entity which were silently dropped because a response could not be returned by a proxy target. This does not include proxy messages that failed because of timeouts.

Quite a few of the original MIB-II snmp group objects were defined as obsolete by RFC 1907. This means that these objects should not be implemented. The reason for marking these objects as obsolete was because it was decided that they are not essential to debugging real problems and that they unnecessarily add to the size of an agent. Considering the number of managed objects in most private MIB trees, this seems kind of dubious. While the objects that had been marked as obsolete may not necessarily aid in debugging problems, some of them are useful in helping to understand how an agent is behaving.

So where does that leave you? Well, most agent implementations out there are still SNMPv1 so for most devices these objects can still be collected. As time moves on, and assuming SNMPv3 gains acceptance, they will disappear.

3.9.3   Information Relating to SNMPv2 Notifications

RFC 1907 defines a group snmpTrap with two objects:

snmpTrapOID: value of the object identifier of the trap or notification that is being sent. The value of this object is the second varbind in SNMPv2-Trap and Inform Request PDUs.

SNMPv1 generic traps have been mapped to the following object identifier values:

coldStart ::= {snmpTraps 1}
warmStart ::= {snmpTraps 2}
linkDown ::= {snmpTraps 3}
linkUp ::= {snmpTraps 4}
authenticationFailure ::= {snmpTraps 5}
egpNeighborLoss ::= {snmpTraps 6}

where snmpTraps has been mapped to the value {snmpMIBObjects 5}.

For example, linkDown will have a value of 1.3.6.1.6.3.1.1.5.3. If the second varbind in an SNMPv2-Trap PDU is this value, the trap is a linkDown.

snmpTrapEnterprise: object identifier of the enterprise associated with the trap being sent. When an SNMPv2 proxy agent maps an SNMPv1 Trap into an SNMPv2-Trap PDU, it will add this variable as the last varbind.

3.9.3.1   SNMPv2 Lock Object

SNMPv2 defines an snmpSet subtree with the value:

{internet (1) snmpV2 (6) snmpModules (3) snmpMIB (1) snmpMIBObjects (1) snmpSet (6)}

There is one object defined under this tree that is used to coordinate SNMP set operations between network management stations.

> **snmpSetSerialNo**: is defined as a TestAndIncr object with read-write access. If a network management application wants to modify or create management data it should first read this object and then include it within an SNMP set operation. This guarantees that another network management application or workstation isn't trying to modify data at the same time.

3.9.4   Interfaces MIB

The Interfaces MIB (RFC 2233) redefines, with a few minor modifications, the interfaces group from MIB-II. It also introduces four new tables, two of which we will discuss here. The Interfaces MIB addresses several weaknesses with the interfaces group. Specifically, it provides for:

- separate counters for broadcast and multicast packets

- 64-bit counters for ifTable 32-bit counters that could wrap quickly at high transmission rates (such as with gigabit Ethernet interfaces).

- interface speeds greater than 2.2 Gbps. The current definition of ifSpeed allows for a maximum transmission rate of 2^{31}-1 (2,147,483,647)).

- a way to map virtual interfaces on top of physical interfaces.

- new interface types. By separating ifType enumerated values from MIB-II, new interface types can be added more easily.

- dynamically adding and deleting interfaces.

An extension to the ifTable, ifXTable, addresses the first three issues. An Interface Stack Table (ifStackTable) addresses the fourth. Minor definition changes to the interfaces group address the remaining issues.

A new description clause for ifIndex allows the numbering scheme for interfaces to not be restricted to 1 through the value of ifNumber. This change supports the dynamic addition and deletion of interfaces.

Other changes to the MIB-II ifTable definitions include

- additional values defined for ifOperStatus. The new values are

  • unknown (4), value if status cannot be determined.
  • dormant (5)
  • notPresent (6), some component is down.
  • lowerLayerDown (7). An interface will have this value if it is stacked on top of a lower-layer interface (such as a frame relay circuit stacked on top of a WAN interface) and the lower-layer interface is down.

- Because of new counters defined in the ifXTable, several objects were deprecated. These objects are ifInNUcastPkts and ifOutNUcastPkts. The object ifSpecific has been deprecated because there was never any real use for it. The object ifOutQLen has also been deprecated.

- ifType has been redefined to be of type IANAifType. Additional values for ifType are assigned by the Internet Assigned Numbers Authority (IANA) by updating the IANAifType-MIB. This MIB is updated periodically and can be found at

  ftp://ftp.iana.org/mib/ianaiftype.mib

Also, a new object, ifTableLastChange, has been added to the interfaces group. This object is defined as a TimeTicks with read-only access and provides the value of sysUpTime at the time the last entry was created or deleted from the ifTable. The value will be 0 if no entries have been added or deleted since the SNMP entity was last restarted.

3.9.4.1   ifXTable

Table 3-20   ifXTable, Indexed by ifIndex

Object	Type	Access
ifName	DisplayString	read-only
ifInMulticastPkts	Counter32	read-only
ifInBroadcastPkts	Counter32	read-only
ifOutMulticastPkts	Counter32	read-only

Table 3-20   ifXTable, Indexed by ifIndex (Continued)

Object	Type	Access
ifOutBroadcastPkts	Counter32	read-only
ifHCInOctets	Counter64	read-only
ifHCInUcastPkts	Counter64	read-only
ifHCInMulticastPkts	Counter64	read-only
ifHCInBroadcastPkts	Counter64	read-only
ifHCOutOctets	Counter64	read-only
ifHCOutUcastPkts	Counter64	read-only
ifHCOutMulticastPkts	Counter64	read-only
ifHCOutBroadcastPkts	Counter64	read-only
ifLinkUpDownTrapEnable	INTEGER	read-write
ifHighSpeed	Gauge32	read-only
ifPromiscuousMode	TruthValue	read-write
ifConnectorPresent	TruthValue	read-write
ifAlias	DisplayString	read-write
ifCounterDiscontinuityTime	TimeStamp	read-only

ifName: used to name the interface. It might be something like "le0" or a simple port number, such as "1" — or even a slot-port number, such a s "1.1." If several entries in the ifTable represent a single interface, then each will have the same value of ifName.

Note: For an agent which responds to SNMP queries for an interface on some other device, then the value of ifName for this interface should be the proxied device's local name for it.

If there is no local name, or this object is for some reason not applicable, then this object will be a zero-length string.

ifInMulticastPkts: count of multicast packets received.

ifInBroadcastPkts: count of broadcast packets received.

ifOutMulticastPkts: count of multicast packets requested to be sent. This includes packets that are discarded due to resource limitations.

ifOutBroadcastPkts: count of broadcast packets requested to be sent. This includes packets that are discarded due to resource limitations.

ifHCInOctets, ifHCInUcastPkts, ifHCInMulticastPkts, ifHCInBroadcastPkts, ifHCOutOctets, ifHCOutUcastPkts, ifHCOutMulticastPkts, ifHCOutBroadcastPkts: high-capacity (64-bit) counter versions of the previously defined 32-bit ifTable counters.

ifLinkUpDownTrapEnable: used to configure whether linkUp/linkDown traps should be generated for this interface. It can be configured to either enabled (1) or disabled (2).

ifHighSpeed: estimate of the interface's current bandwidth in units of 1,000,000 bits per second. For example, an Ethernet interface will have a value of 10, a gigabit interface a value of 1000.

ifPromiscuousMode: used to configure whether an interface is in promiscuous mode. It can be configured to either true (1) or false (2). When an interface is in promiscuous mode it accepts all packets/frames transmitted on the media. When not in promiscuous mode, it accepts only the packets/frames that are addressed to its station. By putting an interface in promiscuous mode, you can see all the packets on the wire — which can be helpful in troubleshooting network problems.

ifConnectorPresent: a value of true (1) indicates that a physical connector is present; otherwise false (2).

ifAlias: text value that a network manager can set. For example, for a frame relay circuit the network manager may set this to the dlci number. Any agent that supports write access to this object is required to keep the value in non-volatile storage.

ifCouterDiscontinuityTime: last value of sysUpTime when one or more of this interface's counters suffered a discontinuity. If no discontinuities have occurred since the agent was last reinitialized, then this value will be zero.

3.9.4.2   ifStackTable

The ifStackTable shows the relationships between different sublayers of network interfaces. In particular, it contains information on which sublayers run "on top of" which other sublayers, where each sub-layer corresponds to a conceptual row in the ifTable.

The ifStackTable allows virtual interfaces to be layered on top of physical interfaces. The MIB definition doesn't make a distinction between physical and virtual interfaces; instead it references higher and lower sublayers. In practice, the higher sublayer will reference a virtual circuit such as a frame relay circuit or an ATM permanent virtual circuit, and the lower sublayer will reference a physical circuit such as a WAN interface.

A row in the ifStackTable has three objects:

ifStackHigherLayer: value of the ifIndex corresponding to the higher sublayer of the relationship (e.g., the virtual interface).

ifStackLowerLayer: value of the ifIndex corresponding to the lower sublayer of the relationship (e.g., the physical interface).

ifStackStatus: a RowStatus object used to add or destroy rows (where appropriate) to this table.

Neither ifStackHigherLayer or ifStackLowerLayer are accessible through the table — both are used as indexes into this table.

As an example, the ifTable has a serial interface with an ifIndex value of 4. Frame relay circuits have been defined to run over this interface, with ifIndex values 2001, 2002, 2003 (each ifIndex references a different dlci). Walking the ifStackStatus objects in the table, we might see

ifStackStatus.0.4 = active
ifStackStatus.4.0 = active
ifStackStatus.2001.4 = active
ifStackStatus.2002.4 = active
ifStackStatus.2003.4 = active

3.9.5   IP Forwarding Table MIB

The IP Routing Table (ipRouteTable) has been replaced by the IP Forwarding MIB (RFC 2096). In reality, most if not all devices that support routing are still implementing the ipRouteTable. Also, there are a quite a few devices which support routing which have not yet implemented the IP CIDR (Classless Inter-Domain Routing) Route Table , which makes both the ipRouteTable and the ipForwardTable obsolete.

One of the major weaknesses of the ipRouteTable is that you can have multiple routing paths to a destination address, but the ipRouteTable is only indexed by the destination address. The ipForwardTable was defined in RFC 1354 to address this problem. The ipCidrRouteTable refines the ipForwardTable by removing the protocol type as an index into the table and adding the subnet mask as an index to the table. It also provides a RowStatus object to standardize adding and removing rows from the table.

So what does all this mean? For the time being you will have to rely on the ipRouteTable, and over time you will need to modify your applications to use the ipCidrRouteTable. We will show the ipCidrRouteTable here.

Table 3-21   ipCidrRouteTable, Indexed by
ipCidrRouteDest.ipCidrRouteMask.ipCidrRouteTos.ipCidrRouteNextHop

Object	Type	Access
ipCidrRouteDest	IpAddress	read-only
ipCidrRouteMask	IpAddress	read-only
ipCidrRouteTos	Integer32	read-only
ipCidrRouteNextHop	IpAddress	read-only
ipCidrRouteIfIndex	Integer32	read-create
ipCidrRouteType	INTEGER	read-create
ipCidrRouteProto	INTEGER	read-only
ipCidrRouteAge	Integer32	read-only
ipCidrRouteInfo	OBJECT IDENTIFIER	read-create
ipCidrRouteNextHopAS	Integer32	read-create
ipCidrRouteMetric1	Integer32	read-create

Table 3-21   ipCidrRouteTable, Indexed by
ipCidrRouteDest.ipCidrRouteMask.ipCidrRouteTos.ipCidrRouteNextHop

Object	Type	Access
ipCidrRouteMetric2	Integer32	read-create
ipCidrRouteMetric3	Integer32	read-create
ipCidrRouteMetric4	Integer32	read-create
ipCidrRouteMetric5	Integer32	read-create
ipCidrRouteStatus	RowStatus	read-create

ipCidrRouteDest: destination IP address of this route.

ipCidrRouteMask: subnet-mask for route. The value of this object logically ANDed with the destination address should be compared to ipCidrRouteDest.

ipCidrRouteTos: the IP Type Of Service (TOS) Field is used to specify the routing policy. A value of zero indicates the default path if no more specific policy applies.

ipCidrRouteNextHop: for a remote route, this is the address of the next system en route to the destination address; otherwise, 0.0.0.0.

ipCidrRouteIfIndex: this identifies the interface through which the next hop is reached by.

ipCidrRouteType: type of route. It can have one of four values:

• other (1)

• reject (2), route which discards traffic as unreachable.

• local (3), route to a directly connected subnetwork. This indicates the next hop if a final destination.

• remote (4), route to a remote destination.

ipCidrRouteProto: mechanism used to learn the route. This has the same enumerations as ipRouteProto, with two additional values added:

- idpr (15) — InterDomain Policy Routing
- ciscoEigrp (16) — Cisco EIGRP

ipCidrRouteAge: number of seconds since route was last updated or determined to be correct.

ipCidrRouteInfo: reference to MIB definitions specific to the particular routing protocol identified by the ipCidrRouteProto value. If this information is not present, its value should be set to the OBJECT IDENTIFIER { 0 0 }.

ipCidrRouteNextHopAS: Autonomous System Number of the Next Hop.

ipCidrRouteMetric1: primary routing metric for this route.

ipCidrRouteMetric2: an alternate routing metric for this route.

ipCidrRouteMetric3: an alternate routing metric for this route.

ipCidrRouteMetric4: an alternate routing metric for this route.

ipCidrRouteMetric5: an alternate routing metric for this route.

ipCidrRouteStatus: a RowStatus object used to add/remove entries to/from this table.

3.10 Summary

This chapter first showed most of the objects defined by MIB-II (RFC 1213) and gave suggestions of how they can be used to do useful stuff. The address translation table and the egp group were ignored because they are in the process of going away and are not really being used anymore.

This chapter next showed the changes that have been made to these MIB groups as they have been moved into other documents. In reality, most (if not all) devices continue to support the standard MIB-II groups. Over time this will change, and the new Interfaces MIB (RFC 2233) and the new IP Forwarding Table MIB (RFC 2096) will be more widely implemented. For now, though, network management applications will need to determine which MIBs a device has implemented and use either the MIB-II definitions from RFC 1213, or the updated MIBs.

CHAPTER 4

SNMPv3 Framework

$\mathbf{T}$his chapter will describe the architecture that the SNMPv3 Framework is defined under. It will also show new textual conventions that have been defined for SNMPv3, along with a new SNMPv3 message format. The goal for this chapter is to prepare the reader for the following SNMPv3 chapters covering notification and proxy forwarding configuration, security, and view-based access control.

4.1 Architecture Overview

An architecture was originally defined by RFC 2271 for describing SNMP Management Frameworks, and the SNMPv3 Framework is a concrete "instantiation" of this architecture. Conceptually SNMPv3 is nothing more than an extension of SNMP to address two major areas, administration and security. A major goal for SNMPv3, though, is to support a module architecture that can be easily extended. This way, for example, if new security protocols are advanced they can be supported by SNMPv3 by defining them as separate modules. Hopefully this will allow us to avoid having to buy books on SNMPv4 in the future.

How important is it to understand this architecture in order to use SNMPv3? Probably not terribly. However, the SNMPv3 Framework is fairly simple and introduces some terminology that will be used later on.

What we used to call SNMP Agents and SNMP Managers, we now call an SNMP entity. An SNMP entity is made up of two pieces: an SNMP engine and SNMP applications.

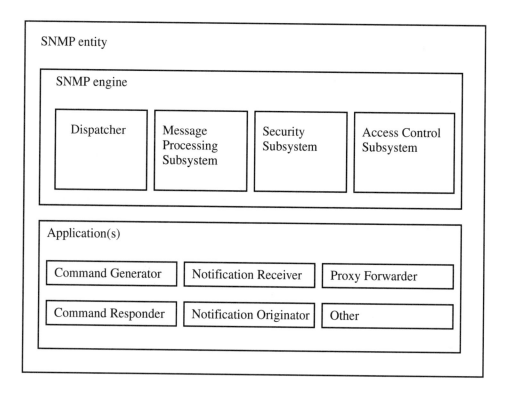

4.1.1   SNMP Engine

As you can see from the above diagram, an SNMP engine is made up of the following components:

- Dispatcher
- Message Processing Subsystem
- Security Subsystem
- Access Control Subsystem

4.1.1.1   Dispatcher

The Dispatcher is responsible for sending and receiving messages. When a message is received, the Dispatcher tries to determine the version number of the message and then passes the message to the appropriate Message Processing Model. If the message cannot be parsed so that the version can be determined, then the snmpInASNParseErrs counter is incremented and the message is discarded. If the version is not supported by the Message Processing Subsystem, then the snmpInBadVersions counter is incremented and the message is discarded. The dispatcher is also responsible for dispatching PDUs to applications, and for selecting the appropriate transports for sending messages.

4.1.1.2   Message Processing Subsystem

The Message Processing Subsystem is made up of one or more Message Processing Models. The following diagram shows a Message Processing Subsystem that supports models for SNMPv3, SNMPv1, SNMPv2c, and something that we will call "Other."

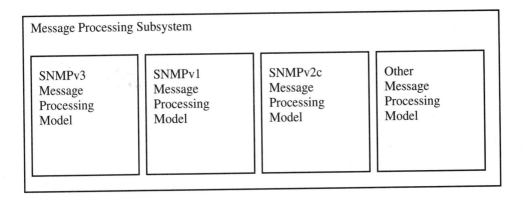

The Message Processing Subsystem is responsible for

1. Preparing messages to be sent.
2. Extracting data from received messages.

Let's walk through a simple case where the Dispatcher receives a valid SNMPv3 message from the line. The Dispatcher determines the version of the message and forwards it to the SNMPv3 Message Processing Model. The SNMPv3 Message Processing Model then processes the message by extracting information from it. It then calls the Security Subsystem to decrypt the data portion of the message (if needed) and make sure the message is properly authenticated. At that point the Dispatcher will forward the PDU portion of the message to the appropriate SNMP application (more about that later).

This architecture allows additional models (like "Other") to be added. These additional models may be enterprise specific or future standards. In any case, the Dispatcher will need to be able to parse the messages to determine the version (and then map the version number to a Message Processing Model).

4.1.1.3   Security Subsystem

The Security Subsystem provides security services such as

1. Authenticating messages.
2. Encrypting/decrypting messages for privacy.

The following diagram shows a Security Subsystem that supports models for SNMPv3, a Community-based Model, and something we will call "Other." The Community-based Model would support SNMPv1 and SNMPv2c.

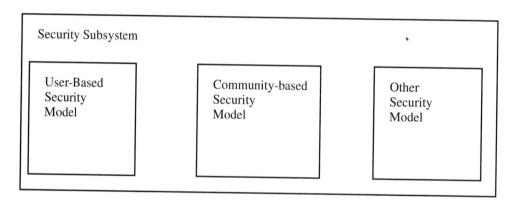

A Security Model defines among other things

1. The security threats against which it protects.
2. The services it provides.
3. The security protocols used to provide services such as authentication and privacy.

The User-Based Security Model will be described in detail in the SNMPv3 security chapter. It protects SNMPv3 messages from the following potential security threats:

• An authorized user sends a message that gets modified in transit by an unauthorized SNMP entity. For example, an authorized user may send a message to set the operational state of a port to up. Someone might maliciously try to capture the message, modify it so the message sets the operational state of the port to testing, and then put the message back on the wire.

- An unauthorized user trying to masquerade as an authorized user. For example, someone might try to perform management operations (such as change the operational state of a port) that they don't have authorization for by pretending to be an authorized user.
- Modifying the message stream. SNMP is typically based on UDP, which is a connection-less transport service. Messages could potentially be captured and reordered, delayed, or possibly replayed at a later time. For example, if a Set operation were captured and replayed in the future, it could conceivably change the desired configuration. By checking the timeliness of messages, this threat can be minimized.
- Eavesdropping. By allowing messages to be encrypted, someone eavesdropping on the line won't be able to make sense of what they see. This feature is essential for carriers that need to protect against sensitive data, such as billing information, from being eaves-dropped on.

The User-Based Security model currently defines the use of HMAC-MD5-96 and HMAC-SHA-96 as the possible authentication protocols and CBC-DES as the privacy protocol. Future authentication and privacy protocols may be added.

SNMPv1 and SNMPv2c Security Models provide only weak authentication (community names) and no privacy.

This architecture allows additional Security Models (like "Other") to be added. These additional models may be enterprise specific or future standards. Authentication and privacy protocols supported by Security Models are uniquely identified using Object Identifiers. Any IETF standard protocols for authentication should have an identifier defined within the snmpAuthProtocols subtree. Any IETF standard protocols for privacy should have an identifier defined within the snmpPrivProtocols subtree. Enterprise specific protocols should have their identifiers defined within the enterprise subtree.

The snmpAuthProtocols subtree is defined as

{iso (1) org (3) dod (6) internet (1) snmpV2 (6) snmpModules (3) snmpFrameworkMIB (10) snmpFrameworkAdmin (1) snmpAuthProtocols (1)} or, 1.3.6.1.6.3.10.1.1

usmHMACMD5AuthProtocol identifies the HMAC-MD5-96 authentication protocol and has the value {snmpAuthProtocols 2}.

usmHMACSHAAuthProtocol identifies the HMAC-SHA-96 authentication protocol and has the value {snmpAuthProtocols 3}.

The snmpPrivProtocols subtree is defined as 1.3.6.1.6.3.10.1.2.

usmDESPrivProtocol identifies the CBC-DES symmetric encryption protocol and has the value {snmpPrivProtocols 2}.

4.1.1.4   Access Control Subsystem

The responsibility of the Access Control Subsystem is straightforward: determine whether access to a managed object should be allowed. Currently one access control model, View-Based Access Control Model (VACM), has been defined. VACM will be described in detail the SNMPv3 View-Based Access Control chapter. As the following diagram shows, the SNMPv3 Framework allows additional Access Control Models to be defined in the future.

```
+-----------------------------------------------------------------------+
| Access Control Subsystem                                              |
|   +------------------+   +------------------+   +------------------+  |
|   | View-Based       |   | Other            |   | Other            |  |
|   | Access           |   | Access           |   | Access           |  |
|   | Control          |   | Control          |   | Control          |  |
|   | Model            |   | Model            |   | Model            |  |
|   |                  |   |                  |   |                  |  |
|   +------------------+   +------------------+   +------------------+  |
+-----------------------------------------------------------------------+
```

As we will be seeing later, with VACM you can control which users and which operations can have access to which managed objects.

So within the SNMPv3 Framework, who calls the Access Control Subsystem? Any SNMP application which needs to access managed objects. Currently that would be any Command Responder or Notification Originator application. What that means in simpler terms:

1. When an SNMP Get, Get-Next, Get-Bulk, or Set PDU is being processed, the Access Control Subsystem needs to be called to make sure the MIB objects specified within the variable bindings are allowed to be accessed.

2. When a Notification (either an SNMPv2-trap or Inform) is being generated, the Access Control Subsystem needs to be called to make sure the MIB objects specified for the variable bindings are allowed to be accessed.

4.1.2   Applications

For SNMPv3, when we refer to applications, we are referring to internal applications within an SNMP entity as opposed to what you might normally think of, such as a network management application to do trending or configuration. These internal applications do things like generate SNMP messages, respond to received SNMP messages, generate notifications, receive notifications, and forward messages between SNMP entitites. Currently there are five types of applications defined:

1. Command Generators — generate SNMP commands to collect or set management data.
2. Command Responders — provide access to management data. For example, processing Get, Get-Next, Get-Bulk and Set PDUs are done by a Command Responder application.
3. Notification Originators — initiate Trap or Inform messages.
4. Notification Receivers — receive and process Trap or Inform messages.
5. Proxy Forwarders — forward messages between SNMP entities.

The SNMPv3 Framework allows other applications to be defined over time. From this list, you can see that Command Generators and Notification Receivers are what we used to think of as part of an SNMP Manager, while Command Responders and Notification Originators are what we used to think of as part of an SNMP Agent.

4.2 New Textual Conventions

4.2.1   SnmpEngineID

This type is used to represent an SNMP engine's administratively unique identifier. Since each SNMP entity contains a single SNMP engine, this will also uniquely identify an SNMP entity within an administrative domain.

An SnmpEngineID resolves to an OCTET STRING between 5 and 32 bytes long. If the first bit of an SnmpEngineID value is 0, then the value was supplied by the vendor and has the following format:

1. The first four octets are set to the device's SNMP management private enterprise number as assigned by the Internet Assigned Numbers Authority (IANA). For example, Cisco's private enterprise number is 9. For a Cisco device the first four octets would be assigned "00000009."
2. The following 8 bytes are assigned in an enterprise-specific method. For example, a ven-

dor may use the IP address of the entity padded with 4 random bytes. Or it may use a MAC address padded with 2 random bytes. Or could use one of several different proprietary methods.

If the first bit of an SnmpEngineID is 1, then the value has the following format:

1. The first four octets are set to the device's SNMP management private enterprise number as assigned by the Internet Assigned Numbers Authority (IANA),with the first bit being set to 1. For example, Cisco's private enterprise number is 9. For a Cisco device the first four octets would be assigned "80000009."
2. The fifth octet is used to indicate how the rest of the octets are used. Its values are

   - 0, reserved.
   - 1, the following four octets are an IPv4 address. The IP address used is the lowest, non-special address assigned to the device.
   - 2, the following sixteen octets are an IPv6 address. The IP address used is the lowest, non-special address assigned to the device.
   - 3, the following six octets are a MAC address. The MAC address used is the lowest MAC address assigned to the device. It is represented in canonical order.
   - 4, the remaining octets are administratively assigned text. The length of the text is enterprise specific and can be at most 27 octets.
   - 5, the remaining octets are administratively assigned hex values. The length of the octet string is enterprise specific and can be at most 27 octets.
   - 6 - 127, reserved.
   - 128 - 255, the meaning of these values is enterprise specific. For example, Cisco could define 128 to refer to a Cisco specific algorithm. BayNetworks on the other hand can define a different meaning for this. The maximum remaining length of the SnmpEngineID can be 27 octets.

As you can see from this the length of a SnmpEngineID can be anywhere between five and thirty-two octets.

4.2.2   SnmpSecurityModel

This type is used to identify a security model being used. It resolves to an INTEGER and has the following values defined:

   - 0, reserved for "any."
   - 1, SNMPv1.
   - 2, SNMPv2c.

- 3, User-Based Security Model (USM).
- 4 - 255, reserved for standards-track security models. These values will be managed by the Internet Assigned Numbers Authority (IANA).
- Values greater than 255 can be used to specify enterprise-specific models. An enterprise-specific security model can be defined as

$$enterprisedNumber * 256 + securityModel$$

For example, given Cisco's enterprise number, 9, Cisco could define enterprise-specific security models with identifiers in the range of 2304 through 2559. This scheme allows enterprises to define up to 255 enterprise-specific security models. This scheme also will support up to 8,388,606 enterprises (given a 32-bit value: first bit needs to be 0, the next 23 bits can be used to identify an enterprise, the final 8 bits are used to define a security model).

In reality, are new security models going to be defined? Very rarely, if ever. Are enterprises going to define their own security models? Possibly, but probably not vendors that have to be concerned with interoperability. Government agencies, though, might take advantage of this.

4.2.3   SnmpMessageProcessingModel

This type is used to identify the message processing model used to process an SNMP message. It resolves to an INTEGER and can have one of the following values:

- 0, SNMPv1.
- 1, SNMPv2c.
- 2, SNMPv2u and SNMPv2*.
- 3, SNMPv3.
- 4 - 255, reserved for standards-track message processing models. These values will be managed by the Internet Assigned Numbers Authority (IANA).
- Values greater than 255 are handled exactly the same way as with the SnmpSecurityModel type to allow enterprise-specific message processing models. An enterprise- specific message processing model can be defined as

$$enterpriseNumber * 256 + messageProcessingModel$$

Again, as with the security model example, since Cisco's enterprise number is 9, Cisco could define enterprise-specific message processing models with identifiers in the range of 2304 through 2559. And as with the security model, this scheme allows enterprises to define up to 255 enterprise-specific message processing models.

4.2.4   SnmpSecurityLevel

This type defines the three security levels that can be used. They are

- noAuthNoPriv (1), SNMP messages are sent without authentication and without privacy.
- authNoPriv (2), SNMP messages are sent with authentication but without privacy.
- authPriv (3), SNMP messages are sent with authentication and with privacy.

4.2.5   SnmpAdminString

This resolves to an OCTET STRING and can be up to 255 bytes long. This is used to represent administrative information, preferably in human-readable form. An SnmpAdminString is encoded in UTF-8 format, which for 7-bit US-ASCII will be identical.

SnmpAdminString is used throughout the SNMPv3 MIBs that we will be looking at in later chapters. It is basically used to represent textual information, such as a user name or an identifier string.

4.2.6   SnmpTagValue

SnmpTagValue resolves to an OCTET STRING. It is expected that its values be human-readable text, such as things like "router" or "host," but can really be any OCTET STRING as long as it doesn't contain a delimeter character (space, tab, carriage return or linefeed).

We'll see in the SNMPv3 applications chapter an example of using SnmpTagValue objects to identify which entities to send notifications and forward messages to. While the general use of an SnmpTagValue object is to select table entries, its use is application and MIB specific.

4.2.7   SnmpTagList

SnmpTagList resolves to an OCTET STRING. It is used to represent a list of tag values. Delimeter characters (space, tab, carriage return, or linefeed) are used to separate tag values in a list. *Note*: Only a single delimeter character should be used between two tag values.

While none of the tag values within the list may be a zero-length OCTET STRING, it is perfectly valid for the SnmpTagList object to be an empty string. This would simply represent a tag list with no tag values. Example values for an SnmpTagList object could be "router Cisco," "router," etc.

We'll see in the SNMPv3 applications chapter an example of using SnmpTagList objects in conjunction with SnmpTagValue objects to identify the target systems to send notifications and forward messages to. Again, as with SnmpTagValue objects, its use is application and MIB specific.

4.2.8   KeyChange

KeyChange resolves to an OCTET STRING. A KeyChange object is used to change the private keys used for authentication and privacy. We'll be looking at how this is done in detail in the SNMPv3 Security chapter.

4.3 The snmpEngine Group

Several MIB variables have been defined to provide information about an SNMP engine. The snmpEngine group is defined under the MIB tree:

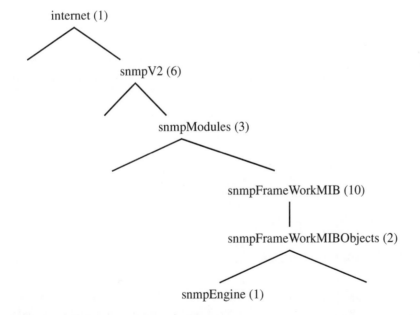

which defines snmpEngine to have the OBJECT IDENTFIER 1.3.6.1.6.3.10.2.1.

Table 4-1   snmpEngine Group

Object	Type	Access
snmpEngineID	SnmpEngineID	read-only
snmpEngineBoots	INTEGER	read-only
snmpEngineTime	INTEGER	read-only
snmpEngineMaxMessageSize	INTEGER	read-only

snmpEngineID: uniquely identifies an SNMP engine within an administrative group. Since there is a one to one mapping between an SNMP engine and an SNMP entity, this is also used to uniquely identify an SNMP entity.

snmpEngineBoots: number of times an SNMP engine has either been started or re-initialized since snmpEngineID was last configured.

snmpEngineTime: number of seconds since the value of the snmpEngineBoots object last changed. If incrementing this value causes it to exceed its maximum value (2147483647, which is roughly 68 years) it will wrap back to zero and snmpEngineBoots will be incremented by one. Future network management applications need to be aware of this or we might end up with a year 2067 problem!

snmpEngineMaxMessageSize: maximum size in octets of an SNMP message which this SNMP engine can send or receive. This is determined by the minimum of the MMS (maximum message size) values supported among all of the transports available to and supported by the engine. This value can range between 484 (any implementation must be able to support an SNMP message size of at least this value) and 2^{31}-1.

4.4 SNMPv3 Message Format

A new format has been defined for SNMPv3 messages. An SNMPv3 message contains among other things an SNMPv2 PDU either encrypted or in plain text, security information, and the context the message should be processed in. The format for the message is

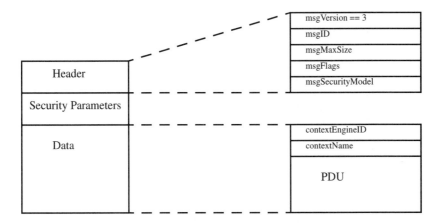

The header is made up of the following:

- msgVersion, a value of 3 identifies the version of the message as an SNMPv3 message.

- msgID (message identifier), this is an integer value that is used to coordinate request and response messages between two SNMP entities. The use of this is similar to the use of the request identifier within a PDU. The request identifier is used by SNMP applications to identify the PDU. The msgID is used by the engine to identify the message which carries a PDU.

Note: One of the security threats that SNMPv3 tries to protect against is where a valid message is captured and replayed later. By guaranteeing that msgID values are not reused and that each message is identified by a unique value, this threat can be eliminated. One possible implementation to generate unique msgID values is to use the low-order bits of snmpEngineBoots as the high-order portion of the msgID value and a counter value for the low-order portion of msgID. This will protect against an SNMP entity generating the same msgID value after a device reboots. It will also guarantee that msgID values won't repeat until after 65,535 messages (2^{16}-1) have been generated.

- msgMaxSize (maximum message size), an integer value which indicates the maximum message size that the sender can support. This value is used to determine how big a response to a request message can be. This can have values ranging from 484 through 2^{31}-1.

- msgFlags (message flags), a 1-byte value that contains flags that indicate whether the message can cause a Report to be generated and the security level the sender had applied to the message before it was sent on the wire. The 3 bits defined are reportableFlag, authFlag, and the privFlag.

If the reportableFlag is set, then a Report PDU can be sent back to the original sender (more on Report PDUs later). All messages that can be responded to (such as a Get PDU or an Inform PDU) are automatically treated as if reportableFlag is set to 1. All messages that are unacknowledged (such as a Report PDU, a Response PDU, or an SNMPv2-trap PDU) are automatically treated as if reportableFlag is set to 0. The reportableFlag is only used if the PDU portion of a message cannot be decoded, for example, if a PDU cannot be decrypted because of an invalid encryption key.

The authFlag and privFlag are used to indicate the security level. This can indicate the message was sent with no authentication and no privacy, authentication and no privacy, or authentication and privacy. The receiver of the message must apply this same security level when the contents are processed.

- msgSecurityModel (message security model), an integer value which identifies the message security model that the sender used to generate this message. The receiver, obviously, must use the same security model to perform security processing for the message. The possible values for this are defined by the SnmpSecurityModel type. Since enterprise-specific security models may be implemented, the mapping of this value to the desired security model within an SNMP engine may need to be done in an implementation-dependent way.

The security parameters provided depend on the security model being used. These values are passed directly to the security model that maps to the msgSecurityModel field in the header portion of the message.

The data portion of the message is either encrypted or in plain text. The data portion is encrypted if the privFlag with the header portion is set. Whether encrypted or in plain text, the data portion contains both context information and a valid SNMPv2c PDU (either Get, Get-Next, Get-Bulk, Set, Response, Inform, Report, or SNMPv2-trap).

The context information includes both a context engine identifier and a context name. Given this information, the proper context for which this PDU should be processed can be determined. *Note*: If a Request PDU (Get, Get-Next, Get-Bulk, Set) contains a context engine identifier that doesn't equal the SNMP engine's administratively unique identifier (snmpEngineID), then the Proxy Forwarder application will attempt to forward the message to the appropriate target. We will see how this is done in the SNMPv3 applications chapter.

4.5 Additional SNMP Statistics

Three additional 32-bit counters are defined under a snmpMPDStats subtree. These counters provide information about the number of packets that an SNMP engine dropped because the packets referenced unknown security models, had invalid or inconsistent components, or had PDUs that could not be processed.

> **snmpUnknownSecurityModels**: the number of received packets that an SNMP engine dropped because they referenced either an unknown or unsupported security model.

> **snmpInvalidMsgs**: the number of received packets that an SNMP engine dropped because they contained either invalid or inconsistent components within the SNMP message.

> **snmpUnknownPDUHandlers**: the number of received packets that an SNMP engine dropped because the PDU could not be processed. Internally, applications must register for a combination of a context engine identifier and a PDU type.

4.6 Reports

Report PDUs were defined for SNMPv2 but never used. For SNMPv3 they provide engine to engine communication and are processed directly by the SNMPv3 Message Processing Model. They allow an SNMP engine to tell another SNMP engine that an error was detected while processing an SNMP message. This (in theory anyway) allows the original SNMP engine to send a corrected SNMP message. Report PDUs are generated to report the following types of problems:

1. A Response message could not be generated.

2. A message was received with the authFlag cleared and the privFlag set.

3. An error occurred while providing authentication and privacy services for an incoming message.

Reports are also used for discovery and time synchronization purposes. An example of this will be shown in the SNMPv3 security chapter.

There have been some concerns addressed over the SNMPv3 mailing list on whether reports open a device up to denial of service attacks. A denial of service attack is where an attacker can use forged unauthenticated reports to confuse a receiving SNMP engine so that it does not talk correctly with other SNMP engines. The problem with dealing with a denial of service threat is distinguishing between intentionally invalid (malicious) messages and normal failures.

While the Report PDU was defined by RFC 1905 as part of SNMPv2, it was never used until SNMPv3. The format for a Report PDU is

0xA8	reqid	0	0	variable bindings

where

- The PDU type 0xA8 indicates a Report PDU.

- reqid is either the request identifier of the message that triggered the report, or zero if the request identifier cannot be extracted (for example, if the PDU cannot be decrypted).

- The variable bindings will contain a single object identifier and its value. This is used to determine the problem that the report is identifying.

4.7 Summary

This chapter provided an overview of the SNMPv3 Framework, including an introduction to the subsystems that make up the framework. It also described new textual conventions that were added for SNMPv3, and the SNMPv3 message format. This chapter finsihed up by providing a description of how Reports are used by SNMPv3.

CHAPTER 5

SNMPv3 Applications

This chapter will examine the SNMP applications that
have so far been defined by the Internet-Draft for SNMP Applications. The main objective for
this chapter, though, will be to show how to use new MIB tables defined for SNMPv3 to configure notifications and proxy forwarding.

With SNMPv1 there was no standard way for defining which IP addresses to send traps to
or to forward proxy messages to. Some vendors implemented proprietary MIB tables, others
required trap or proxy information to be configured through a command line interface.

MIB objects have been defined for SNMPv3 to allow notification and proxy forwarding
configuration to be done remotely and in a standard way. This chapter will describe these MIB
objects and show how to use them to configure an SNMP entity for generating notification messages and proxy forwarding.

5.1 Command Generator Applications

A command generator application generates SNMP commands to collect or set management information. It will initiate SNMP Get, Get-Next, Get-Bulk, and Set requests, along with
processing the responses to those requests.

When receiving a response to a request, the received values of messageProcessingModel,
securityModel, securityName, contextEngineID, contextName, and pduVersion must match
what was used in the original request. If they don't, the response will be discarded. A response
will also be discarded if the request identifier from the PDU does not match what was used in
the original request.

5.2 Command Responder Applications

A command responder application provides access to management data. It will process a received SNMP Get, Get-Next, Get-Bulk, or Set request if the contextEngineID specified in the request matches the local SNMP engine. The command responder application will perform the appropriate operation, using the access control that has been configured, and generate a response message back to the originator.

The access control module determines a MIB view to use based on the securityLevel, securityModel, securityName, contextName, and operation type (read, write, or notify). Each object within the request's variable bindings will be tested to see if it can be accessed based on the MIB view.

If the access control module cannot find a MIB view for

- the operation type, or
- the combination of securityModel and securityName, or
- the combination of contextName, groupName (determined by securityName and security-Model), securityModel, and securityLevel

then a response will be sent using the original request PDU, but replacing the error status with an authorizationError code and setting error index to zero.

If the access control module returns an error indicating that some undefined error occurred, then a response will be sent using the original request PDU but setting the error status value to genErr.

If the access control module returns an error indicating that contextName is not found within vacmContextTable (more on this in the SNMPv3 view-based access control chapter), then no response PDU will be sent. Instead the snmpUnknownContexts counter will be incremented.

If the context named by contextName is unavailable, then again no response PDU will be sent. Instead the snmpUnavailableContexts counter will be incremented. Most likely this condition will never be encountered for most (if not all) implementations.

5.3 Notification Originator Applications

A notification originator application generates SNMP notification messages (with either an SNMPv2-Trap or Inform PDU). Later in this chapter we will show MIB tables that allow you to configure the target addresses to send the notifications to, whether the notification message should contain an SNMPv2-Trap or Inform PDU, and what timeout and retry counts to use for Inform PDUs. MIB tables also allow you to set up filters based on target addresses and NOTIFI-CATION-TYPE object identifiers.

5.4 Notification Receiver Applications

Notification receiver applications receive notification messages. Whether a notification receiver application receives SNMPv2-Trap and/or Inform PDUs depends on what it has registered for.

If a notification receiver application receives an Inform PDU, it will generate a response to the originator using the request identifier and variable-bindings from the original Inform PDU, setting the error-status and error-index to zero.

5.5 Proxy Forwarder Applications

First, before we look at what a proxy forwarder application does let's first define what we mean by "proxy". Historically, an "SNMP proxy agent" could have meant any of the following:

a. Something that forwards SNMP requests to other SNMP entities. In order to perform this forwarding it may be required to translate an SNMP request from one SNMP version to another; or possibly from one transport domain to another.
b. Something that translates an SNMP operation into some non-SNMP protocol.
c. Something that translates a single object that actually represents an aggregate of multiple objects.

The definition that a proxy forwarder application uses is close to (a). A proxy forwarder application forwards requests and/or notifications to other SNMP entities according to the context of the original message and without any regard to the managed objects specified within the message's variable-bindings. A proxy forwarder will also forward the responses from these forwarded messages back to the SNMP entity that sent the original message. *Note*: As part of this forwarding messages may be translated from one SNMP version to another. Messages may also be translated from one transport domain to another.

How does a proxy forwarder application know which messages it needs to forward? As we will be seeing later, MIB tables have been defined to specify the context of an incoming message, and how to map that incoming message to one or more target addresses. As entries are added or removed from these tables, the proxy forwarder application is responsible for registering or unregistering the remote SNMP engine identifiers (and the type of messages) it will forward messages to. *Note*: A proxy forwarder application *CAN NOT* register to forward messages to its own SNMP engine.

The following diagram demonstrates how proxy forwarding of a request message (Get, Get-Next, Get-Bulk, Set) works:

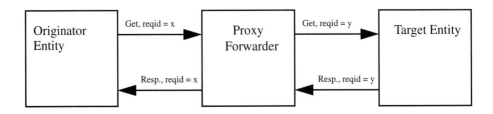

This example shows an SNMP entity sending a Get PDU with a request identifier equal to *x* to an SNMP entity acting as a proxy. The proxy forwarder application will translate the context of the incoming message to a target address and will then forward the message to the target. In forwarding the message, the proxy forwarder application will create a new PDU. A unique request-id, *y*, will be used. This is done so that the proxy forwarder application can correlate a response message to the request. If the SNMP version of the incoming message is different than the SNMP version used for the target entity, then the proxy forwarder application may need to perform further translation on the Get PDU.

Note: If the incoming message cannot be translated to a target address, then the snmpProxyDrops counter will be incremented. This may result in a Report being generated to the original SNMP entity.

Getting back to the example: the target will receive the forwarded Get PDU and will process the message, sending back a Response with request identifier = *y*. The proxy forwarder application will receive the response and match the request identifier, *y*, to the original Get PDU message. A new Response PDU will be created using a request identifier value of *x*. The rest of the values of the new PDU will match the Response PDU, unless there is an SNMP version mismatch between the incoming and outgoing Response PDUs. If there is, some translation may be needed. The new Response PDU will be sent to the SNMP entity that sent the original Get PDU.

Note: If an incoming Response PDU is received by a proxy forwarder application where the request identifier cannot be matched to a cached value, the message will be discarded.

Now let's look at how proxy forwarding of an Inform PDU works:

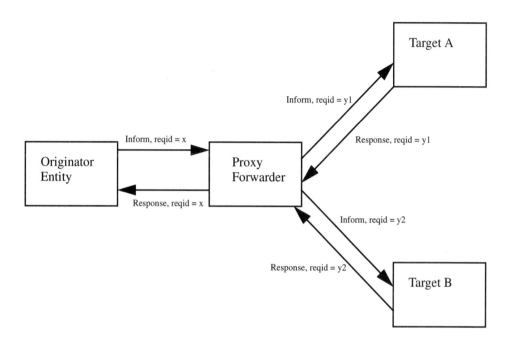

This example shows an SNMP entity sending an Inform PDU with a request identifier equal to x to an SNMP entity acting as a proxy. While a proxy forwarder application maps a request message to a single target, a notification (either Inform or SNMPv2-Trap) may be mapped to several target addresses. In this example, the context of the incoming Inform message is mapped to two addresses: Target A and Target B. As with the previous example, new PDUs will be created with unique request identifiers generated. The new Inform PDUs will be forwarded to Target A and Target B. Both Target A and Target B will process the Inform and send back responses.

When the proxy forwarder application receives a Response from any of the target addresses, it will generate a Response back to the SNMP entity that sent the original Inform. The request identifier and variable-bindings will match the original Inform. The error-status and error-index values for the Response will be set to zero.

What happens if the proxy forwarder application times out since none of the targets responded to the Inform? If this happens, processing for the Inform is halted. It is then up to the original SNMP entity to resend an Inform.

A proxy forwarder application deals with an SNMPv2-Trap PDU in a similar fashion but doesn't have to bother with handling responses back to the original sender.

Note: As with the previous example, some translation may be needed if the SNMP versions of the incoming and outgoing messages don't match. Also, if a proxy forwarder applica-

tion cannot map an Inform message to a target address, then the snmpProxyDrops counter will
be incremented. If an SNMPv2-Trap cannot be mapped to a target address, the incoming message is simply dropped.

As a final example, let's look at what happens if a target systems sends a Report back to a
proxy forwarder application:

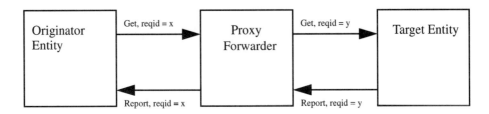

In this example, a Get PDU is forwarded to a target. The target, however, determines a
problem, such as the wrong security level being used, and sends a Report back to the proxy forwarder application. If the SNMP version of the original Get message supports Report PDUs, the
Report will be forwarded back to the SNMP entity that generated the original Get PDU.

5.6 MIB Tables for Configuring Notifications and Proxy Forwarding

New MIB tables have been defined for configuring to whom to send notification messages
and to whom to forward SNMP proxy messages. These new tables can be broken into three
groups.

Management Target MIBs

• snmpTargetAddrTable defines target addresses used for generating notifications and proxy
  forwarding. Each row contains an identifier into a parameters table which defines the
  SNMPv3 parameters to use in generating a message. Each row also contains a list of tag
  values which are used by the notification and proxy tables.
• snmpTargetParamsTable defines the SNMPv3 parameters to use in generating messages.
  This includes things like which Message Processing Model, Security Model, Security
  Level and Security Name to use.

Notification MIBs

- snmpNotifyTable selects targets to send notifications to and defines whether to send an Inform or an SNMPv2-Trap PDU. Each row in this table contains a tag value which is used to identify rows within snmpTargetAddrTable.
- snmpNotifyFilterProfileTable associates a notification filter profile with a set of target parameters — and indirectly with target addresses.
- snmpNotifyFilterTable provides filters which are used to determine whether a notification should be sent to a particular target. The way this is done is fairly complex and will be described later in the chapter.

Proxy MIB

- snmpProxyTable is the only table defined under this group and is used to identify the incoming messages to forward and to select the target address or addresses to forward these messages to.

A MIB object, snmpTargetSpinLock, is provided so that two or more managers don't try to modify these tables at the same time. Like the previous locks that we have looked at, it is defined as a TestAndIncr type with read-write access.

Two 32-bit MIB Counter objects are also provided, snmpUnavailableContexts and snmpUnknownContexts. As we saw earlier,

- snmpUnknownContexts provides the number of packets received by an SNMP engine that were dropped because the context contained in the message was unknown.
- snmpUnavailableContexts provides the number of packets received by an SNMP engine that were dropped because the context contained in the message was unavailable. In all likelihood, this counter value will not increase and few, if any, implementations will define or implement an unavailable context.

5.6.1 Management Target MIBs

The snmpTargetAddrTable is used to specify target addresses that are to be used in the generation of SNMP messages. Each row specifies an index into the snmpTargetParamsTable. The same address can appear more than once in this table. This could cause the same message to be generated to the same target address, but using a different set of SNMP parameters.

Table 5-1   snmpTargetAddrTable, indexed by snmpTargetAddrName

Object	Type	Access
snmpTargetAddrName	SnmpAdminString	not-accessible
snmpTargetAddrTDomain	TDomain	read-create
snmpTargetAddrTAddress	TAddress	read-create
snmpTargetAddrTimeout	TimeInterval	read-create
snmpTargetAddrRetryCount	Integer32	read-create
snmpTargetAddrTagList	SnmpTagList	read-create
snmpTargetAddrParams	SnmpAdminString	read-create
snmpTargetAddrStorageType	StorageType	read-create
snmpTargetAddrRowStatus	RowStatus	read-create

snmpTargetAddrName: a unique identifier used to index this table.

snmpTargetAddrTDomain: specifies the transport type of the address defined by snmpTargetAddrTAddress.

snmpTargetAddrTAddress: specifies the target address. The format of this value depends on the snmpTargetAddrTDomain value. For example, if snmpTargetAddrT-Domain specifies UDP, then this value will be a 6-byte OCTET STRING, where the first 4 bytes specify the IP address, and last 2 bytes specify the UDP port number.

snmpTargetAddrTimeout: when a message is generated which requires a response (for example, an Inform or when forwarding a Get, Get-Next, etc.), a timeout value is used for retransmissions or timing out an operation. This value can be used as either the timeout value or to derive the timeout value. This is implementation specific. For example a method could be used to derive the timeout value based on this value and the current retry count. Another example could be if a message is being generated that requires both authentication and privacy, then the timeout value may be increased to account for the added processing that's needed. In the simplest case where this value is used as the timeout value, it should represent the largest expected round-trip delay for communicating with the target address. The default value for this is 1500 (15 seconds).

snmpTargetAddrRetryCount: specifies a default number of retries to be attempted when a response isn't received for a generated message. An application may use its own retry count, in which case this value will be ignored.

snmpTargetAddrTagList: a list of tag values that tie this table to both the snmpNotifyTable and the snmpProxyTable. These tag values are used to identify target addresses to send notifications to and forward messages to.

snmpTargetAddrParams: identifies a row in the snmpTargetParamsTable. This in effect specifies the SNMP parameters to use when generating a message.

snmpTargetAddrStorageType: specifies how a row in this table should be stored. The default is for it to be stored in nonVolatile memory.

snmpTargetAddrRowStatus: a RowStatus object used for adding and removing rows to/from this table. A row cannot be made active until snmpTargetAddrTDomain, snmpTargetAddrTAddress, and snmpTargetAddrParams have all been set. Also, snmpTargetAddrTDomain and snmpTargetAddrTAddress cannot be modified while the row is active (the row would first have to be put in notInService).

The snmpTargetParamsTable specifies the SNMP parameters that should be used when generating a message to a target. A single row within this table can be referenced by more than one target address, and similarly, more than one row in this table can be used by the same target address.

Table 5-2 snmpTargetParamsTable, Indexed by snmpTargetParamsName

Object	Type	Status
snmpTargetParamsName	SnmpAdminString	not-accessible
snmpTargetParamsMPModel	SnmpMessageProcessingModel	read-create
snmpTargetParamsSecurityModel	SnmpSecurityModel	read-create

Table 5-2   snmpTargetParamsTable, Indexed by snmpTargetParamsName

Object	Type	Status
snmpTargetParamsSecurityName	SnmpAdminString	read-create
snmpTargetParamsSecurityLevel	SnmpSecurityLevel	read-create
snmpTargetParamsStorageType	StorageType	read-create
snmpTargetParamsRowStatus	RowStatus	read-create

snmpTargetParamsName: a unique identifier used to index this table. It is also used to connect this table to the snmpTargetAddrTable, snmpNotifyFilterProfile-Table, and the snmpProxyTable.

snmpTargetParamsMPModel: the Message Processing Model to use when generating an SNMP message. For example, a value of 3 specifies SNMPv3's Message Processing Model should be used.

snmpTargetParamsSecurityModel: the Security Model to use when generating SNMP messages. For example, a value of 3 specifies the User-Based Security Model.

snmpTargetParamsSecurityName: identifies the Principal on whose behalf SNMP messages will be generated.

snmpTargetParamsSecurityLevel: identifies the Security Level to be used when generating SNMP messages. For example, a value of 2 would specify authentication with no privacy.

snmpTargetParamsStorageType: specifies how a row in this table should be stored. The default is for it to be stored in nonVolatile memory.

snmpTargetParamsRowStatus: a RowStatus object used for adding and removing rows to/from this table. A row cannot be made active until snmpTargetParamsMP-Model, snmpTargetParamsSecurityModel, snmpTargetParamsSecurityName, and snmpTargetParamsSecurityLevel have all been set. Also, none of those objects can be modified while the row is active (the row would first have to be put in notInService).

5.6.2   Notification MIBs

The snmpNotifyTable is used to specify the target addresses to send notifications to. Whether a notification gets sent to a target address depends on whether a filter has been set up to include or exclude a target. After we go over the Notification MIBs, we will go over the algorithm used to determine which targets to generate notifications to.

Table 5-3   snmpNotifyTable, Indexed by snmpNotifyName

Object	Type	Access
snmpNotifyName	SnmpAdminString	not-accessible
snmpNotifyTag	SnmpTagValue	read-create
snmpNotifyType	INTEGER	read-create
snmpNotifyStorageType	StorageType	read-create
snmpNotifyRowStatus	RowStatus	read-create

snmpNotifyName: a unique identifier used to index this table.

snmpNotifyTag: a tag value used to select entries in snmpTargetAddrTable.

snmpNotifyType: specifies whether to generate an SNMPv2-Trap PDU (1) or an Inform PDU (2). If an SNMP entity does not support Informs, then this object may be treated as read-only.

snmpNotifyStorageType: specifies how a row in this table should be stored. The default is for it to be stored in nonVolatile memory.

snmpNotifyRowStatus: a RowStatus object used for adding and removing rows to/from this table.

The snmpNotifyFilterProfileTable is a short table used to tie the snmpTargetParamsTable to the snmpNotifyFilterTable. The reason why this is needed will be made clearer soon.

Table 5-4   snmpNotifyFilterProfileTable, indexed by snmpTargetParamsName

Object	Type	Access
snmpNotifyFilterProfileName	SnmpAdminString	read-create
snmpNotifyFilterProfileStorType	StorageType	read-create
snmpNotifyFilterProfileRowStatus	RowStatus	read-create

snmpNotifyFilterProfileName: this value is used as an index into the notify filter table (snmpNotifyFilterTable).

snmpNotifyFilterProfileStorType: specifies how a row in this table should be stored. The default is for it to be stored in nonVolatile memory.

snmpNotifyFilterProfileRowStatus: a RowStatus object used for adding and removing rows to/from this table. A row in this table cannot be made active until snmpNotifyFilterProfileName has been set.

The snmpNotifyFilterTable defines filters that are used to determine whether a notification should be sent to a target address. This table is indexed partially by a notify filter profile name, and partially by an object identifier. A target address is mapped to a notify filter profile name through one level of indirection:

1. Given a target address, get its associated params name.
2. Using the params name as an index, find a corresponding entry within the snmpNotifyFil-terProfileTable. If an entry exists, the profile name is given by the snmpNotifyFilterPro-fileName object.

Table 5-5   snmpNotifyFilterTable, Indexed by
snmpNotifyFilterProfileName.snmpNotifyFilterSubtree

Object	Type	Access
snmpNotifyFilterSubtree	OBJECT IDENTIFIER	not-accessible
snmpNotifyFilterMask	OCTET STRING	read-create

Table 5-5   snmpNotifyFilterTable, Indexed by
snmpNotifyFilterProfileName.snmpNotifyFilterSubtree (Continued)

Object	Type	Access
snmpNotifyFilterType	INTEGER	read-create
snmpNotifyFilterStorageType	StorageType	read-create
snmpNotifyFilterRowStatus	RowStatus	read-create

snmpNotifyFilterSubtree: a MIB subtree that is used to determine whether a notification matches this profile. How this is done will be described later.

snmpNotifyFilterMask: a bit mask used in conjunction with snmpNotifyFilterSubtree to determine whether a notification matches this profile. Each bit of this value corresponds to a subidentifier position. The most-significant bit corresponds to the first subidentifier position, the next significant bit corresponds to the second subidentifier position, and so on. When trying to match an OBJECT IDENTIFIER to an snmpNotifyFilterSubtree value, each subidentifier of both values must be equal if the corresponding bit in snmpNotifyFilterMask is a one (you can think of a zero bit value as being treated as a wild card).

As an example, the NOTIFICATION-TYPE for linkDown is 1.3.6.1.6.3.1.1.5.3. An snmpNotifyFilterSubtree value of 1.3.6.1.6.3.1.1.5.3 and an snmpNotifyFilterMask value of "3FF" (0011 1111 1111) will match a linkDown Trap OID. If the snmpNotifyFilterSubtree value was 1.3.6.1.6.3.1.1.5.0, then a snmpNotifyFilterMask value of "3FE" (0011 1111 1110) would not only match a linkDown Trap OID but also coldStart, warmStart, linkUp, authenticationFailure, and egpNeighborLoss Trap OIDs.

Note: If the number of bits in the bit mask is less than the number of subidentifiers in snmpNotifyFilterSubtree, then the bit mask is extended with ones so that the lengths match. If the value of snmpNotifyFilterMask is a zero-length string, this extension rule causes a bit mask of all ones to be used (which means snmpNotifyFilterSubtree will have to be the exact value of an object identifier for a match to occur).

snmpNotifyFilterType: is used to indicate whether a notification should be sent. This can have one of two values: included (1) or excluded (2). How this is used will be described a little later.

snmpNotifyFilterStorageType: specifies how a row in this table should be stored. The default is for it to be stored in nonVolatile memory.

snmpNotifyFilterRowStatus: a RowStatus object used for adding and removing rows to/from this table.

5.6.3   How Notifications Work

When an event such as a link going down is detected, a notification originator application needs to go through each entry in the snmpNotifyTable looking for entries within the snmpTargetAddrTable with matching tag values. If notification filters have not been configured (i.e., the snmpNotifyFilterProfileTable is empty) then things are simplified greatly — notifications may be sent to each address where a snmpTargetAddrTable entry is found with a matching tag value. What I mean by "may be sent" is that whether or not a notification is sent depends on whether the Notification Originator application is granted access by the View-Based Access Control Model (VACM) to each of the variable-bindings used by the notification. We will be looking at the VACM in detail in a later chapter.

If notification filters have been configured, then things get quite a bit more complex. In order to determine which target addresses notifications "may" be sent to, the following steps will need to be taken for each matching snmpTargetAddrTable entry.

Note: i will be used to reference the snmpNotifyTable entry. j will be used to reference the snmpTargetAddrTable entry. Also, whether a notification is actually sent depends on whether the VACM allows access to the notification's variable-bindings.

1. Use the snmpTargetAddrParams.j value to index the snmpNotifyFilterProfileTable.

2. If an entry doesn't exist within the snmpNotifyFilterProfileTable, then a notification can be sent (if the VACM allows access to the variable-bindings) to the target address snmpTargetAddrTAddress.j using the SNMP parameters referenced by snmpTargetAddrParams.j. Whether the notification contains an Inform or SNMPv2-Trap PDU depends on the value of snmpNotifyType.i. We're done.

3. At this point an entry exists within the snmpNotityFilterProfileTable. Set p to the filter profile name (snmpNotifyFilterProfileName).

snmpTargetAddrTable

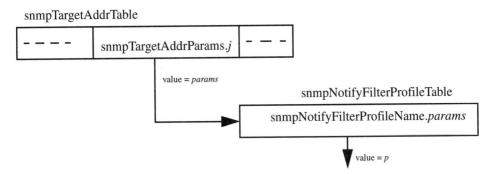

value = *params*

4. Read all entries from the snmpNotifyFilterTable that are indexed by *p.**.
5. If no entries were read, then don't send a notification to the target address. We're done.
6. For each entry compare the subtree object with trap.oid. The subidentifiers that need to match are defined by the mask object. If a match occurs, save the entry in a collection called oidmatches.

snmpNotifyFilterTable

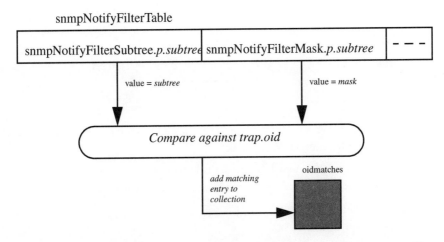

7. For each entry compare the subtree object with each of the traps variable bindings. The subidentifiers that need to match are defined by the mask object. If a match occurs, save the entry in an array of collections, vbmatches[varbind] (where varbind is the trap variable-binding that was used).

snmpNotifyFilterTable

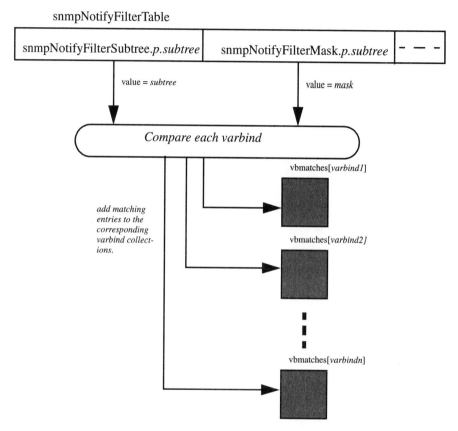

8. If oidmatches is empty, then none of the entries matched the trap.oid. In this case a notification cannot be sent out. We're done.

9. Find the entry within oidmatches with the longest and lexicographically largest subtree value. If the filter type for that entry is excluded, then a notification cannot be sent out. We're done.

oidmatches

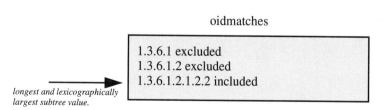

10. For each varbind within trap.variablebindings check to see if vbmatches[varbind] has any entries. If it does, find the entry with the longest and lexicographically largest subtree value. If the filter type for that entry is excluded, then a notification cannot be sent out. We're done.

11. Send a notification (if VACM allows access to the variable-bindings) to the target address snmpTargetAddrTAddress.*j* using the SNMP parameters referenced by snmpTargetAddrParams.*j*. Whether the notification contains an Inform or SNMPv2-Trap PDU depends on the value of snmpNotifyType.*i*.

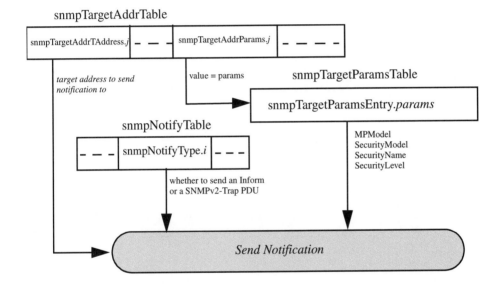

It is possible that an event can cause several notification messages to be sent to the same target address since

    a. The same target address can be in more than one entry within the snmpTargetAddrTable.

    b. An entry within the snmpTargetAddrTable can have a tag list that maps to several entries within the snmpNotifyTable.

The following pseudocode also illustrates how a notification originator application chooses the target addresses to send notifications to

```
// Cycle through each row in snmpNotifyTable. The foreach
// statement will cycle through each entry within snmpNotifyTable,
// assigning i to each instance identifier in turn.

foreach i in snmpNotifyTable
{
    tag <- snmpNotifyTag.i

    // Cycle through each row in snmpTargetAddrTable.

    foreach j in snmpTargetAddrTable
    {
        if (tag not in snmpTargetAddrTagList.j)
            continue

        params <- snmpTargetAddrParams.j
        if (snmpNotifyFilterProfileName.params doesn't exist)
        {
            SendNotification(snmpTargetAddrTAddress.j,
                snmpNotifyType.i,
                params,
                trap.oid,
                trap.variablebindings)
            continue
        }

        pname <- snmpNotifyProfileName.params
        entries <- all snmpNotifyFilterTable entries matching
                   instance pname.*
        if (entries == "")
        {
            continue
        }

        matches <- ""
        foreach varbind in trap.variablebindings
        {
            oidmatches[varbind] <- ""
        }

        foreach entry in entries
        {
            subtree <- snmpNotifyFilterSubtree.entry
            mask <- snmpNotifyFilterMask.entry
            if (CompareOID(trap.oid, mask, subtree) == true)
            {
              add entry to matches
            }
```

```
            foreach varbind in trap.variablebindings
            {
              if (CompareOID(varbind, mask, subtree) == true)
              {
                add entry to oidmatches[varbind]
              }
            }
        }

        if (matches == "")
        {
            // Target is excluded since there were no matches.

            continue
        }

        flag <- false
        n <- LargestMatch(matches)
        if (snmpNotifyFilterType.n == included)
        {
            flag <- CheckIfVarbindsIncluded(oidmatches, trap)
        }

        if (flag == true)
        {
            // A notification is being sent since a filter
            // included the trap.oid, and none of the trap's
            // variable bindings were excluded.

            SendNotification(snmpTargetAddrTAddress.j,
                snmpNotifyType.i,
                params,
                trap.oid,
                trap.variablebindings)
        }
    }
}
```

The CheckIfVarbindIncluded procedure will return false if the longest and lexicographically largest matching entry for any of the trap's variable-bindings has a type value of excluded. *Note*: If there were no matching entries for any of the trap's variable-bindings, then the procedure will return true.

The pseudocode for CheckIfVarbindIncluded is as follows:

```
procedure Boolean::CheckIfVarbindIncluded(oidmatches, trap)
```

```
{
    // This procedure will return true if no varbinds
    // had matched, or if longest and lexicographically
    // largest matching entry for each varbind is included.

    foreach varbind in trap.variablebindings
    {
        if (oidmatches[varbind] != "")
        {
            n <- LargestMatch(oidmatches[varbind])
            if (snmpNotifyFilterType.n == excluded)
            {
                return false
            }
        }
    }
    return true
}
```

The procedure CompareOID will compare an OBJECT IDENTIFIER (either a trap.oid or a varbind.oid) with a subtree value to see if they match. For the two objects to match, each subidentifier within the objects must be equal if the corresponding bit within the mask is a 1. For example, if the most-significant bit within the mask value is a 1, then the first subidentifiers must be equal. If the least-significant bit is a 1, then the last subidentifiers must be equal. If the OBJECT IDENTIFIER and the subtree match, then CompareOID will return true; otherwise it will return false.

The procedure LargestMatch will search through a collection of entries for the entry with the longest and lexicographically largest subtree value. LargestMatch will return the instance of that entry.

The procedure SendNotification will send a notification message to a specified target address. SendNotification is passed five parameters:

1. target address to send the notification to.
2. notify type, which specifies whether an Inform or an SNMPv2-Trap PDU should be used.
3. an index into the snmpTargetParamsTable. This specifies the SNMP parameters to use in generating this message.
4. the trap.oid value used for snmpTrapOID.0 (the second variable binding within the Inform or SNMPv2-Trap PDU).
5. the object instances to be included within the variable bindings.

5.6.4   Notification Example

Let's walk through an example where we have configured target addresses, notification entries, and notification filters.

First, let's show snmpTargetAddrTable configured with three entries:

Table 5-6   snmpTargetAddrTable Example

	addr1	addr2	addr3
snmpTargetAddrName	addr1	addr2	addr3
snmpTargetAddrTDomain	snmpUDPDomain	snmpUDPDomain	snmpUDPDomain
snmpTargetAddrTAddress	158.101.121.1/162	158.101.121.2/162	158.101.121.3/162
snmpTargetAddrTagList	monitor HP	monitor	HP admin
snmpTargetAddrParams	p1	p1	p2
snmpTargetAddrStorageType	nonVolatile (3)	nonVolatile (3)	nonVolatile (3)
snmpTargetAddrRowStatus	active (1)	active (1)	active (1)

The entries configured within the snmpTargetAddrTable reference two entries within the snmpTargetParamsTable, p1 and p2. We have configured snmpTargetParamsTable as follows:

Table 5-7   snmpTargetParamsTable Example

	p1	p2
snmpTargetParamsName	p1	p2
snmpTargetParamsMPModel	SNMPv3 (3)	SNMPv3 (3)
snmpTargetParamsSecurityModel	USM (3)	USM (3)
snmpTargetParamsSecurityName	secure-admin	admin
snmpTargetParamsSecurityLevel	authPriv (3)	authNoPriv (2)
snmpTargetParamsStorageType	nonVolatile (3)	nonVolatile (3)
snmpTargetParamsRowStatus	active (1)	active (1)

Now let's show an snmpNotifyTable configured with two entries:

Table 5-8   snmpNotifyTable Example

	n1	n2
snmpNotifyName	n1	n2
snmpNotifyTag	HP	monitor
snmpNotifyType	inform (2)	trap (1)
snmpNotifyStorageType	nonVolatile (3)	nonVolatile (3)
snmpNotifyRowStatus	active (1)	active (1)

To keep things simple at first, let's assume both snmpNotifyFilterProfileTable and snmp-NotifyFilterTable are empty.

Let's look at what happens when an event which can trigger a notification is detected. The first entry in snmpNotifyTable, n1, has a tag value of "HP" and a type value of inform. Two entries within snmpTargetAddrTable have the tag "HP" within their tag lists. These entries are indexed by addr1 and addr3 and have associated target addresses of 158.101.121.1 and 158.101.121.3. This will cause SNMP messages with an Inform PDU to be sent to 158.101.121.1 and 158.101.121.3.

The SNMP message sent to 158.101.121.1 will be generated using the SNMP parameters (MPModel = SNMPv3, SecurityModel = USM, SecurityName = secure-admin, SecurityLevel = `authPriv`).

The SNMP message sent to 158.101.121.3 will be generated using the SNMP parameters (MPModel = SNMPv3, SecurityModel = USM, SecurityName = admin, SecurityLevel = `authNoPriv`).

The next entry in snmpNotifyTable, n2, has a tag value of "monitor" and a type value of trap. Two entries within snmpTargetAddrTable have the tag value "monitor" within their tag lists. These entries are indexed by addr1 and addr2. This will cause SNMP messages with an SNMPv2-Trap PDU to be sent to 158.101.121.1 and 158.101.121.2.

As with the other notification sent to 158.101.121.1, this one will also be generated with the same SNMP parameters. Since addr2 references the same row within the snmpTargetParamsTable, the message sent to 158.101.121.2 will also be generated with the same SNMP parameters.

So as a result of an event being detected, both SNMPv2-Trap and Inform messages were sent to 158.101.121.1, an SNMPv2-Trap message sent to 158.101.121.2, and an Inform message sent to 158.101.121.3.

Now that we have covered a *simple* example, let's see what happens if we have configured notify filters.

First we'll show an snmpNotifyFilterProfileTable that has been configured with two entries:

Table 5-9   snmpNotifyFilterProfileTable example

	p1	p2
snmpNotifyFilterProfileName	nf1	nf2
snmpNotifyFilterProfileStorType	nonVolatile (3)	nonVolatile (3)
snmpNotifyFilterProfileRowStatus	active (1)	active (2)

Note that the indexes for this table are the same that were used for the snmpTargetParamsTable. The important value in this table is the notify filter profile name.

We'll now show an snmpNotifyFilterTable that has been configured with three entries. The first entry will be associated with the filter profile name, nf1, and will be used to include any trap.oids directly under the snmpTraps subtree. This will cause notifications to be generated to any target addresses that map to the filter profile name nf1 if coldStart, warmStart, linkDown, linkUp, authenticationFailure, or egpNeighborLoss events are detected. The next two entries in the table will be associated with filter profile name nf2. These two entries will cause a notification to be generated to any target address that maps to the filter profile name nf2 if a linkDown event is detected on any interface except Interface 8.

Note: The NOTIFICATION-TYPE OBJECT IDENTIFIER for

linkDown is 1.3.6.1.6.3.1.1.5.3

snmpTraps is 1.3.6.1.6.3.1.1.5

The OBJECT IDENTIFIER for ifIndex is 1.3.6.1.2.1.2.2.1.1.

Table 5-10   snmpNotifyFilterTable Example

	nf1.1.3.6.1.6.3.1.1.5.0	nf2.1.3.6.1.6.3.1.1.5.3	nf2.1.3.6.1.2.1.2.2.1.1.8
snmpNotifyFilterSubtree	1.3.5.1.6.3.1.1.5.0	1.3.6.1.6.3.1.1.5.3	1.3.6.1.2.1.2.2.1.1.8
snmpNotifyFilterMask	03FE	03FF	07FF
snmpNotifyFilterType	included (1)	included (1)	excluded (2)
snmpNotifyFilterStorageType	nonVolatile (3)	nonVolatile (3)	nonVolatile (3)
snmpNotifyFilterRowStatus	active (1)	active (1)	active (1)

Now let's look at what happens if a linkUp event is detected.

As we saw before, the first entry in snmpNotifyTable, n1, has a tag value of "HP" that maps to two entries within snmpTargetAddrTable, addr1 and addr3. For addr1, using the snmpTargetAddrParams value, p1, we get the filter profile name, nf1. Now searching through the snmpNotifyFilterTable we find that the first entry (and only the first entry) matches the notify filter profile name nf1 and the linkUp OBJECT IDENTIFIER. This will cause an SNMP message with an Inform PDU to be sent to 158.101.121.1.

The snmpTargetAddrTable entry for addr3 has an snmpTargetAddrParams value of p2. This gives us a notify filter profile name, nf2 (snmpNotifyFilterProfileName.p2 = nf2). No entries exist within the snmpNotifyFilterTable that match the notify filter profile name nf2 and the linkUp OBJECT IDENTIFIER. No notification will be sent to 158.101.121.3.

Also, as we saw before the next entry in snmpNotifyTable, n2, has a tag value of "monitor" that maps to two entries within snmpTargetAddrTable, addr1 and add2. Both of these entries have snmpTargetAddrParams values of p1. As we have already seen, this will be accepted by the notify filtering and SNMP messages with an SNMPv2-Trap PDU will be sent to 158.101.121.1 and 158.101.121.2.

If a linkDown event is detected, everything will work as before except for the filtering for addr3. Here the second entry in the snmpNotifyFilterTable will match the notify filter profile name nf2 and the OBJECT IDENTFIER for linkDown. The snmpNotifyFilterType value for that entry is included so for the moment it looks as if an Inform message will be generated to 158.101.121.3. However, if the ifIndex object for the trap is for interface 8, then that object will match the third entry in the snmpNotifyFilterTable which will cause the notification to be excluded.

As we can see from these examples, configuring notifications can get complicated when we add filters. As we can also see from the last example, the way trap objects are filtered is somewhat limiting. Instead of filtering on a specific instance of an object, what would probably be more useful would be to filter on the value of an object. In the last example what I would probably want to do is exclude any linkDown trap for an interface that has been configured to be administratively down. This way I wouldn't generate a notification for the normal action of configuring a port to be down. With the notification mechanism that has been defined, you can't do that. The next section will examine this a little more.

5.6.5   Configuring Notifications

As we have seen in the previous section, configuring notifications can get complicated. It doesn't have to be though. In most environments devices will be configured to send notifications to one host system. Also, trap filtering can be done more powerfully and completely by the network management application that is receiving and analyzing traps than by the mechanism defined by the SNMP Notification MIBs. The overall cost of management can be lowered if the complexity is added to the application that is receiving and analyzing the notifications than to the configuration of the notifications. The reasons for this are straightforward:

1. There can be thousands of devices in a network that may need to be configured to send notifications.

2. Even though you may (and should!) have an application to perform a bulk configuration of all your devices, a user may still end up configuring notifications through some other means (either through a command line interface, or possibly by using a MIB browser).

3. The more complicated a configuration is, the more prone to errors any modifications to that configuration will be.

4. Any sort of complicated configuration will need to be routinely checked to make sure it is consistent and correct.

Are there any reasons why you might want to have notification filtering done within the device? Well, there are two possible scenarios that I can think of but I don't think either is worth adding the extra complexity for.

    a. A device could be routinely sending out a large number of notifications. In order to cut down on the bandwidth that device is consuming with these notifications, you might want to filter out the notifications that are really nothing more than noise. As I have stated before not all devices are equal. Some do a good job of sending out mostly useful (or at least conceivably useful) notifications; others can send out a lot of useless information. Could a device be sending out so many notifications that it is affecting network performance? I guess anything is possible, especially if the notifications end up going over a low-speed line.

b. In order to preserve bandwidth, you could conceivably configure filters so some notifications are sent as SNMPv2-Traps and other more critical notifications are sent as Informs. I don't think this is worth the configuration complexity — you would probably be better off simply configuring all notifications to be sent as Informs if you want any to be sent as Informs.

The simplest way to configure a device to send notifications is to have a single row in the snmpNotifyTable that specifies whether you want SNMPv2-Trap or Inform PDUs to be used. For that entry, assign a tag value of something like "trap." Then for each target address that you want to send a notification to (and most likely that will be only one target), search for that address in the snmpTargetAddrTable. If the address is found, check to see if the tag list contains the tag value "trap." If it doesn't, add the tag value "trap" to the tag list. If the address isn't found in the snmpTargetAddrTable, first add an entry in the snmpTargetParamsTable if a suitable one doesn't already exist, and then add an entry into the snmpTargetAddrTable specifying the target domain, target address, SNMP parameters index, and a tag list value of "trap."

As long as snmpNotifyFilterProfileTable is empty, this is all you need to do.

Note: In this example we are trying to keep things simple by guaranteeing there is only one entry in the snmpNotifyTable. If there is more than one entry or we find an entry with values that we are not expecting, then we will delete it. This may have consequences if a conflicting network management application is trying to do something else, but again what we are trying to do is demonstrate a simple way to configure notifications.

Our pseudocode will reference the following routines that we will describe here but not provide any pseudocode for.

- CreateSnmpSession(*addr*) simply creates an SNMP session to the device specified by *addr*. This session is used as the context for Get, Get-Next, and Set operations.

- SnmpGetNext(*pdu*) generates an SNMP Get-Next message to the device specified by CreateSnmpSession. This will return the Response PDU.

- SnmpSet(*pdu*) generates an SNMP Set message to the device specified by CreateSnmpSession. This will return the Response PDU.

- GetVarBindValue(*pdu*, *n*) returns the object value at position *n* within *pdu*.

- GetVarBindInstance(*pdu*, *n*, *oid*) gets the instance portion of the OBJECT IDENTIFIER at position *n* within *pdu*. Use *oid* as the base OBJECT IDENTIFIER.

- CheckPDU(*response*, *orig*) is used after a Get-Next to make sure the objects within the response PDU, *response*, are still under the same tree as the original PDU, *orig*. This will return true if they are, false otherwise.

- GetUniqueInstance(*rowStatusOID*) is passed a RowStatus object and will return the instance for a new row that has been created with `createAndWait`.

- MakeTAddress(*addr*, *port*) returns a 6-byte octet representing the 4-byte IP address and the 2-byte port number.

The following pseudocode demonstrates configuring the target address to send notifications to.

```
// Configure device to send notifications to address1.
//
// First, make sure snmpNotifyTable is configured
// with only one entry, tagged by 'trap'. Note.
// the variable trapType indicates whether to use Inform (2)
// or SNMPv2-Trap (1) PDUs.

CreateSnmpSession(device)

ConfigureNotifyTable(trapType)

// Next, walk the snmpTargetAddrTable to see if address1
// is in the table.

inTableFlag <- false
flag <- true
responsePDU <- {snmpTargetAddrTAddress, snmpTargetAddrTagList,
                snmpTargetAddrRowStatus}
origPDU <- responsePDU
while (flag)
{
    pdu <- SnmpGetNext(responsePDU)
    responsePDU <- pdu
    flag <- CheckPDU(pdu, origPDU)

    if (flag == false)
        continue

    addr <- GetVarBindValue(pdu, 1)
    taglist <- GetVarBindValue(pdu, 2)
    status <- GetVarBindValue(pdu, 3)
```

```
        if (status != 'active')
           continue

        if (addr == address1)
        {
           inTableFlag <- true
           flag <- false
           if (InTagList('trap', taglist) == false)
           {
               inst <- GetVarBindInstance(
                   pdu,
                   2,
                   snmpTargetAddrTagList)

               AddToTagList(inst, taglist, 'trap')
           }
        }
     }

  if (inTableFlag == false)
  {
     // Add address1 to the snmpTargetAddrTable using
     // the following SNMP parameters:
     // SnmpMessageProcessingModel = mp
     // SnmpSecurityModel = sm
     // Security Name = sn
     // SnmpSecurityLevel = sl

     AddToTargetTable(address1, mp, sm, sn, sl)
  }
```

The ConfigureNotifyTable procedure simply makes sure there is one entry in the snmpNotifyTable, that the entry has the tag value "trap," and that the snmpNotifyType object for the entry has the value specified by the trapType parameter (either 1 to generate SNMPv2-Trap PDUs or 2 to generate Inform PDUs).

The following pseudocode shows the logic for the procedure ConfigureNotifyTable:

```
procedure Void::ConfigureNotifyTable(trapType)
{
     // Read snmpNotifyTable. There should only be one
     // entry. If there are more than one entry, delete
     // them and set the remaining entry to have a tag
     // value of 'trap' and a type value of trapType.
     // If the table is empty, add a new entry.

     validFlag <- false
```

```
flag <- true
responsePDU <- {snmpNotifyTag, snmpNotifyType,
          snmpNotifyRowStatus}
origPDU <- responsePDU
while (flag)
{
    pdu <- SnmpGetNext(responsePDU)
    responsePDU <- pdu
    flag <- CheckPDU(pdu, origPDU)

    if (flag == false)
        continue

    status <- GetVarBindValue(pdu, 3)
    if (status != 'active')
        continue

    // An entry has been found. If a valid one
    // has already been found, delete this one,
    // else check if this one is valid.

    if (validFlag == true)
    {
        inst <- GetVarBindInstance(
            pdu,
            1,
            snmpNotifyTag)
        SnmpSet(snmpNotifyRowStatus.inst <- destroy)
        continue
    }

    // Check to see if type and tag values are what we want.

    tag <- GetVarBindValue(pdu, 1)
    type <- GetVarBindValue(pdu, 2)

    if ((tag == 'trap') && (type == trapType))
    {
        validFlag <- true
        continue
    }

    // Remove entries that don't match what we're looking for.

    inst <- GetVarBindInstance(
            pdu,
            1,
            snmpNotifyTag)
```

```
        SnmpSet(snmpNotifyRowStatus.inst <- destroy)
    }

    if (validFlag == false)
    {
        // At this point snmpNotifyTable is empty. Add
        // an entry using a tag value of 'trap', a type
        // value of trapType. Use an instance value 'e1'.

        setpdu <- {snmpNotifyTag.e1 <- tag,
                snmpNotifyType.e1 <-type,
                snmpNotifyRowStatus.e1 <- createAndGo}
        SnmpSet(setpdu)
    }
}
```

The pseudocode for AddToTagList is shown below. It's fairly straightforward, except it demonstrates using the TestAndIncr object, snmpTargetSpinLock, to guarantee that two managers are not trying to modify the tag list value at the same time. If that happened, the SNMP Set operation within the ModifyTagList procedure would return an error status of inconsistentValue.

```
procedure Void::AddToTagList(inst, taglist, tag)
{
    // Add the tag value to the taglist for
    // snmpTargetAddrTagList. The lock (snmpTargetSpinLock)
    // must be used when modifying snmpTargetAddrTagList to
    // make sure two managers aren't trying to modify the object
    // at the same time.

    newtaglist <- taglist + ' ' + tag
    while (true)
    {
        status <- ModifyTagList(inst, newtaglist)

        // If a new tag list has been set, break out of the
        // while loop, otherwise try again after some random
        // time.

        if (status == true)
            break
        WaitRandomTime()
    }
}
```

```
procedure Boolean::ModifyTagList(inst, val)
{
    // Try modifying the value of snmpTargetAddrTagList.inst.
    // If successful, return true, else return false.

    pdu <- SnmpGet(snmpTargetSpinLock.0)
    lockVal <- GetVarBindValue(pdu, 1)

    setpdu <- {snmpTargetSpinLock.0 <- lockVal,
            snmpTargetAddrTagList <- val}

    pdu <- SnmpSet(setpdu)

    status <- GetErrorStatus(pdu)
    if (status == 'noError')
        return true

    return false
}
```

The AddToTargetTable procedure takes five parameters: the target address to add to snmpTargetAddrTable, and the SNMP parameters (Message Processing Model, Security Model, Security Name, and Security Level) to use when generating a message to the target system. AddToTargetTable will first check to see if an entry already exists within snmpTargetParamsTable that matches the specified SNMP parameters. If one does, its index will be used in creating a new row in snmpTargetAddrTable. If an entry doesn't exist, one will be created, and again, that index will be used when creating a new row in snmpTargetAddrTable.

The pseudocode for AddToTargetTable is presented below.

```
procedure Void::AddToTargetTable(addr, mp, sm, sn, sl)
{
    // First try to locate an entry within snmpTargetParamsTable
    // where the Message Processing Model = mp
    //          Security Model = sm
    //          Security Name = sn
    //          Security Level = sl

    foundFlag <- false
    flag <- true

    responsePDU <- {snmpTargetParamsMPModel,
            snmpTargetParamsSecurityModel,
            snmpTargetParamsSecurityName,
            snmpTargetParamsSecurityLevel,
            snmpTargetParamsRowStatus}
```

```
origPDU <- responsePDU

while (flag)
{
    pdu <- SnmpGetNext(responsePDU)
    responsePDU <- pdu
    flag <- CheckPDU(pdu, origPDU)

    if (flag == false)
        continue

    // An entry has been found. Check to see if it
    // matches the desired parameters.

    mpmodel <- GetVarBindValue(pdu, 1)
    securitymodel <- GetVarBindValue(pdu, 2)
    securityname <- GetVarBindValue(pdu, 3)
    securitylevel <- GetVarBindValue(pdu, 4)
    status <- GetVarBindValue(pdu, 5)

    if (status != 'active')
        continue

    if ((mpmodel == mp) && (securitymodel = sm) &&
        (securityname = sn) && (securitylevel == sl))
    {
        // A matching set of parameters have been
        // found. Set params to the instance of that row
        // and set foundFlag to true and flag to false (get
        // out of while loop).

        params <- GetVarBindInstance(
                pdu,
                1,
                snmpTargetParamsMPModel)

        foundFlag <- true
        flag <- false
        continue
    }
}

if (foundFlag == false)
{
    params <- GetUniqueInstance(snmpTargetParamsRowStatus)
    AddParamsRow(params, mp, sm, sn, sl)
}
```

```
        inst <- GetUniqueInstance(snmpTargetAddrRowStatus)
        AddTargetRow(inst, addr, params, 'trap')
}

procedure Void::AddParamsRow(inst, mp, sm, sn, sl)
{
        // A row indexed by inst has already been created
        // in the snmpTargetParamsTable with the RowStatus
        // set to 'createAndWait'. Fill in the rest of the
        // values and set the RowStatus to 'active'.

        setpdu <- {snmpTargetParamsMPModel.inst <- mp,
                snmpTargetParamsSecurityModel.inst <- sm,
                snmpTargetParamsSecurityName.inst <- sn,
                snmpTargetParamsSecurityLevel.inst <- sl,
                snmpTargetParamsRowStatus.inst <- active}

        SnmpSet(setpdu)
}


procedure Void::AddTargetRow(inst, addr, params, tag)
{
        // A row indexed by inst has already been created
        // in the snmpTargetAddrable with the RowStatus
        // set to 'createAndWait'. Fill in the rest of the
        // values and set the RowStatus to 'active'.

        taddr <- MakeTAddress(addr, 162)

        setpdu <- {snmpTargetAddrTDomain.inst <- snmpUDPDomain,
                snmpTargetAddrTAddress.inst <- taddr,
                snmpTargetAddrTagList.inst <- tag,
                snmpTargetAddrParams.inst <- params,
                snmpTargetParamsRowStatus.inst <- active}

        SnmpSet(setpdu)
}
```

As we have just demonstrated, if we avoid notification filtering within the device, we can keep notification configuration relatively simple. If you want to use filtering to control which traps are shown to a network manager, it makes more sense to perform the filtering within the network management application that is receiving and analyzing the traps. Not only can the filtering be done more intelligently (for example, you can filter based on trap object values) but it can also be used to keep track of state information. If a network management application receives one hundred link up/down traps for an interface during a twenty-four hour period, it would be much more useful to show a single line in a report that indicates how many transitions that interface has seen over the last twenty-four hours, what percentage of time during the last twenty-four hours that interface has been up, its current state, and how long it has been in that state than to simply dump to the user the one hundred events.

If you do decide you want to filter out certain notifications within the device, you need to add notify filters that include all the subtrees you care about and then add specific notify filters to exclude the notifications you want to filter out.

If for some reason you want to have some notifications sent as SNMPv2-Traps and a set of critical notifications sent as Informs, then you need to do the following:

1. Two entries need to be created in snmpNotifyTable: one to generate SNMPv2-Traps, the other to generate Informs.
2. For each target address that you want to send notifications to, you'll need two entries in the snmpTargetAddrTable. Each entry must reference a different snmpTargetParamsTable row. The corresponding rows in snmpNotifyFilterProfileTable must reference one of two notify filter profile names. For now, let's call these profile names "inform" and "trap."
3. Filters for the 'inform' profile name need to be added to snmpNotifyFilterTable. These filters must include all notifications that should be sent as Informs and exclude all notifications that should be sent as SNMPv2-Traps.
4. Filters for the 'trap' profile name need to be added to snmpNotifyFilterTable. These filters must include all notifications that should be sent as SNMPv2-Traps and exclude all notifications that should be sent as Informs.

5.6.6   Proxy MIB

The snmpProxyTable allows you to configure which target addresses to forward SNMP messages to.

Table 5-11   snmpProxyTable, Indexed by snmpProxyName

Object	Type	Access
snmpProxyName	SnmpAdminString	no-accessible
snmpProxyType	INTEGER	read-create
snmpProxyContextEngineID	SnmpEngineID	read-create
snmpProxyContextName	SnmpAdminString	read-create

Table 5-11   snmpProxyTable, Indexed by snmpProxyName (Continued)

Object	Type	Access
snmpProxyTargetParamsIn	SnmpAdminString	read-create
snmpProxySingleTargetOut	SnmpAdminString	read-create
snmpProxyMultipleTargetOut	SnmpTagValue	read-create
snmpProxyStorageType	StorageType	read-create
snmpProxyRowStatus	RowStatus	read-create

snmpProxyName: a unique identifier used to index this table.

snmpProxyType: defines the type of message that may be forwarded by this entry. This can have one of the following values:

- read (1) allows SNMP messages with Get, Get-Next, and Get-Bulk PDUs to be forwarded.

- write (2) allows SNMP messages with Set PDUs to be forwarded.

- trap (3) allows SNMP messages with SNMPv2-Trap PDUs to be forwarded.

- inform (4) allows SNMP messages with Inform PDUs to be forwarded.

snmpProxyContextEngineID: the contextEngineID contained in messages that may be forwarded using this entry.

snmpProxyContextName: the contextName contained in messages that may be forwarded by this entry. *Note*: This object is optional. If an implementation chooses not to use it, then the contextName contained in a message is ignored.

snmpProxyTargetParamsIn: the value of this object is used as an index into the snmpTargetParamsTable. An incoming message must have the same SNMP parameters as the corresponding row within the snmpTargetParamsTable for it to be forwarded by this entry.

snmpProxySingleTargetOut: the value of this object is used as an index into the snmpTargetAddrTable, which selects the target address to forward the incoming message to. This is used when forwarding an incoming read or write request.

snmpProxyMultipleTargetOut: this tag value is used to select target addresses to forward the incoming message to. This is used when forwarding either a trap or inform.

snmpProxyStorageType: specifies how a row in this table should be stored. The default is for it to be stored in nonVolatile memory

snmpProxyRowStatus: a RowStatus object used for adding and removing rows to/ from this table. A row cannot be made active until snmpProxyType, snmpProxy-ContextEngineID, snmpProxyContextName, snmpProxyTargetParamsIn, snmp-ProxySingleTargetOut, and snmpProxyMultipleTargetOut have all been set. Also, none of these objects may be modified while the row is active (the row would first have to be put in notInService).

5.6.7   How Proxy Forwarding Works

If an SNMP message is received with a contextEngineID which matches a value that a proxy forwarder application had registered for, then the following steps will be taken to determine which target address or addresses to forward the message to:

1. Search snmpProxyTable for all entries which match the incoming message. An entry matches an incoming message if snmpProxyContextEngineID matches the message's contextEngineID, snmpProxyContextName (if supported) matches the message's context-Name, the SNMP parameters for the message match the values referenced by snmpProxyTargetParamsIn, and the type of message matches snmpProxyType (a Get, Get-Next, Get-Bulk will match a value of `read` (1), a Set will match `write` (2), an SNMPv2-Trap will match `trap` (3), and an Inform will match `inform` (4)).

2. If the incoming message is a Get, Get-Next, Get-Bulk, or Set, then choose from the matching entries the one whose snmpProxyName value is the lexicographically smallest. The snmpProxySingleTargetOut object for this entry provides the index into the snmpTar-getAddrTable for the target address to forward the incoming message to. The SNMP parameters to use are specified by this row's snmpTargetAddrParams object.

3. If the incoming message is an SNMPv2-Trap or an Inform, then use each matching entry's tag value to locate the target addresses within snmpTargetAddrTable to forward the message to.

Note: As stated earlier, a proxy forwarder application cannot register the local snmpEngineID as one of the contextEngineIDs that it wants to forward messages for.

The following pseudocode also illustrates how a proxy forwarder application chooses the target address or addresses to forward an incoming message to.

```
// First, parse information from the incoming message, incoming.

info <- ParseMessage(incoming)

// Next search for entries within the snmpProxyTable that
// match the incoming message.

matches <- ''
foreach inst in snmpProxyTable
{

    type <- snmpProxyType.inst
    contextid <- snmpProxyContextEngineID.inst
    contextname <- snmpProxyContextName.inst
    params <- snmpProxyTargetParamsIn.inst

    if ((type != info.type) || (contextid != info.contextid))
        continue

    if (ContextNameImplemented() == true)
        if (contextname != info.contextname)
            continue

    // So far type, contextEngineID, and contextName (if supported)
    // matches, now check that the SNMP parameters match.

    if (snmpTargetParamsMPModel.params != info.mp)
        continue
    if (snmpTargetParamsSecurityModel.params != info.sm)
        continue
    if (snmpTargetParamsSecurityName.params != info.sn)
        continue
    if (snmpTargetParamsSecurityLevel != info.sl)
        continue
    add inst to matches
```

```
}

if ((info.type == read) || (info.type == write))
    ProcessProxySingle(incoming, matches)
else
    ProcessProxyMultiple(incoming, matches)
```

The procedure ProcessProxySingle is called if the incoming message is a Get, Get-Next, Get-Bulk, or Set. It will choose from the matching entries the one with the lexicographically smallest snmpProxyName. The target address to forward the message to will be selected from the corresponding snmpProxySingleTargetOut value.

The pseudocode for ProcessProxySingle is as follows.

```
procedure Void::ProcessProxySingle(incoming, matches)
{
    if (matches == '')
        return

    name <- ''
    foreach inst in matches
    {
        // Initialize name if it hasn't been
        // initialized yet.

        if (name == '')
            name <- inst

        // Check if a lexicographically smaller snmpProxyName
        // value has been seen.

        if (name > inst)
            name <- inst
    }

    target <- snmpProxySingleTargetOut.name

    taddr <- snmpTargetAddrTAddress.target
    params <- snmpTargetAddrParams.target

    SendProxyMessage(incoming, taddr, params)
}
```

The procedure ProcessProxyMultiple is called if the incoming message is an SNMPv2-Trap or an Inform. For each of the matching entries found within snmpProxyTable, it will use the tag value associated with the matching entry to find target addresses within snmpTargetAddrTable to forward the notification to.

The pseudocode for ProcessProxyMultiple is as follows.

```
procedure Void::ProcessProxyMultiple(incoming, matches)
{
    if (matches == '')
        return

    foreach inst in matches
    {
        // Get the tag value associated with the matching
        // entry. Then use the tag value to locate target
        // addresses within snmpTargetAddrTable.

        tag <- snmpProxyMultipleTargetOut.inst

        foreach inst2 in snmpTargetAddrTable
        {
            taddr <- snmpTargetAddrTAddress.inst2
            taglist <- snmpTargetAddrTagList.inst2
            params <- snmpTargetAddrParams.inst2

            if (params == '')
              continue
            if (InTagList(tag, taglist) == false)
              continue
            if (CheckForTargetParamsEntry(params) == false)
              continue

            // At this point, an entry has been found in
            // snmpTargetAddrTable whose tag list contains tag,
            // and whose snmpTargetAddrParams objects references
            // a valid row within snmpTargetParamsTable. Forward
            // the incoming message to this target.

            SendProxyMessage(incoming, taddr, params)
        }
    }
}
```

5.6.8   Proxy Forwarding Example

For this example let's configure snmpTargetAddrTable with two entries; one so we can forward read requests to a router, another so we can forward traps to a SUN workstation.

Table 5-12   snmpTargetAddrTable Proxy Example

	addr1	addr2
snmpTargetAddrName	addr1	addr2
snmpTargetAddrTDomain	snmpUDPDomain	snmpUDPDomain
snmpTargetAddrTAddress	158.101.121.1/161	158.101.121.2/162
snmpTargetAddrTagList	router	workstation
snmpTargetAddrParams	p1	p2
snmpTargetAddrStorageType	nonVolatile (3)	nonVolatile (3)
snmpTargetAddrRowStatus	active (1)	active (1)

We'll use the same snmpTargetParamsTable from the notification example. Now let's configure the snmpProxyTable with two entries and walk through examples of forwarding both a Get and an SNMPv2-Trap message.

Table 5-13   snmpProxyTable example

	proxy1	proxy2
snmpProxyName	proxy1	proxy2
snmpProxyType	1	3
snmpProxyContextEngineID	80 00 00 09 01 9e 65 79 01	80 00 00 2a 01 9e 65 79 02
snmpProxyContextName	admin	monitor
snmpProxyTargetParamsIn	p1	p2
snmpProxySingleTargetOut	addr1	
snmpProxyMultipleTargetOut		workstation
snmpProxyStorageType	nonVolatile (3)	nonVolatile (3)
snmpProxyRowStatus	active (1)	active (1)

Note: The contextEngineID value "80 00 00 09 01 9e 65 79 01" is interpreted as follows: the first 4 bytes (80 00 00 09) specify that the value is determined algorithmically and that the enterprise is Cisco's. The next byte, 01, indicates that the next 4 bytes represent an IP address (95 65 79 01 => 158.101.121.1). The contextEngineID value "80 00 00 2a 01 9e 65 79 02" is interpreted similarly, with the first 4 bytes (80 00 00 2a) specifying that the value is determined algorithmically and that the enterprise is Sun's. The IP address represented by "9e 65 79 02" translates to 158.101.121.2.

When an SNMP entity receives an incoming message with a contextEngineID that doesn't match its local engine ID, it will check to see if a proxy forwarder application has registered to forward messages for that contextEngineID. For this example, an incoming Get-Request message with a contextEngineID value of "80 00 00 09 01 9e 65 79 01" has been received. Since that contextEngineID had been registered by a proxy forwarder application, snmpProxyTable is searched for a matching entry. The first entry ends up matching the type, contextEngineID, and the contextName. The SNMP parameters referenced by p1 end up matching the SNMP parameters used in the incoming message.

Since only one matching entry was found, that entry is used to determine the forwarding address (otherwise, we'd have to pick the matching entry that has the lexicographically smallest snmpProxyName value). The snmpProxySingleTargetOut value is addr1. Using that to index the snmpTargetAddrTable, we get a target address of 158.101.121.1, port 161. We further get an snmpTargetAddrParams value of p1.

The incoming message that was received will be forwarded to 158.101.121.1 using the SNMP parameters referenced by p1.

The next example is when we receive an incoming SNMPv2-Trap message with a contextEngineID value of "80 00 00 2a 01 9e 65 79 02." Again, since that contextEngineID value had been registered by a proxy forwarder application, snmpProxyTable will be searched for matching entries. The second entry ends up matching the type, contextEngineID, and the contextName. The SNMP parameters referenced by p2 end up matching the SNMP parameters used in the incoming message.

The snmpProxyMultipleTargetOut specifies a tag "workstation." Searching through the snmpTargetAddrTable, one entry is found with a tag value of "workstation." The SNMPv2-Trap message will be forwarded to the corresponding IP address, 158.101.121.2, using the SNMP parameters referenced by p2. Notifications can be forwarded to more than one target. If the snmpTargetAddrTable had more entries labeled with the tag "workstation," the SNMPv2-Trap message would be forwarded to those additional targets.

5.6.9   Configuring Proxy Forwarding

Configuring proxy forwarding for read/write messages is fairly straightforward:

a. If the target address doesn't exist within snmpTargetAddrTable, then add both an entry to the snmpTargetParamsTable (if needed) and snmpTargetAddrTable.

b. The SNMP parameters used by the incoming message must map to a row within snmpTargetParamsTable. If a row with these parameters does not exist, a new row must be added to the table.

c. Add two entries to the snmpProxyTable — one for read requests (Get, Get-Next, and Get-Bulk) and one for write requests (Set). Each entry must specify the contextEngineID of the target device that the message will be forwarded to. If the proxy forwarder application supports using the contextName, then the contextName must also be specified. Set the snmpProxyTargetParamsIn object for both entries to reference SNMP parameters for the incoming message.

The following pseudocode illustrates this.

```
procedure Void::ConfigureProxyReadWrite(info, addr, mp, sm, sn, sl)
{
    // info is a structure containing all necessary
    // information about the incoming message. It would
    // be defined by a C structure as follows:
    //
    // struct IncomingInfo {
    //      int type;
    //      SnmpEngineID contextid;
    //      SnmpAdminString contextname;
    //      SnmpMessageProcessingModel mp;
    //      SnmpSecurityModel sm;
    //      SnmpAdminString sn;
    //      SnmpSecurityLevel sl;
    // }
    //
    // addr is the target address to forward the
    // incoming message to.
    // mp, sm, sn, sl specify the SNMP parameters (Message
    // Processing Model, Security Model, Security Name,
    // and Security Level) to use when forwarding the message
    // to the target address.

    // LookupTargetParams will return either the index
    // of a matching row or an empty string.
```

```
params <- LookUpTargetParams(mp, sm, sn, sl)

if (params == '')
{
    // if a row doesn't exist with the necessary
    // SNMP parameters needed to forward the incoming
    // message to the target, create a new row in
    // snmpTargetParamsTable.

    params <- GetUniqueInstance(snmpTargetParamsRowStatus)
    AddParamsRow(params, mp, sm, sn, sl)
}

// LookupTargetAddr will return either the index
// of a matching row or an empty string.

target <- LookUpTargetAddr(addr, params)

if (target == '')
{
    target <- GetUniqueInstance(snmpTargetAddrRowStatus)
    AddTargetRow(target, addr, params, '')
}

// At this point an entry for the target address exists in the
// snmpTargetAddrTable, and is indexed by target.
//
// Check to see if an entry exists within snmpTargetParamsTable
// that matches the SNMP parameters of the incoming message. If
// not, add one.

params <- LookUpTargetParams(info.mp, info.sm, info.sn,
          info.sl)

if (params == '')
{
    // if a row doesn't exist with the necessary
    // SNMP parameters needed to recognize the incoming
    // message, create a new row in snmpTargetParamsTable.

    params <- GetUniqueInstance(snmpTargetParamsRowStatus)
    AddParamsRow(params,
          info.mp, info.sm, info.sn, info.sl)
}

// Check to see if rows already exist within snmpProxyTable
// to forward incoming read/write messages for the specified
```

```
// contextEngineID and contextName. If rows do exist, destroy
// them.
//
// Add new rows to the snmpProxyTable.

foreach type {read, write}
{
    inst <- LookUpProxy(type,
            info.contextid,
            info.contextname,
            params)

    if (inst != '')
    {
        pdu <- {snmpProxyRowStatus.inst <- destroy}
        SnmpSet(pdu)
    }

    // Add a row into snmpProxyTable.

    name <- GetUniqueInstance(snmpProxyRowStatus)
    pdu <- {snmpProxyType.name <- type,
        snmpProxyContextEngineID.name <- info.contextid,
        snmpProxyContextName.name <- info.contextname,
        snmpProxyTargetParamsIn.name <- params,
        snmpProxySingleTargetOut.name <- target,
        snmpProxyMultipleTargetOut.name <- ''
        snmpProxyRowStatus.name <- active}

    SnmpSet(pdu)
    }
}
```

The procedure LookUpTargetAddr is passed an IP address and an index for snmpTarget-ParamsTable. It will return either an index for a matching row within snmpTargetAddrTable or an empty string. LookUpTargetParams is passed a Message Processing Model, a Security Model, a Security Name, and a Security Level and will return either an index for snmpTarget-ParamsTable if a matching row is found or an empty string. LookUpProxy is passed a message type (read, write, trap, or inform), a contextEngineID, a contextName, and an index for snmpTargetParamsTable. It will similarly return either an index for a matching row within snmpProxyTable or an empty string.

Configuring proxy forwarding for trap/inform messages is similar to what we have just seen for read/write messages with the following differences:

a. Notification messages can be forwarded to a list of targets as opposed to a single target. The target addresses to use are specified by a tag value. This tag value must be added to each corresponding snmpTargetAddrTable row's tag list

b. The snmpProxyMultipleTargetOut object needs to be set to this tag value. The snmpProxySingleTargetOut object will be set to an empty string.

The following pseudocode illustrates this.

```
procedure Void::ConfigureProxyTrapInform(info, addrList,
        mp, sm, sn, sl)
{
    // info is a structure containing all necessary
    // information about the incoming message. It would
    // be defined by a C structure as follows:
    //
    // struct IncomingInfo {
    //     int type;
    //     SnmpEngineID contextid;
    //     SnmpAdminString contextname;
    //     SnmpMessageProcessingModel mp;
    //     SnmpSecurityModel sm;
    //     SnmpAdminString sn;
    //     SnmpSecurityLevel sl;
    // }
    //
    // addrList is a list of target addresses to
    // forward the incoming notification message to.
    //
    // mp, sm, sn, sl specify the SNMP parameters (Message
    // Processing Model, Security Model, Security Name,
    // and Security Level) to use when forwarding the message
    // to the target addresses.

    // LookupTargetParams will return either the index
    // of a matching row or an empty string.

    params <- LookUpTargetParams(mp, sm, sn, sl)

    if (params == '')
    {
        // if a row doesn't exist with the necessary
        // SNMP parameters needed to forward the incoming
        // message to the target, create a new row in
        // snmpTargetParamsTable.
```

```
      params <- GetUniqueInstance(snmpTargetParamsRowStatus)
      AddParamsRow(params, mp, sm, sn, sl)
}

// For each target address within addrList check to
// see if a corresponding row exists within
// snmpTargetAddrTable. If a row doesn't exist, add one.

foreach addr in addrList
{
    target <- LookUpTargetAddr(addr, params)

    if (target == '')
    {
        target <- GetUniqueInstance(snmpTargetAddrRowStatus)
        AddTargetRow(target, addr, params, '')
    }
}

// At this point entries exist in snmpTargetAddrTable
// for each target address within addrList.
//
// Check to see if an entry exists within snmpTargetParamsTable
// that matches the SNMP parameters of the incoming message. If
// not, add one.

params <- LookUpTargetParams(info.mp, info.sm, info.sn,
          info.sl)

if (params == '')
{
    // if a row doesn't exist with the necessary
    // SNMP parameters needed to recognize the incoming
    // message, create a new row in snmpTargetParamsTable.

    params <- GetUniqueInstance(snmpTargetParamsRowStatus)
    AddParamsRow(params,
        info.mp, info.sm, info.sn, info.sl)
}

// Check to see if rows already exist within snmpProxyTable
// to forward incoming trap/inform messages for the specified
// contextEngineID, contextName, and SNMP parameters. If rows
// do exist, destroy them.
//
// Add new rows to the snmpProxyTable. A tag value is used to
// map the proxy entry to target addresses. Use the
// snmpProxyName value as the tag value and add it to each
```

```
        // target addresses's tag list.

        foreach type {trap, inform}
        {
            inst <- LookUpProxy(type,
                    info.contextid,
                    info.contextname,
                    params)

            if (inst != '')
            {
                pdu <- {snmpProxyRowStatus.inst <- destroy}
                SnmpSet(pdu)
            }

            // Add a row into snmpProxyTable.

            name <- GetUniqueInstance(snmpProxyRowStatus)
            pdu <- {snmpProxyType.name <- type,
                  snmpProxyContextEngineID.name <- info.contextid,
                  snmpProxyContextName.name <- info.contextname,
                  snmpProxyTargetParamsIn.name <- params,
                  snmpProxySingleTargetOut.name <- '',
                  snmpProxyMultipleTargetOut.name <- name,
                  snmpProxyRowStatus.name <- active}

            SnmpSet(pdu)

            // Add name to each target addresses's tag list.

            foreach addr in addrList
            {
                target <- LookUpTargetAddr(addr, params)
                pdu <- {snmpTargetAddrTagList.target}
                response <- SnmpGet(pdu)
                taglist <- GetVarBindValue(response, 1)
                AddToTagList(target, taglist, name)
            }
        }
    }
```

5.7 Summary

While this chapter discussed SNMPv3 Applications, the focus was on how notifications
and proxy forwarding work. To that end, pseudocode was provided to try to make notification

and proxy forwarding configuration simple. What we saw with notification configuration, we can either keeps it simple or we can make it complex. The more complex we make it, the higher the overall management cost is going to be since we are going to have to spend more time trying to fix configuration mistakes, and in trying to validate that configurations are consistent and correct.

CHAPTER 6

SNMPv3 Security

$\mathbf{T}$his chapter examines the User-based Security Model that has been defined for SNMPv3.

In order to feel that an SNMP operation is secure, we would like to ask the following questions:

1. Has the message been altered?
2. Is the message coming from a valid user?
3. Has the message been maliciously delayed?
4. Is the message being replayed?
5. Can sensitive information be protected against eavesdroppers?
6. Is the user allowed to access the MIB objects specified in the message?

The User-based Security Model addresses the first five questions. The View-based Access Control, which we discuss in the next chapter, answers the final question.

6.1 Authoritative and Non-authoritative

When an SNMP Request or notification message is sent from one SNMP entity to another, one of the entities is considered authoritative, the other non-authoritative. For the most part, the authoritative entity is the one we used to think of in SNMPv1 days as an SNMP agent. Or putting it another way, the authoritative entity

• receives and responds to requests

• generates SNMPv2-Traps

The one exception to this is that the entity that receives an Inform message is considered authoritative. The reason why one of the entities needs to be authoritative will be shown later when we talk about timeliness.

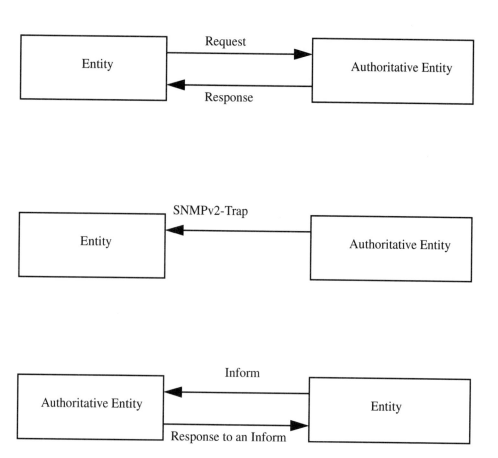

6.2 Security Parameters

Each SNMPv3 message contains security parameters which are encoded as an octet string. The meaning of these security parameters depends on the Security Model being used. For the User-based Security Model, the security parameters represent the following ASN.1 sequence:

```
USMSecurityParametersSyntax DEFINITIONS IMPLICIT TAGS ::= BEGIN

    UsmSecurityParameters ::=
        SEQUENCE {
            -- global User-based security parameters
            msgAuthoritativeEngineID      OCTET STRING,
            msgAuthoritativeEngineBoots   INTEGER (0..2147483647),
            msgAuthoritativeEngineTime    INTEGER (0..2147483647),
            msgUserName                   OCTET STRING (SIZE(0..32)),

            -- authentication protocol specific parameters
            msgAuthenticationParameters   OCTET STRING,

            -- privacy protocol specific parameters
            msgPrivacyParameters          OCTET STRING
        }
    END
```

The ASN.1 sequence will be encoded using the Basic Encoding Rules (BER). The msg-AuthoritativeEngineID object identifies the authoritative SNMP engine involved in the message exchange. The msgAuthoritativeEngineBoots and msgAuthoritativeEngineTime objects are used for timeliness checking (as we'll be seeing later). For both the HMAC-MD5-96 and HMAC-SHA-96 authentication protocols, the msgAuthenticationParameters will contain a 12-byte octet string that will be used as an electronic *fingerprint* to authenticate the message. This will be described in detail later in this chapter. The meaning of the msgPrivacyParameters object for the CBC-DES Symmetric Encryption Protocol will also be described later in this chapter.

Finally, both the msgUserName and msgAuthoritativeEngineID objects are needed to identify the secret keys used for the message.

6.3 Discovery

A simple discovery method has been built in to the User-based Security Model to allow a non-authoritative SNMP entity to learn the snmpEngineID value of the authoritative entity it wishes to communicate with.

The non-authoritative entity simply sends a Request message to the authoritative entity with

- a securityLevel of noAuthNoPriv
- a msgUserName of zerolength
- a msgAuthoritativeEngineID value of zerolength

• an empty variable-bindings

The authoritative entity responds by sending a Report message. Its local snmpEngineID value will be supplied within the msgAuthoritativeEngineID field. The Report PDU will include the usmStatsUnknownEngineIDs counter in its variable-bindings.

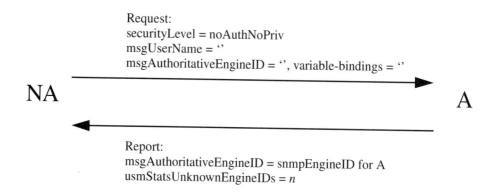

6.4 Timeliness

For messages to be considered authenticated, they must be received in a timely manner. This is to protect against a message being intentionally delayed or replayed by a malicious party. Timeliness is guaranteed by using what amounts to a loosely synchronized clock.

In every secure SNMPv3 communication between two engines, one engine is considered authoritative, the other non-authoritative. The authoritative engine maintains a "clock" value that is used for synchronization. It is the responsibility of the non-authoritative engine to learn this "clock" value and keep track of it.

This "clock" value is made up of two values: engineBoots and engineTime. Remember, engineBoots is the number of times the engine has rebooted, and engineTime is the number of seconds that has passed since the engine has last rebooted. If engineTime ever wraps, engine-Boots will be incremented as if a reboot has occurred.

The non-authoritative engine initially learns the authoritative engine's engineBoots and engineTime values by sending a Request message to the authoritative engine with msgAuthoritativeEngineBoots and msgAuthoritativeEngineTime both set to zero. The authoritative engine responds by sending a Report message which contains the up to date values of snmpEngine-Boots and snmpEngineTime.

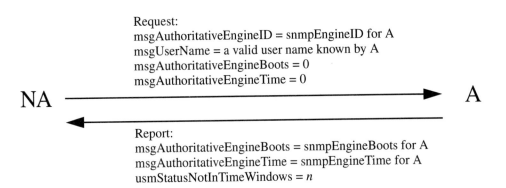

Request:
msgAuthoritativeEngineID = snmpEngineID for A
msgUserName = a valid user name known by A
msgAuthoritativeEngineBoots = 0
msgAuthoritativeEngineTime = 0

NA ———————————————————————▶ A

◀———————————————————————

Report:
msgAuthoritativeEngineBoots = snmpEngineBoots for A
msgAuthoritativeEngineTime = snmpEngineTime for A
usmStatusNotInTimeWindows = n

Once the non-authoritative engine learns the snmpEngineBoots and snmpEngineTime values for an authoritative engine, it will need to keep track of these values. Future messages sent to the authoritative engine will contain the non-authoritative engine's *idea* of what the snmpEngineBoots and snmpEngineTime values are for the authoritative engine. The authoritative engine will compare these with its actual values. If the values are within a 150-second time window, then the message is considered timely. If it falls outside of that window, the message is discarded and an error counter will be incremented.

To make this explanation a little simpler, we will refer to the authoritative engine's snmpEngineBoots and snmpEngineTime values as $boots_A$ and $time_A$. The non-authoritative engine's local notion of these values will be referred as $boots_L$ and $time_L$.

When an authoritative engine receives a message: $boots_L$ and $time_L$ are determined from the msgAuthoritativeEngineBoots and msgAuthoritativeEngineTime fields. The authoritative engine will decide that a message falls outside the 150-second time window if any of the following occur:

- $boots_A$ has been set to 2147483647. This indicates that the authoritative engine has detected a serious problem and needs to be manually reconfigured.
- $boots_A$ and $boots_L$ are not equal.
- $time_A$ and $time_L$ differ by more than 150 seconds.

When a non-authoritative engine receives a message: $boots_A$ and $time_A$ are determined from the msgAuthoritativeEngineBoots and msgAuthoritativeEngineTime fields.
If either

- $boots_A$ is greater than $boots_L$, or
- $boots_A$ equals $boots_L$, but $time_A$ is greater than $time_L$

then the non-authoritative engine will update its $boots_L$ and $time_L$ values with the values extracted from the msgAuthoritativeEngineBoots and msgAuthoritativeEngineTime fields.

A non-authoritative engine will further discard a message for being outside of the Time Window if any of the following conditions are true:

- $boots_L$ equals 2147483647. This indicates that the *authoritative* engine has detected a serious problem and needs to be manually reconfigured. Remember, $boots_L$ can be updated from the extracted msgAuthoritativeEngineBoots field.
- $boots_L$ is greater than $boots_A$.
- $boots_L$ equals $boots_A$, but $time_L$ is more than 150 seconds greater than $time_A$.

There is still the possibility of messages being maliciously replayed within the 150 second time window. This is protected as follows:

For a Response message:

> Every message has a message identifier. An entity that originates an SNMP Request is responsible for matching a response it receives with an outstanding request by using the message identifier. Let's assume two responses are received within a 150-second time window with the same message identifier *id*. The first response will match an outstanding request with *id*. When the response is later replayed, the matching request has already been removed from the internal cache — *id* will no longer match any outstanding requests and the replayed response will be discarded.

For a Request message:

> Entities receiving Request messages cannot utilize the message identifier for protecting against replays. However if a Request message is replayed that is simply retrieving values, then no real damage can be done. Set operations can be protected against replays by including a TestAndIncr object within the Set's variable-bindings.

Note: Timeliness checks are performed only if authentication is being used. Without autnetication, a malicious individual could alter the "clock" information provided in the message making any sort of timeliness check and clock synchronization useless.

6.5 Keys

Secret keys are used by both the authentication and privacy protocols.

For authentication:

When an SNMP entity wants to send an SNMP Request to an authoritative entity, *X*, it will use a secret authentication key that both it and *X* know about to create a *fingerprint* of the message. When *X* receives the message, it will also calculate a *fingerprint* by using the same secret authentication key. If the *fingerprints* match, the message has been authenticated.

For privacy:

This is similar to authentication. Both sides share a secret privacy key and use this key to both encrypt and decrypt messages.

Key management:

An authoritative engine needs secret keys for each user. As we will be seeing later, the secret keys for a user will be able to be set remotely through SNMP.

On the SNMP manager side, there should be a simple way to map a user to a secret key. As we'll be seeing, secret keys are going to be represented by long octet strings. Humans, though, deal better with textual information than long random hex values.

We're going to propose a solution that will map a user name to a textual password — and then map the password to what amounts to random octet string (or key). Furthermore, an SNMP manager may need to access thousands of devices in a network. Instead of a user having to maintain a different password for each device, we will show a solution proposed by the Internet-Draft USM document for using one password for each user, but still deriving unique secret keys for each authoritative entity. This means that if the secret key for a user and an authoritative entity is somehow discovered, none of the other authoritative entities will be compromised.

The Internet-Draft USM document provides the following C procedure (only slightly modified and truncated here) to convert a password into a 16-byte octet string that can be used by the HMAC-MD5-96 authentication protocol:

```
void password_to_key_md5(
    u_char *password,    /* IN */
    u_int   passwordlen, /* IN */
    u_char *engineID,    /* IN  - pointer to snmpEngineID  */
    u_int   engineLength, /* IN  - length of snmpEngineID */
    u_char *key) /* OUT - pointer to caller 16-octet buffer */
{
    MD5_CTX    MD;
    u_char     *cp, password_buf[64];
    u_long     password_index = 0;
    u_long     count = 0, i;
```

```
MD5Init (&MD);    /* initialize MD5 */

// Generate 1 Megabyte of data by using the supplied
// password. Call MD5Update with 64 byte chunks.

while (count < 1048576) {
    cp = password_buf;
    for (i = 0; i < 64; i++) {
        // Fill a buffer with the characters in the supplied
        // password. When the end of the password is reached
        // cycle back to the beginning.

        *cp++ = password[password_index++ % passwordlen];
    }
    MD5Update (&MD, password_buf, 64);
    count += 64;
}

MD5Final (key, &MD);              /* tell MD5 we're done */
}
```

The procedures MD5Init, MD5Update, and MD5Final are defined in RFC 1321. The procedure password_to_key_md5 simply runs 1 megabyte worth of data through an MD5 hashing algorithm. The 1 megabyte of data is generated 64 bytes at a time by cycling through each character of the password. *Note*: Passwords such as "four," "fourfour," and "fourfourfour" will generate the same results since the code

```
for (i = 0; i < 64; i++) {
    *cp++ = password[password_index++ % passwordlen];
}
```

will cause the 64-byte buffer password_buf to be loaded with identical values. Passwords should not have repeating blocks of characters. The longer the password the better!

Calling password_to_key_md5 will produce a 16-byte octet string that we'll call *ku*. The next step is to produce a localized or specific version of *ku* for an authoritative entity. The way we'll do that is to build an octet string by concatenating *ku* to both ends of the snmpEngineID value for an authoritative entity, and then running this octet string through an MD5 hashing algorithm. We'll call this localized key, *kul*. The following pseudocode calculates the localized key, *kul*, for a given user and an authoritative entity:

```
procedure OctetString::GetLocalizedKeyMD5(userName, addr)
{
    // userName specifies the user to generate the key for.
```

```
    // addr is the IP address of the authoritative engine

    password <- GetPassword(userName)
    passwordLen <- LengthOf(password)
    engineID <- GetEngineID(addr)
    engineIDLen <- LengthOf(engineID)

    // Call password_to_key_md5 passing the password,
    // password length, pointer to an octet string
    // containing the engineID, length os the engineID, and
    // a pointer to a buffer that will derived key, ku. Note.
    // ku will need to point to a 16-byte buffer.

    password_to_key_md5(password, passwordLen, &engineID,
            engineIDLEn, &ku)

    // Note. The + operator for octet string results
    // in a concatenation operation. The result of
    // ku + engineID + ku is the concatentation of those
    // octet strings.

    kul <- MD5(ku + engineID + ku)
    return kul
}
```

Producing keys for the HMAC-SHA-96 authentication protocol is done in a similar way. We still want to map a user to a password and then to a key (in this case the key will be a 20-byte octet string), and we still want to produce localized versions of the key for each authoritative engine.

The following C code is taken from the Internet-Draft USM document (slightly modified and truncated here):

```
void password_to_key_sha(
    u_char *password,     /* IN */
    u_int   passwordlen, /* IN */
    u_char *engineID,    /* IN  - pointer to snmpEngineID  */
    u_int   engineLength,/* IN  - length of snmpEngineID */
    u_char *key) /* OUT - pointer to caller 20-octet buffer */
{
    SHA_CTX     SH;
    u_char      *cp, password_buf[72];
    u_long      password_index = 0;
    u_long      count = 0, i;

    SHAInit (&SH);   /* initialize SHA */
```

```
// Generate 1 Megabyte of data by using the supplied
// password. Call SHAUpdate with 64 byte chunks.

while (count < 1048576) {
    cp = password_buf;
    for (i = 0; i < 64; i++) {
        // Fill a buffer with the characters in the supplied
        // password. When the end of the password is reached
        // cycle back to the beginning.

        *cp++ = password[password_index++ % passwordlen];
    }
    SHAUpdate (&SH, password_buf, 64);
    count += 64;
}

SHAFinal (key, &SH);                /* tell SHA we're done */
return;
}
```

The pseudo code to produce a localized key for HMAC-SHA-96 is as follows:

```
procedure OctetString::GetLocalizedKeySHA(userName, addr)
{
    // userName specifies the user to generate the key for.
    // addr is the IP address of the authoritative engine

    password <- GetPassword(userName)
    passwordLen <- LengthOf(password)
    engineID <- GetEngineID(addr)
    engineIDLen <- LengthOf(engineID)

    // Call password_to_key_sha passing the password,
    // password length, pointer to an octet string
    // containing the engineID, length os the engineID, and
    // a pointer to a buffer that will derived key, ku. Note.
    // ku will need to point to a 20-byte buffer.

    password_to_key_sha(password, passwordLen, &engineID,
            engineIDLen, &ku)

    // Note. The + operator for octet string results
    // in a concatenation operation. The result of
    // ku + engineID + ku is the concatentation of those
```

```
// octet strings.

kul <- SHA(ku + engineID + ku)
return kul
}
```

The same procedures that were used used to generate the MD5 and SHA authentication keys can be used to generate the privacy keys for DES. Since DES keys are 16 bytes, if the SHA procedure is used, the 20-byte output would need to be truncated to 16 bytes.

Changing Key Values:

Key values can be changed through SNMP. The more often key values are changed, the less likely that a key can be discovered. Obviously, the most secure practice would be to change a key value after every exchange, but the overhead involved on both the management side and for the device could end up being overwhelming. A good practice might be to change the key values every day or every week.

To remotely change a key used by the HMAC-MD5-96 authentication algorithm, go through the following steps:

1. Generate a new password for a user.

2. Get the localized key value by calling the GetLocalizedKeyMD5 procedure.

3. Generate a value, *random*, a 16-byte random octet string.

4. Calculate a value, *delta*, as follows:

```
// oldkul represents the previous localized key.
// kul represents the new localized key value.
// Concatenate the oldkul with the random 16-byte
// octet string and run this value through an MD5
// hashing algorithm. Save the results as temp.

temp <- MD5(oldkul + random)
for (i = 0; i < 16; i++) {
    delta[i] = temp[i] XOR kul[i]
}
```

5. Concatenate *random* and *delta* to form a 32-byte octet string. This octet string can now be used to remotely configure an authoritative entity's secret key. The MIB

objects that need to be set will be shown when we later go over the USM MIB. A remote entity will go through the following logic to calculate a new key value given *random* and *delta*.

```
// oldkul represents the previous localized key.
// Given a 16-byte octet string, random, and a
// 16-byte octet string, delta, calculate a new
// localized key value by reverse engineering
// the steps taken to calculate delta.
//
// Note.if (a XOR b == c) then (a XOR c == b)
//
// First calculate an MD5 hash on the octet string
// formed by appending random to the previous key value.

temp <- MD5(oldkul + random)

// Next calculate the new localized key by XORing each
// byte of temp and delta.

for (i = 0; i < 16; i++) {
    kul[i] = temp[i] XOR delta[i]
}
```

What we're in effect doing is using the previous and new key values to calculate a *delta* value. Then we pass the remote entity both the *random* and *delta* values which it uses in combination with the previous key to calculate the new key. The *random* and *delta* values won't help anyone eavesdropping on the line calculate the new secret key unless they know the previous key. This allows us to update keys without worrying about privacy.

To remotely change a key used by the HMAC-SHA-96 authentication algorithm, we will go through almost identical steps:

1. Generate a new password for a user.

2. Get the localized key value by calling the GetLocalizedKeySHA procedure.

3. Generate a value, *random*, a 20-byte random octet string.

4. Calculate a value, *delta*, as follows:

```
// oldkul represents the previous localized key.
// kul represents the new localized key value.
```

```
// Concatenate the oldkul with the random 20-byte
// octet string and run this value through an MD5
// hashing algorithm. Save the results as temp.

temp <- SHA(oldkul + random)
for (i = 0; i < 20; i++) {
    delta[i] = temp[i] XOR kul[i]
}
```

5. Concatenate *random* and *delta* to form a 40-byte octet string. This octet string can now be used to remotely configure an authoritative entity's secret key. Again, we will show the MIB objects that need to be set when we go over the USM MIB. A remote entity will go through the following logic to calculate a new key value given *random* and *delta*.

```
// oldkul represents the previous localized key.
// Given a 20-byte octet string, random, and a
// 20-byte octet string, delta, calculate a new
// localized key value by reverse engineering
// the steps taken to calculate delta.
//
// Note.if (a XOR b == c) then (a XOR c == b)
//
// First calculate a SHA hash on the octet string
// formed by appending random to the previous key value.

temp <- SHA(oldkul + random)

// Next calculate the new localized key by XORing each
// byte of temp and delta.

for (i = 0; i < 20; i++) {
    kul[i] = temp[i] XOR delta[i]
}
```

6.6 USM MIB

The USM MIB defines

- OBJECT IDENTIFIERs for specifying standard authentication and privacy protocols. These will be shown when the usmUserTable is described.
- USM Error Statistics.
- The usmUserTable, which is a table of valid users for the User-based Security Model.

• A TestAndIncr object, usmUserSpinLock, used to coordinate Set operations to the usmUserTable.

The following 32-bit counters have been defined to provided error statistics for the User-based Security Model:

usmStatsUnsupportedSecLevels: counts the number of packets received by an SNMP engine that were dropped because the requested security level is not supported.

usmStatsNotInTimeWindows: counts the number of packets received by an SNMP engine which were dropped because they were outside an authoritative SNMP engine's time window. Remember, in any exchange where timeliness is checked, one entity will be authoritative, one will be non-authoritative.

For the authoritative engine, this will happen if any of the following occurs:

1. The local value of snmpEngineBoots is 2147483647.
2. The value of msgAuthoritativeEngineBoots doesn't equal the local value of snmpEngineBoots.
3. The value of msgAuthoritativeEngineTime differs from the local value of snmpEngineTime by more than 150 seconds.

For the non-authoritative engine, this will happen if any of the following occurs:

1. The local notition of the value of snmpEngineBoots for the authoritative engine is 2147483647.
2. The value of msgAuthoritativeEngineBoots is less than the local notion of snmpEngineBoots for the authoritative engine.
3. The value of msgAuthoritativeEngineBoots matches the local notion of snmpEngineBoots, but the value msgAuthoritativeEngineTime is more than 150 seconds less than the local notion of snmpEngineTime for the authoritative engine.

Note: If an authoritative SNMP engine has a problem where it cannot determine its snmpEngineBoots value, then it must set its snmpEngineBoots value to 2147483647. It will latch at this value. This will cause all received messages to be dropped because they will be determined to be outside the time window. In order to fix this, an SNMP engine must be reconfigured manually, either with a new snmpEngineID value, or with new secret values for authentication and privacy for all known users to that SNMP engine.

usmStatusUnknownUserNames: counts the number of packets received by an SNMP engine which were dropped because they referenced an unknown user. A user is unknown by the User-based Security Model if a row cannot be found within the usmUserTable that is indexed by the values of the authoritative engine identifier and user name provided by the security parameters (msgAuthoritativeEngineID.msgUserName).

usmStatsUnknownEngineIDs: counts the number of packets received by an SNMP engine which were dropped because they referenced an unknown engine identifier. An engine identifier is unknown if the value of the msgAuthoritativeEngineID field in the security parameters is unknown.

usmStatsWrongDigests: counts the number of packets received by an SNMP engine which were dropped because the authentication failed (the *fingerprint* or digest calculated by the authoritative engine doesn't match what's in the message).

usmStatsDecryptionErrors: counts the number of packets received by an SNMP engine which were dropped because they could not be decrypted.

The usmUserTable maintains authentication and privacy information for each user. Each row in the table is indexed by an SNMP engine identifier and a user name. For most network devices which receive requests or send notifications, the SNMP engine identifier used will be its own local value. However, if an entity is expected to send requests to a remote device, a row may exist using the SNMP engine identifier for the remote device.

Each row specifies the authentication protocol (if any) and the encryption protocol (if any) to use when exchanging SNMP messages for a specific user. Each row also contains authentication and encryption KeyChange objects to allow secret keys to be changed remotely.

Finally, new rows are created by cloning them from existing rows. However, before a newly created row can be made active the secret keys for authentication and encryption must be changed (if either authentication or encryption are being used) by modifying the appropriate KeyChange object.

Note: At least one "template" row must be created and have its secret keys configured through some means other than SNMP (most likely through a command line interface) so that new rows can be cloned from it.

Table 6-1   usmUserTable, Indexed by usmUserEngineID.usmUserName

Object	Type	Access
usmUserEngineID	SnmpEngineID	not-accessible
usmUserName	SnmpAdminString	not-accessible
usmUserSecurityName	SnmpAdminString	read-only
usmUserCloneFrom	RowPointer	read-create
usmUserAuthProtocol	AutonomousType	read-create
usmUserAuthKeyChange	KeyChange	read-create
usmUserOwnAuthKeyChange	KeyChange	read-create
usmUserPrivProtocol	AutonomousType	read-create
usmUserPrivKeyChange	KeyChange	read-create
usmUserOwnPrivKeyChange	KeyChange	read-create
usmUserPublic	OCTET STRING	read-create
usmUserStorageType	StorageType	read-create
usmUserStatus	RowStatus	read-create

usmUserEngineID: for devices that behave as what we used to think of as an SNMP agent, this will simply be the snmpEngineID value of the local entity. However if the local entity can generate SNMP Request messages, then this row may reference a remote snmpEngineID that this entity may send SNMP Requests to.

usmUserName: the name of a user. This should be a textual string between 1 and 32 bytes long. The usmUserEngineID along with the usmUserName is used to index into this table.

usmUserSecurityName: the name of a user in a Security Model independent format. Normally, the securityName will be the same value as the userName.

usmUserCloneFrom: a new row is created by "cloning" it from an already existing row. What this means is that if you want to add a new row in the table, this object must be set to point to an already existing row. The objects, usmUserAuthProtocol and usmUserPrivProtocol, are copied from the cloned row. Also the initial values of the secret authentication key and the secret encryption key are set from the cloned row.

If a new row employs authentication (usmUserAuthProtocol set to something other than usmNoAuthProtocol), then the secret authentication key must be changed by setting usmUserAuthKeyChange before the row can be made active.

Similarly, if the new row employs privacy (usmUserPrivProtocol set to something other than usmNoPrivProtocol), then the secret encryption key must be changed by setting usmUserPrivKeyChange before the row can be made active.

usmUserAuthProtocol: specifies the authentication protocol to use. The following values have so far been defined:

Table 6-2   usmUserAuthProtocol Values Defined So Far

Authentication Protocol	Value	OBJECT IDENTIFIER
None	usmNoAuthProtocol	1.3.6.1.6.3.10.1.1.1
HMAC-MD5-96	usmHMACMD5AuthProtocol	1.3.6.1.6.3.10.1.1.2
HMAC-SHA-96	usmHMSCSHAAuthProtocol	1.3.6.1.6.3.10.1.1.3

If an initial set operation tries to set usmUserAuthProtocol to an unknown or unsupported protocol, then the set operation will fail and a `wrongValue` error will be returned.

If a set operation later tries to change the value to anything other than `usmNoAuthProtocol`, the set operation will fail and an `inconsistentValue` error will be returned.

Since privacy requires authentication, if an encryption protocol has been configured for this row, then this value cannot be set to `usmNoAuthProtocol`. Trying to do so will cause the set operation to fail and an `inconsistentError` to be returned.

Finally, if the usmUserAuthProtocol associated with the row that this one was cloned from is set to `usmNoAuthProtocol`, then this object will also be set to have no authentication protocol.

usmUserAuthKeyChange: this KeyChange object is used to change a user's secret authentication key. If the HMAC-MD5-96 authentication protocol is being used, then this value will be a 32-byte OCTET STRING. If the HMAC-SHA-96 authentication protocol is being used, then this value will be a 40-byte OCTET STRING. We have already seen several examples of using a KeyChange object to modify a secret key value. When creating a new row in usmUserTable, if this object is set before usmUserCloneFrom, then the set operation will fail with an `inconsistentName` error. Reading this object returns a zero-length string.

usmUserOwnAuthKeyChange: this KeyChange object behaves exactly the same as usmUserAuthKeyChange, except that in order for the set operation to succeed the msgUserName embedded within the SNMP message's security parameters must match the usmUserName object for this row. This is an interesting property. The access control for this object can be set to allow anyone to write this object, but in fact it can only be used by the user associated with the row. For example, while user *X* can set the object usmUserOwnAuthKeyChange.*engineid.X*, if *X* tries setting the object usmUserOwnAuthKeyChange.*engineid.Y*, the set operation will fail and a `noAccess` error will be returned.

usmUserPrivProtocol: specifies the privacy protocol to use. The following values have so far been defined:

Table 6-3   usmUserPrivProtocol Values defiNed So Far

Privacy Protocol	Value	OBJECT IDENTIFIER
None	`usmNoPrivProtocol`	1.3.6.1.6.3.10.1.2.1
CBC-DES	`usmDESPrivProtocol`	1.3.6.1.6.3.10.1.2.2

If an initial set operation tries to set usmUserPrivProtocol to an unknown or unsupported protocol, then the set operation will fail and a `wrongValue` error will be returned.

If a set operation later tries to change the value to anything other than `usmNo-PrivProtocol`, the set operation will fail and an `inconsistentValue` error will be returned.

Since privacy requires authentication, an encryption protocol cannot be configured if the associated usmUserAuthProtocol object has been set to `usmNoAuthProtocol`. If an initial set operation tries to set usmUserPrivProtocol to anything other than `usmNoPrivProtocol` and usmUserAuthProtocol to `usmNoAuthProtocol`, then the set operation will fail and an `inconsistentError` will be returned.

Finally, if the usmUserPrivProtocol associated with the row that this one was cloned from is set to `usmNoPrivProtocol`, then this object will also be set to have no encryption protocol.

usmUserPrivKeyChange: this KeyChange object is used to change a user's secret encryption key. For the CBC-DES protocol, this value should be set to a 32-byte OCTET STRING. When creating a new row in usmUserTable, if this object is set before usmUserCloneFrom, then the set operation will fail with an `inconsistentName` error. Reading this object returns a zero-length string.

usmUserOwnPrivKeyChange: this KeyChange object behaves exactly the same as usmUserPrivKeyChange, except that in order for the set operation to succeed the msgUserName embedded within the SNMP message's security parameters must match the usmUserName object for this row. This is an interesting property. The access control for this object can be set to allow anyone to write this object, but in fact it can only be used by the user associated with the row. For example, while user X can set the object usmUserOwnPrivKeyChange.*engineid.X*, if X tries setting the object usmUserOwnPrivKeyChange.*engineid.Y*, the set operation will fail and a `noAccess` error will be returned.

usmUserPublic: this object can be used to validate that a set operation to change a private authentication or encryption key succeeded. The way this is done is when setting a KeyChange object, add a varbind in the Set operation to modify the associated usmUserPublic object. Remember, either all the variable-bindings are set or none are. After the set operation, read the usmUserPublic object to see if its value has changed. If it has, the KeyChange object must have also been set. *Note*: If you get a `noError` response to setting a KeyChange object, you know the Set operation succeeded. This object is needed in the case where a KeyChange object was successfully changed, but the Response PDU got lost.

usmUserStorageType: specifies how a row in this table should be stored. The default is for it to be stored in nonVolatile memory.

Note: Rows that are stored as `permanent` must minimally allow write-access to the following objects:

• usmUserAuthKeyChange, usmUserOwnAuthKeyChange

• usmUserPrivKeyChange , usmUserOwnPrivKeyChange

• usmUserPublic

This is so that secret keys for authentication and encryption can still be changed.

Note: A value of `readOnly` cannot be used for a row configured for either authentication or encryption. This is necessary so that authentication and encryption keys can always be changed.

usmUserStatus: a RowStatus object used for adding and removing rows to/from this table. A row cannot be made active until usmUserCloneFrom is set. Further, if a row employs authentication, then the row cannot be made active until the authentication key has been changed (usmUserAuthKeyChange has been set). Along the same lines, if a row employs privacy, then usmUserPrivKeyChange must be set before the row can be made active.

As an example, let's configure usmUserTable with a row that can be used as a template for creating new rows. This "template" row will be configured for HMAC-MD5-96 authentication and CBC-DES encryption. *Note*: The octet string value 80 00 00 09 01 9e 65 79 01 will represent the snmpEngineID for the local entity.

Table 6-4   Template Row in usmUserTable

	80000009019e657901.template
usmUserEngineID	80000009019e657901
usmUserName	template
usmUserSecurityName	template
usmUserCloneFrom	0.0
usmUserAuthProtocol	usmHMACMD5AuthProtocol
usmUserAuthKeyChange	' '
usmUserOwnAuthKeyChange	' '
usmUserPrivProtocol	usmDESPrivProtocol
usmUserPrivKeyChange	' '
usmUserOwnPrivKeyChange	' '
usmUserPublic	OCTET STRING
usmUserStorageType	permanent
usmUserStatus	active

We will be showing pseudocode which demonstrates adding a new row for user "admin". This new row will use MD5 authentication and no encryption. *Note*: The pseudocode will reference the following procedures which we will describe here but will not provide any implementation details for.

- GetAuthKey returns an authentication key for a given engine identifier and user name.
- GetPrivKey returns an encryption key for a given engine identifier and user name.
- GetPassword returns the authentication password for a user name.
- GetEngineID returns the snmpEngineID value for an address.
- LengthOf returns the length of a string.
- SetPassword associates an authentication password with a user name.
- SetPasswordDES associates an encryption password with a user name.
- WaitRandomTime simply waits some random amount of time before continuing.
- RandomOctetString is passed an argument n and returns a random OCTET STRING of length n.

- RandomNumber returns a random integer.
- ObjectExists is passed a PDU and a position *n* as arguments. If the variable-binding at the position *n* has a value `noSuchObject` or `noSuchInstance`, then ObjectExists will return false; otherwise it will return true.
- RaiseException simply raises an exception that needs to be caught somewhere up the call stack.

```
// template is a structure containing information
// about the template to use when creating a new
// row within UsmUserTable.
//
// It can be defined by the following C structure:
//
//      struct templateInfo {
//          ObjectIdentifier inst
//          OctetString intitialAuthKey;
//          OctetString initialPrivKey;
//      }

template.inst <- 80000009019e657901.template
template.initialAuthKey <-
   GetAuthKey(80000009019e657901.template)
template.initialPrivKey <-
   GetPrivKey(80000009019e657901.template)

// For this pseudo code we'll introduce a java-like
// exception handling syntax, and define several specific
// exceptions that we will be looking for.

try
{
    AddNewUser(addr, admin,
            GetPassword(admin), true,
            '', false, template)
}
catch(SetOperationFailedException)
{
    // Add logic to handle the case where
    // a set operation to destroy an already
    // existing row fails.
}
catch(NewRowFailException)
{
```

```
      // Add logic to handle the case where the initial
      // set operation to create the row fails.
   }
   catch(SetActiveFailedException)
   {
      // Add logic to handle the case where the set operation
      // to transition the row to 'active' fails.
   }
   catch(SetAuthFailedException)
   {
      // Add logic to handle the case where a set operation
      // to configure authentication failed.
   }
   catch(SetPrivFailedException)
   {
      // Add logic to handle the case where a set operation
      // to configure privacy failed.
   }
   catch(UnderContructionException)
   {
      // Add logic to handle the case where an entry exists
      // for the user we are trying to add, but the entry is
      // not active (most likely another manager is in the
      // process of also adding this user).
   }
```

AddNewUser is passed the following arguments: an address of a remote device to configure, the new user name, the password to use in generating a new secret authentication key, a boolean indicating whether MD5 authentication should be used, the password to use in generating a new secret encryption key, a boolean indicating whether encryption should be used, and a structure which provides information about the template row that the new row will be cloned from.

AddNewUser will raise an exception if an error occurs during a set operation.

The logic for AddNewUser is as follows:

1. Check to see if a row already exists for the new user within usmUserTable. If it does and the row is active, then try to modify the row to match the given parameters and return. If a

row exists but it isn't in the `active` state, then this entry might be under construction by another manager. In this case raise an UnderConstructionException.

2. Try creating a new row, cloning it from the row specified by the template structure, and placing the row in the `createAndWait` state. If any error was detected, raise a NewRowFailException.

3. Try to configure both the authentication and privacy according to the arguments passed to AddNewUser. A procedure SetAuthentication will be provided for configuring authentication. This will be called within a while loop so that conflicts with usmUserSpinLock can be handled. A procedure SetPrivacy will be provided for configuring privacy. This will similarly be called within a while loop so that conflicts with usmUserSpinLock can be handled. Both of these routines will generate exceptions if unexpected errors are detected during a set operation.

4. Finally, set the new row's status to `active`.

```
procedure void::AddNewUser(addr, userName,
      password, md5Flag, despasswd, desFlag, template)
{
    // This procedure will add a new user to the usmUserTable.
    //
    //    addr:     The address of the device to modify. The
    //              snmpEngineID value for this address will be
    //              used.
    //    userName:User name to add.
    //    password:Textual string used to map a secret
    //              authentication key.
    //    md5Flag: If true, use the MD5 authentication protocol.
    //              Otherwise, use no authentication.
    //    despasswd: Textual string used to map a secret privacy
    //              key.
    //    desFlag: If true, use the DES encryption protocol.
    //              Otherwise, use no encryption.
    //    template:Is a structure containing information
    //              about the template to use.
    //
    // First check if a row for the engine identifier and
    // userName already exists within the table. If it does,
    // call a routine to modify the row and return.

    engineID <- GetEngineID(addr)

    pdu <- {usmUserStatus.engineID.userName}
    responsePDU <- SnmpGet(pdu)
    if (ObjectExists(responsePDU, 1))
    {
```

```
            // A row already exists within usmUserTable for
            // engineID.userName. If the RowStatus is not active
            // then raise an UnderConstructionException. Otherwise
            // try to modify the existing row to match the
            // parameters if possible.

            status <- GetVarBindValue(responsePDU, 1)
            if (status != 'active')
              RaiseException(UnderConstructionException)

            ModifyUser(addr, userName,
                    password, md5Flag,
                    despasswd, desFlag)
            return
        }

    // If we get to this point we know a row does not
    // exist within usmUserTable for engineID.userName.
    //
    // Create a new row that clones from the template row.

    // Note. template.inst indexes the template row within
    // the usmUserTable to use for cloning this new row.

    // Set ninst to the new instance, tinst to the template
    // instance.

    ninst <- engineID.userName
    tinst <- template.inst
    setpdu <- {
          usmUserCloneFrom.ninst <- usmUserSecurityName.tinst,
          usmUserStatus.ninst <- 'createAndWait'}

    responsePDU <- SnmpSet(setpdu)
    status <- GetErrorStatus(responsePDU)
    if (status != 'noError')
    {
        RaiseException(NewRowFailException)
    }

    // At this point a new row has been added. Configure the
    // desired authentication and privacy information, and then
    // set the row to active.

    while (true)
    {
        flag <- SetAuthentication(addr,
                    userName, ninst, template,
```

```
                    md5Flag, password)
      if (flag == true)
         break
      WaitRandomTime()
   }

   while (true)
   {
      flag <- SetPrivacy(addr,
                  userName, ninst, template,
                  desFlag, despasswd)
      if (flag == true)
         break
      WaitRandomTime()
   }

   pdu <- {usmUserStatus.ninst <- 'active'}
   responsePDU <- SnmpSet(pdu)
   if (GetErrorStatus(reponsePDU) != 'noError')
   {
      RaiseException(SetActiveFailedException)
   }
}
```

The procedure SetAuthentication is passed the following arguments: the address of the device to configure, the new user name, the index for the new row, a structure containing information about the row that the new row has been cloned from, a boolean indicating whether MD5 authentication should be configured, and a password to use to generate a new secret authentication key. SetAuthentication will use usmUserSpinLock to guarantee that two or more managers are not trying to write to usmUserTable at the same time. If a conflict is detected with usmUser-SpinkLock, SetAuthentication will return false. This will allow the calling routine to try again after some random time. If any other error is detected during a set operation, SetAuthentication will raise an exception. Otherwise SetAuthentication will return true.

The pseudocode for SetAuthentication is provided below.

```
procedure Boolean::SetAuthentication(addr,
      userName, index, template, flag, password)
{
   // If flag is false, set usmUserAuthProtocol to
   // usmNoAuthProtocol and return.
   // Otherwise, set usmUserAuthKeyChange so that the
   // new password is used.

   if (flag == false)
```

```
{
   pdu <- {usmUserAuthProtocol.index <- usmNoAuthProtocol}
   responsePDU <- SnmpSet(pdu)
   if (GetErrorStatus(responsePDU) != 'noError')
   {
      RaiseException(SetAuthFailedException)
   }
   return
}

// We will use the GetLocalizedKeyMD5 procedure defined
// earlier to translate the new password into a localized
// key (kul). After that we need to generate the random and
// delta components of a KeyChange object so that we
// can change the secret key to kul.
//
// The usmUserSpinLock object will be used so that two
// managers can't try to set usmUserAuthKeyChange at the
// same time. Also, usmUserPublic will be set to a random
// value. We can then verify that the set succeeded
// by reading usmUserPublic and verifying that it's
// value was properly changed.

pdu <- {usmUserSpinLock.0,
      usmUserPublic.index}
responsePDU <- SnmpGet(pdu)

lockVal <- GetVarBindValue(reponsePDU, 1)
public <- GetVarBindValue(responsePDU, 2)

// Update the password for userName. Then
// calculate the new key value. Finally, generate
// a 16-byte random OCTET STRING and calculate
// the 16-byte delta portion. Concatenate random
// and delta to form the KeyChange value.

SetPassword(userName, password)
newkey <- GetLocalizedKeyMD5(userName, addr)

random <- RandomOctetString(16)
temp <- MD5(template.initialAuthKey + random)
for (i = 0; i < 16; i++) {
    delta[i] = temp[i] XOR newkey[i]
}

n <- RandomOctetString(8)
while (n == public)
{
```

```
        n <- RandomOctetString()
}

pdu <- {usmUserSpinLock.0 <- lockVal,
      usmUserAuthKeyChange.index <- random + delta,
      usmUserPublic.index <- n}
responsePDU <- SnmpSet(pdu)


status <- GetErrorStatus(responsePDU)


// If an error status of 'noError' is returned, we know
// the Set operation succeeded and we don't need to bother
// with usmUserPublic. However, if we didn't get a
// response back we need to look at usmUserPublic to
// understand whether the Set operation succeeded and
// to know the state of the key. Through most of the pseudo
// code in this book we have been ignoring timeouts. In this
// case we will check usmUserPublic to know if the
// KeyChange object was set.

if (status == 'timeout')
{
    getPDU <- SnmpGet(usmUserPublic.index)
    public <- GetVarBindValue(getPDU, 1)
    if (n != public)
    {
      RaiseException(SetAuthFailedException)
    }
}

// If the set operation returned an inconsistentValue
// error, then a lock conflict occurred. Return false.

if (status == 'inconsistentValue')
{
    return false
}

// If any other error was returned then raise
// an exception to indicate that the authentication
// configuration failed.

if (status != 'noError')
{
    RaiseException(SetAuthFailedException)
}
```

```
        return true
    }
```

The procedure SetPrivacy is going to be virtually identical to SetAuthentication. *Note*: CBC-DES uses a 16-byte secret key. It will call a procedure GetLocalizedKeyDES to translate a password to a localized key. This procedure will be identical to GetLocalizedKeyMD5, except for the password that is used.

The pseudocode for SetPrivacy is presented below.

```
procedure Boolean::SetPrivacy(addr,
        userName, index, template, flag, password)
{
    // If flag is false, set usmUserPrivProtocol to
    // usmNoPrivProtocol and return.
    // Otherwise, set usmUserPrivKeyChange so that the
    // new password is used.

    if (flag == false)
    {
        pdu <- {usmUserPrivProtocol.index <- usmNoPrivProtocol}
        responsePDU <- SnmpSet(pdu)
        if (GetErrorStatus(responsePDU) != 'noError')
        {
          RaiseException(SetPrivFailedException)
        }
        return
    }

    // We will use a procedure GetLocalizedKeyDES to
    // generate a localized key value(kul). GetLocalizedKeyDES
    // will be virtually identical to the GetLocalizedKeyMD5
    // procedure we have shown earlier. The only difference
    // between the two procedures is the password that is used.
    // Note. This is because both CBC-DES and MD5 use 16-byte
    // secret keys.
    //
    // After we have caluated a new secret key we need to
    // generate the random and delta components of a KeyChange
    // object so that we can change the secret key to kul.
    //
    // The usmUserSpinLock object will be used so that two
    // managers can't try to set usmUserPrivKeyChange at the
    // same time. Also, usmUserPublic will be set to a random
    // value. In the case of a timeout, we can determine whether
    // the set succeeded by reading usmUserPublic and verifying
```

```
// that it's value was properly changed.

pdu <- {usmUserSpinLock.0,
    usmUserPublic.index}
responsePDU <- SnmpGet(pdu)

lockVal <- GetVarBindValue(reponsePDU, 1)
public <- GetVarBindValue(responsePDU, 2)

// Update the password for userName. Then
// calculate the new key value. Finally, generate
// a 16-byte random OCTET STRING and calculate
// the 16-byte delta portion. Concatenate random
// and delta to form the KeyChange value.

SetPasswordDES(userName, password)
newkey <- GetLocalizedKeyDES(userName, addr)

random <- RandomOctetString(16)
temp <- MD5(template.initialAuthKey + random)
for (i = 0; i < 16; i++) {
    delta[i] = temp[i] XOR newkey[i]
}

n <- RandomNumber()
while (n == public)
{
    n <- RandomNumber()
}
pdu <- {usmUserSpinLock.0 <- lockVal,
    usmUserPrivKeyChange.index <- random + delta,
    usmUserPublic.index <- n}
responsePDU <- SnmpSet(pdu)

// If an error status of 'noError' is returned, we know
// the Set operation succeeded and we don't need to bother
// with usmUserPublic. However, if we didn't get a
// response back we need to look at usmUserPublic to
// understand whether the Set operation succeeded and
// to know the state of the key. Through most of the pseudo
// code in this book we have been ignoring timeouts. In this
// case we will check usmUserPublic to know if the
// KeyChange object was set.

if (status == 'timeout')
{
    getPDU <- SnmpGet(usmUserPublic.index)
    public <- GetVarBindValue(getPDU, 1)
```

```
        if (n != public)
        {
          RaiseException(SetAuthFailedException)
        }
    }

    // If the set operation returned an inconsistentValue
    // error, then a lock conflict occurred. Return false.

    status <- GetErrorStatus(responsePDU)
    if (status == 'inconsistentValue')
    {
        return false
    }

    // If any other error was returned then raise
    // an exception to indicate that the privacy
    // configuration failed.

    if (status != 'noError')
    {
        RaiseException(SetPrivFailedException)
    }

    return true
}
```

Finally, the procedure ModifyUser can be defined simply by using SetAuthentication and SetPrivacy.

```
procedure void::ModifyUser(addr, userName, password, md5Flag,
            despasswd, desFlag)
{
    engineID <- GetEngineID(addr)
    index <- engineID.userName

    // Set up template so it has the current secret
    // authentication and privacy keys.

    template.inst <- index
    template.initialAuthKey <- GetAuthKey(index)
    template.initialPrivKey <- GetPrivKey(index)

    while (true)
    {
        flag <- SetAuthentication(addr,
                userName, index, template,
```

```
                          md5Flag, password)
            if (flag == true)
               break
            WaitRandomTime()
        }

        while (true)
        {
            flag <- SetPrivacy(addr,
                        userName, index, template,
                        desFlag, despasswd)
            if (flag == true)
               break
            WaitRandomTime()
        }
    }
```

This wraps up our example of adding a new row to the usmUserTable. There were several procedures that were referenced in our example which have previously been defined within the SNMPv3 applications chapter.

6.7 Authentication

Authentication within the User-based Security Model allows an entity to verify whom the message is from and whether the message has been altered. It further allows for the timeliness checks that we saw earlier. By assuring that messages are received in a timely fashion, you can reduce the threat of a message being delayed or replayed by a malicious party.

So far two authentication protocols have been defined: HMAC-MD5-96, which is based on MD5, and HMAC-SHA-96, which is based on SHA-1.

Authentication uses a secret key to produce a *fingerprint* of the message. The *fingerprint* is included within the message. The entity that receives the message uses the same secret key to validate that the *fingerprint* is correct. If it is, and assuming the message was received in a timely fashion, then the message has been authenticated. Otherwise the message will be discarded. This *fingerprint* is called a Message Authentication Code (MAC).

For the HMAC-MD5-96 authetication protocol the MAC is produced in the following way:

First, set the msgAuthenticationParameters field (within the security parameters) to an OCTET STRING of 12 zero octets.

Create a variable extendedKey, which is the secret authentication key appended with 48 zero octets. Next, go through the following logic to calculate a 12-octet MAC.

```
for (i = 0; i < 64; i++)
{
    K1[i] <- extendedKey[i] XOR 0x36
}

for (i = 0; i < 64; i++)
{
    K2[i] <- extendedKey[i] XOR 0x5C
}

// Prepend K1 to the message. Run this through an MD5 hash.
// Prepend K2 to the results of the previous step and run
// this value through an MD5 hash.

temp <- MD5(K2 + MD5(K1 + message))

// Since temp is the result of an MD5 hash, its value
// is a 16-byte OCTET STRING. Use the first 12-bytes
// as the Message Authentication Code (MAC).

MAC <- temp[0 .. 11]
```

Finally, replace the msgAuthenticationParameters field with the MAC.

When an entity receives a message, it will verify the MAC by duplicating the same steps. Namely, it will save the 12-byte MAC and then replace the msgAuthenticationParameters field with an OCTET STRING of 12 zero octets. It will then create an extended key and go through identical logic to calculate a MAC. If the calculated MAC equals what was originally in the msg-AuthenticationParameters field, then the message was authenticated.

For the HMAC-SHA-96 authentication protocol, the MAC is produced in a similar way. A variable, extendedKey, is created by appending 44 zero octets to the secret key (*Note*: The secret key for HMAC-SHA-96 will be 20 octets, so this will make extendedKey 64 octets — the same length as for HMAC-MD5-96). K1 and K2 are calculated the same as for HMAC-MD5-96. The 12-byte MAC will be calculated by

```
// Prepend K1 to the message. Run this through an SHA hash.
// Prepend K2 to the results of this and run this value through
// an SHA hash.
```

```
temp <- SHA(K2 + SHA(K1 + message))

// Since temp is the result of an SHA hash, its value
// is a 20-byte OCTET STRING. Use the first 12-bytes
// as the Message Authentication Code (MAC).

MAC <- temp[0 .. 11]
```

6.8 Privacy

The User-based Security Model uses the CBC-DES Symmetric Encryption Protocol for privacy. This protocol uses a 16-byte secret key. The secret key can be generated using either the GetLocalizedKeyMD5 or GetLocalizedKeySHA procedures that have been shown earlier. Since GetLocalizedKeySHA returns a 20-byte OCTET STRING, if that method is used to generate a localized secret privacy key, only the first 16 bytes should be used. Also, the routines should probably be modified so that different passwords are used to generate the authentication and privacy secret keys.

Whether encryption is used or not for a user is identified by the usmDESPrivProtocol object. If encryption is being used, the msgPrivacyParameters field will contain an 8-byte OCTET STRING that represents a "salt" value for the initialization vector used in DES encryption.

The "salt" value is generated by concatenating the 32-bit snmpEngineBoots value with a 32-bit counter value that the encryption engine maintains. This 32-bit counter will be initialized to some arbitrary value at boot time.

The 16-byte secret privacy key is made up of 8 bytes that make up the DES key and 8 bytes used as a preinitialization vector. The DES key is actually made up of 56 bits; the least-significant bit in each byte is disregarded.

The initialization vector that is used by the DES algorithm is the result of the 8-byte pre-initialization vector XOR-ed with the 8-byte "salt".

Only the data portion of an SNMP message will be encrypted (the header and security paramaters will not be). We'll call this data portion the "plaintext." The plaintext portion needs to be a multiple of 8 octets. If it isn't, it will be padded at the end (it doesn't matter what is used to pad it).

This plaintext will be divided into 64-bit blocks. The plaintext for each block is XOR-ed with the "ciphertext" of the previous block. The result is then encrypted, added to the encrypted PDU portion of the message, and used as the "ciphertext" for the next block. For the first block, the initialization vector is used as the "ciphertext."

When an "encrypted" message is received, the following steps are taken to process it:

1. If the length of the data portion is not a multiple of 8 bytes, the message is discarded.

2. The first "ciphertext" block is decrypted. The decryption result is XOR-ed with the initialization vector, and the result is the first plaintext block.

3. The rest of the "ciphertext" blocks are treated similarly. They are decrypted, with the results being XOR-ed with the previous "ciphertext" block to obtain the plaintext block.

6.9 Final Thoughts

While SNMPv3 fills a huge security hole by providing both authentication and privacy, there is a cost involved. More processing time is going to be consumed calculating the MAC for authentication and decrypting messages. There is also going to be a management cost in configuring the security information, and in periodically validating that the security information is consistent.

Time and experience will tell what this true cost is going to be. If the cost is too high, the security features won't be used, or at best, will be used in limited situations.

Several questions that a network manager may want to ask to help access this cost:

1. Is the added authentication and encryption processing affecting the performance of the network devices?

2. How much delay is this going to add in getting a respone to a request?

3. How many SNMP messages a second do the network devices need to handle? How many SNMP messages a second can they handle with authentication and privacy turned on?

4. Is network management being distributed? How difficult is it going to be to maintain user passwords on all the distributed management stations?

5. How difficult is it going to be to routinely update passwords and configure the network devices?

Again, as devices supporting SNMPv3 are deployed, we will learn the true cost for using authentication and encryption for SNMP messages. This cost will determine how widely used the security features will be, and ultimately how widely used SNMPv3 will be.

SNMPv3 View-based Access Control

Access control in the SNMP framework means controlling the management information that users can access. The View-based Access Control Model accomplishes this by associating users to MIB views. A MIB view defines the management information that should be included and excluded from the view.

7.1 VACM MIB Overview

The VACM (View-based Access Control Model) MIB consist of several tables that are used to determine whether an SNMP operation is allowed to access certain managed objects. A quick overview of its tables are

- vacmContextTable: defines the locally available contexts. This table is read-only and can not be configured by SNMP.
- vacmSecurityToGroupTable: maps a securityModel and securityName to a groupName.
- vacmAccessTable: maps a groupName, context, and security information into a MIB view.
- vacmViewTreeFamilyTable: defines whether an OBJECT IDENTIFIER can be accessed for a given MIB view.

Before we look at these tables in any detail, let's run through how they are used to determine whether a MIB object can be accessed.

When either a notification message needs to be generated or Get, Get-Next, Get-Bulk, or Set Request is received, a check needs to be made for whether the user has the right to access the

MIB objects specified within the PDU's variable-bindings. In order to do this we need to be able to map a user to a MIB view, where a MIB view defines the MIB objects that can be accessed. Also, we might want to use different MIB views depending on the security model being used, or on whether encryption or authentication is being used. For example, if encryption is not being used we might need to prevent sensitive data from being accessed to protect against eavesdroppers. Finally, different MIB views may be needed based on whether we're performing a read operation (Get, Get-Next, Get-Bulk), a write operation (Set), or generating a notification.

The following steps are taken to determine whether the MIB objects specified within a PDU's variable-bindings can be accessed:

1. Use the vacmSecurityToGroupTable to map the message's securityModel and securityName to a groupName.

2. Use the vacmAccessTable to map a groupName, context, securityModel, and securityLevel into a MIB view. The MIB view that will be used is dependent on whether the message is a notification, performing a read operation (Get, Get-Next, Get-Bulk), or performing a write operation (Set).

3. Use the vacmViewTreeFamilyTable to check whether the MIB objects within the PDU's variable-bindings can be accessed according to the MIB view.

The following diagram shows these steps:

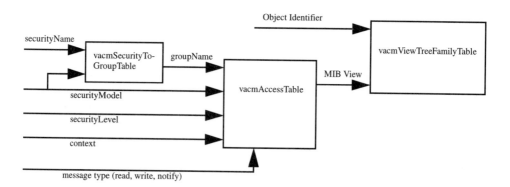

When a Get, Get-Next, Get-Bulk, or Set Request is received, a Command Responder application will call the View-based Access Control Subsystem for each of the MIB objects within the PDU's variable-bindings to determine whether access is allowed. The following table shows both the codes that the View-based Access Control Subsystem can return to a Command Responder application, and the action the Command Responder application will take:

Table 7-1 Status Codes Returned by the View-based Access Control Subsystem + Actions Performed by the Command Responder Application

Code	Description	Action
accessAllowed	A MIB view was found and access is granted.	Continue processing SNMP message.
notInView	A MIB view was found but access is denied. This could be because the MIB object was explicitly excluded, or didn't fall under any included subtree families within vacmViewTreeFamilyTable.	For a Get Request, a `noSuchInstance` exception will be put in the Response PDU. For a GetNext or GetBulk request, the instance will simply be skipped. For a Set Request, generate a Response PDU using the values from the originally received PDU but replacing the error status with a `noAccess` code and the error index with a value of 0.
noSuchView	No MIB view was found within vacmAccessTable.	Generate a Response PDU using the values from the originally received PDU but replacing the error status with an `authorizationError` code and the error index with a value of 0.
noSuchContext	The contextName was not found within vacmContextTable.	Increment the snmpUnknownContexts counter — do not generate a Response PDU.
noGroupName	The securityModel and securityName could not be mapped into a groupName.	Generate a Response PDU using the values from the originally received PDU but replacing the error status with an `authorizationError` code and the error index with a value of 0.

Table 7-1   Status Codes Returned by the View-based Access Control Subsystem + Actions Performed by the Command Responder Application (Continued)

Code	Description	Action
noAccessEntry	A row could not be found within vacmAccessTable which matches the groupName, contextName, securityModel, and securityLevel.	Generate a Response PDU using the values from the originally received PDU but replacing the error status with an `authorizationError` code and the error index with a value of 0.
otherError	Some other undefined error occurred.	Generate a Response PDU using the values from the originally received PDU but replacing the error status with a `genError` code.

Additionally, if for some reason the context referenced by the contextName is unavailable, the snmpUnavailableContexts counter will be incremented and the Command Responder application will not generate a Response PDU.

A Notification Originator application will also call the View-based Access Control Subsystem for each of the MIB objects within the PDU's variable-bindings to determine whether access is allowed. If any code other than `accessAllowed` is returned, the notification will not be sent to the management target.

7.2 vacmContextTable

The vacmContextTable is a read-only table of the locally available contexts. If a contextName used in a message doesn't exist within vacmContextTable, then access for the MIB objects within the message's PDU will be denied.

Table 7-2   vacmContextTable, Indexed by vacmContextName

Object	Type	Access
vacmContextName	SnmpAdminString	read-only

vacmContextName: can be between 0 and 32 bytes long. This value represents a locally available context. A zero-length contextName represents the default context.

Note: Currently this table must be configured through some other means than SNMP. It is possible (and even likely) that in the future additional MIB objects could be defined to allow this table to be configured remotely through SNMP.

7.3 vacmSecurityToGroupTable

The vacmSecurityToGroupTable maps a security model and security name to a group name. The group name will be used as part of an index into the vacmAccessTable.

It will obviously be easier to configure access for a few "categories" or groups, then for each individual user. To keep the overall configuration simple (and manageable) we would like to map all the users into a few groups, such as a "restricted" group or "full access" group. That way we will eventually end up mapping a few groups into MIB views, as opposed to trying to map a larger number of users into MIB views. Also, we want to be able to base the group mapping (and eventually the MIB view mapping) on the security model (USM, SNMPv1, etc.) being used.

Table 7-3   vacmSecurityToGroupTable, Indexed by vacmSecurityModel.vacmSecurityName

Object	Type	Access
vacmSecurityModel	SnmpSecurityModel	not-accessible
vacmSecurityName	SnmpAdminString	not-accessible
vacmGroupName	SnmpAdminString	read-create
vacmSecurityToGroupStorageType	StorageType	read-create
vacmSecurityToGroupStatus	RowStatus	read-create

vacmSecurityModel: security model along with a security name is used to index a row in this table. *Note*: The any (0) value cannot be used.

vacmSecurityName: an OCTET STRING between 1 and 32 bytes that is used to identify the user. Normally, the userName and securityName will be the same value. If not, a security name can be mapped to a user name by the usmUserTable.

vacmGroupName: a group name that is used as part of an index into the vacmAccessTable.

vacmSecurityToGroupStorageType: specifies how a row in this table should be stored. The default is for it to be stored in nonVolatile memory.

vacmSecurityToGroupStatus: a RowStatus object used for adding and removing rows to/from this table.

7.4 vacmAccessTable

The vacmAccessTable maps a group name, security information, a context, and a message type (read operation, write operation, or notification) into a MIB view. Given a MIB view we can determine whether a managed object is allowed to be accessed.

Table 7-4   vacmAccessTable, Indexed by
vacmGroupName.vacmAccessContextPrefix.vacmAccessSecurityModel.vacmAccessSecurityLevel

Object	Type	Access
vacmAccessContextPrefix	SnmpAdminString	not-accessible
vacmAccessSecurityModel	SnmpSecurityModel	not-accessible
vacmAccessSecurityLevel	SnmpSecurityLevel	not-accessible
vacmAccessContextMatch	INTEGER	read-create
vacmAccessReadViewName	SnmpAdminString	read-create
vacmAccessWriteViewName	SnmpAdminString	read-create
vacmAccessNotifyViewName	SnmpAdminString	read-create
vacmAccessStorageType	StorageType	read-create
vacmAccessStatus	RowStatus	read-create

vacmAccessContextPrefix: an OCTET STRING between 0 and 32 bytes. This is used to match against a contextName. Depending on the value of vacmAccessContextMatch, this must match a contextName exactly, or it must match the first part (prefix) of a contextName.

vacmAccessSecurityModel: a securityModel to match against.

vacmAccessSecurityLevel: a securityLevel to match against. All values less than or equal to a specific securityLevel will match.

vacmAccessContextMatch: specifies whether a contextName needs to match exactly or whether only the first part of the contextName needs to match.

• `exact` (1), contextName and vacmAccessContextPrefix must match exactly.
• `prefix` (2), vacmAccessContextPrefix must match the first part of contextName.

The default value for this is `exact`.

vacmAccessReadViewName: MIB view to use for a read operation (Get, Get-Next, Get-Bulk). This can be an OCTET STRING between 0 and 32 bytes long. If the value is an empty string, then access will not be allowed. Also, if no instance of vacmViewTreeFamilyViewName has this value, then access will not be allowed. The default value for this is an empty string.

vacmAccessWriteViewName: MIB view to use for a write operation (Set). This can be an OCTET STRING between 0 and 32 bytes long. If the value is an empty string, then access will not be allowed. Also, if no instance of vacmViewTreeFamilyViewName has this value, then access will not be allowed. The default value for this is an empty string.

vacmAccessNotifyViewName: MIB view to use for a notification. This can be an OCTET STRING between 0 and 32 bytes long. If the value is an empty string, then access will not be allowed. Also, if no instance of vacmViewTreeFamilyViewName has this value, then access will not be allowed. The default value for this is an empty string.

vacmAccessStorageType: specifies how a row in this table should be stored. The default is for it to be stored in nonVolatile memory.

vacmAccessStatus: a RowStatus object used for adding and removing rows to/from this table.

In order to select a row from this table given a group name, g, a securityModel, sm, a securityLevel, sl, and a context c, find all rows where

1. g equals the vacmGroupName value, **AND**
2. either c matches vacmAccessContextPrefix - or vacmAccessContextMatch equals `prefix` and vacmAccessContextPrefix is a prefix of c, **AND**
3. vacmSecurityModel either equals sm or 'any', **AND**
4. vacmSecurityLevel is equal to or less than sl

If only one row is found then we're done. Otherwise we need to go through the following steps to whittle the matching rows down (if after any step only one row is left, then we're done):

a. If any rows have vacmSecurityModel matching the sm, discard all rows where vacmSecurityModel equals `any`.
b. If any rows have vacmAccessContextPrefix matching c exactly, discard all rows where vacmAccessContextPrefix is only a prefix of c.
c. Discard all entries where vacmAccessContextPrefix is shorter than the longest one left in the set of matching entries.
d. Select the entry with the highest securityLevel.

7.5 vacmViewTreeFamilyTable

The vacmViewTreeFamilyTable identifies whether an object is allowed to be accessed within a given MIB view. Each row within this table specifies a MIB view, a MIB subtree, and whether an object that is within the MIB subtree should be included or excluded. If an object is included, then access to it is granted. If it is excluded, then access is denied.

To determine whether an object is in a particular MIB view, the object must be compared with each of the MIB view's active entries. If the none of the entries match, then the object is not in the MIB view and access to it will be denied.

If a single match is found, then the object is included or excluded based on the vacmViewTreeFamilyType value. If more than one match is found, the entry whose vacmViewTreeFamilySubtree value has the most subidentifiers will be chosen. If this still doesn't resolve to a single row, then the entry with the lexicographically largest value of vacmViewTreeFamilySubtree will be chosen.

A TestAndIncr object, vacmViewSpinLock, is provided to coordinate Set operations to vacmViewTreeFamilyTable.

Table 7-5 vacmViewTreeFamilyTable, Indexed by
vacmViewTreeFamilyViewName.vacmViewTreeFamilySubtree

Object	Type	Access
vacmViewTreeFamilyViewName	SnmpAdminString	not-accessible
vacmViewTreeFamilySubtree	OBJECT IDENTIFIER	not-accessible
vacmViewTreeFamilyMask	OCTET STRING	read-create
vacmViewTreeFamilyType	INTEGER	read-create
vacmViewTreeFamilyStorageType	StorageType	read-create
vacmViewTreeFamilyStatus	RowStatus	read-create

vacmViewTreeFamilyViewName: an OCTET STRING between 1 and 32 bytes that represents a MIB view. This associates the vacmViewTreeFamilyTable to the vacmAccessTable through the vacmAccessReadViewName, vacmAccessWriteViewName, and vacmAccessNotifyViewName objects.

vacmViewTreeFamilySubtree: a MIB subtree which when used in conjunction with vacmViewTreeFamilyMask defines a view subtree.

vacmViewTreeFamilyMask: a bit mask used in conjunction with vacmViewTreeFamilySubtree to determine whether an OBJECT IDENTIFIER falls under a view subtree. Each bit of this value corresponds to a sub-identifier position. The most significant bit corresponds to the first subidentifier position, the next significant bit corresponds to the second subidentifier position, and so on. When trying to determine if an OBJECT IDENTIFIER falls under a vacmViewTreeFamilySubtree, each subidentifier of the vacmViewTreeFamilySubtree value must match the OBJECT IDENTIFIER subidentifier if the corresponding bit in vacmViewTreeFamilyMask is a one (you can think of a zero bit value as being treated as a wild card).

For example, a vacmViewTreeFamilySubtree value representing MIB-II, 1.3.6.1.2.1, and a vacmViewTreeFamilyMask value of "3F" (0011 1111) will catch any MIB-II object.

Note: If the number of bits in the bit mask is less than the number of subidentifiers in vacmViewTreeFamilySubtree, then the bit mask is extended with ones so that the lengths match. If the value of vacmViewTreeFamilyMask is a zero-length string, this extension rule causes a bit mask of all ones to be used (which means each subidentifier within vacmViewTreeFamilySubtree must match each subidentifier within an OBJECT IDENTIFIER).

vacmViewTreeFamilyType: used to determine whether access to a MIB object is granted or denied.

- `included` (1), if included then a MIB object can be accessed.
- `excluded` (2), if excluded then access to a MIB object is denied.

The default is value is `included`.

vacmViewTreeFamilyStorageType: specifies how a row in this table should be stored. The default is for it to be stored in nonVolatile memory.

vacmViewTreeFamilyStatus: a RowStatus object used for adding and removing rows to/from this table.

7.6 Example Configuration

An authoritative SNMP engine which supports the View-based Access Control Model should be initially configured to support one of the following:

1. A minimum security configuration that allows access to all objects under the internet (1.3.6.1) subtree.
2. A semi-secure configuration which allows access to objects under the System group, SNMP group, snmpEngine subtree, snmpMPDStats subtree, and the usmStats subtree.
3. A no access configuration which will deny access to all MIB objects.

The no access configuration is accomplished by leaving all the VACM MIB tables empty.

To set up for either minimum security or semi-secure configuration, we need to add an entry in the vacmContextTable with vacmContextName set to the empty string. Next, we need to add one entry to the vacmSecurityToGroupTable to map a user name "initial" to a group name "initial."

Table 7-6　Example vacmSecurityToGroupTable Configuration

	3.initial
vacmSecurityModel	3 (USM)
vacmSecurityName	"initial"
vacmGroupName	"initial"
vacmSecurityToGroupStorageType	nonVolatile
vacmSecurityToGroupStatus	active

Note: This entry will only match messages that are using the User-based Security Model.

Next, we are going to add three entries to the vacmAccessTable. One entry will be for mapping a message with no authentication and will cause any access for a write operation to be denied. The other two entries will be for authentication without privacy, and authentication with privacy. Both of these entries will provide identical access rights.

Table 7-7　Example vacmAccessTable Configuration

	initial.3.1	**initial.3.2**	**initial.3.3**
vacmGroupName	initial	initial	initial
vacmAccessContextPrefix	""	""	""
vacmAccessSecurityModel	3 (USM)	3 (USM)	3 (USM)
vacmAccessSecurityLevel	1 (noAuthNoPriv)	2 (authNoPriv)	3 (authPriv)
vacmAccessContextMatch	exact	exact	exact
vacmAccessReadViewName	restricted	internet	internet
vacmAccessWriteViewName	""	internet	internet
vacmAccessNotifyViewName	restricted	internet	internet
vacmAccessStorageType	nonVolatile	nonVolatile	nonVolatile
vacmAccessStatus	active	active	active

The MIB views that will be configured depend on the whether we're configuring for minimum security or semi-secure. If we're configuring for minimum security, we need to add two rows to the vacmViewTreeFamilyTable.

Table 7-8   vacmViewTreeFamilyTable for minimum security

	internet.1.3.6.1	**restricted.1.3.6.1**
vacmViewTreeFamilyViewName	internet	restricted
vacmViewTreeFamilySubtree	1.3.6.1	1.3.6.1
vacmViewTreeFamilyMask	""	""
vacmViewTreeFamilyType	1 (included)	1 (included)
vacmViewTreeFamilyStorageType	nonVolatile	nonVolatile
vacmViewTreeFamilyStatus	active	active

Note: From this configuration, if authentication is not being used then:

• MIB access will be denied for any write operation.
• Any MIB object under the internet subtree (1.3.6.1) can be accessed for a read operation.
• Any MIB object under the internet subtree can be accessed in generating a notification.

If authentication is being used, then any MIB object under the internet subtree can be accessed for a read or write operation, or for generating a notification.

If we're configuring for the semi-secure configuration, we need to add six rows to the vacmViewTreeFamilyTable. One row will be for the "internet" view, the other five will be for the "restricted" view. The restricted view allows access to objects that fall under the following subtrees: System Group (1.3.6.1.2.1.1), SNMP Group (1.3.6.1.2.1.11), snmpEngine (1.3.6.1.6.3.10.2.1), snmpMPDStats (1.3.6.1.6.3.11.2.1), and usmStats (1.3.6.1.6.3.15.1.1).

Each of the rows for the "restricted" view will be identical except for the vacmViewTreeFamilySubtree value. Table 7-9 shows the "restricted" view row for the System Group subtree. Rows need to be added for the SNMP Group, snmpEngine subtree, snmpMDPStats subtree, and usmStats subtree.

Table 7-9 vacmViewTreeFamilyTable for Semi-secure Configuration

	internet.1.3.6.1	restricted.1.3.6.1.2.1.1
vacmViewTreeFamilyViewName	internet	restricted
vacmViewTreeFamilySubtree	1.3.6.1	1.3.6.1.2.1.1
vacmViewTreeFamilyMask	""	""
vacmViewTreeFamilyType	1 (included)	1 (included)
vacmViewTreeFamilyStorageType	nonVolatile	nonVolatile
vacmViewTreeFamilyStatus	active	active

7.7 Testing for Whether Access is Allowed

The following pseudocode determines whether a MIB object can be accessed:

```
procedure Boolean::IsAccessAllowed(sn, sm, sl, c, op, oid)
{
    // This procedure determines whether access is
    // allowed to a MIB object.
    //
    // sn:  securityName from SNMP message
    // sm:  securityModel from SNMP message
    // sl:  securityLevel from SNMP message
    // c:   context from PDU
    // op:  Operation type of PDU - either r, w, or n (for read,
    //      write, or notify)
    // oid: OBJECT IDENTIFIER to test
    //
    // This will return true if access is allowed to oid,
    // otherwise it will return false.

    // Map securityName and securityModel to a group name

    pdu <- {vacmGroupName.sm.sn}
    respPDU <- SnmpGet(pdu)
    if (!ObjectExists(respPDU, 1))
    {
```

```
                    // securityModel and securityName do not resolve
                    // to a groupName. Return false, indicating that
                    // access is denied to oid.

                    return false
                }

                groupName <- GetVarBindValue(respPDU, 1)

                // Map groupName, context, securityModel, securityLevel,
                // and operation type to a MIB view

                mibView <- GetMibView(groupName, c, sm, sl, op)
                if (mibView == '')
                {
                    // If no MIB view was found, deny access to oid.

                    return false
                }

                return GetAccess(mibView, oid)
            }
```

GetMibView will search through the vacmAccessTable for the best possible matching row given a groupName, contextName, securityModel, and securityLevel. The steps that are taken to select valid rows were described in the vacmAccessTable section, as were the steps that are used to find the best match from all the valid rows.

If no valid matches are found, GetMibView will return the empty string and IsAccessAllowed will end up returning false. Otherwise, based on whether the SNMP operation is a read, write, or notify, the associated MIB view will be returned.

```
            procedure SnmpAdminString::GetMibView(gn, c, sm, sl, op)
            {
                // Return either a MIB view or an empty string.
                //
                // gn:  groupName
                // c:   context
                // sm:  securityModel
                // sl:  securityLevel
                // op:  operation type

                flag <- true
                responsePDU <- {vacmAccessContextMatch.gn}
                origPDU <- responsePDU
```

```
while (flag)
{
   // Read all entries in the vacmAccessTable that
   // are indexed by the groupName. Build a list of
   // rows that match the context, securityModel,
   // and securityLevel.

   pdu <- SnmpGetNext(responsePDU)
   responsePDU <- pdu
   flag <- CheckPDU(pdu, origPDU)

   if (flag == false)
     continue

   // Get the ContextPrefix, SecurityModel, and
   // SecurityLevel values from the instance.

   inst <- GetVarBindInstance(
           pdu,
           1,
           vacmAccessContextMatch.gn)

   // From the instance, parse the contextPrefix,
   // securityModel, and securityLevel values.
   //
   // VacmAccessInstanceStruct can be defined
   // by the following C structure:
   //
   //   struct VacmAccessInstanceStruct {
   //      SnmpAdminString context;
   //      SecurityModel sm;
   //      SecurityLevel sl;
   //   }

   info <- new(VacmAccessInstanceStruct)
   ParseVacmAccessInstance(inst, &info)
   m <- GetVarBindValue(pdu, 1)

   // Test whether either the context names match,
   // or row's contextName matches the first part of
   // the contextName (if m == 'prefix').

   if (c == info.context)
     contextExactFlag <- true
   else if ((m == 'prefix') && IsPrefix(info.context, c))
     contextExactFlag <- false
   else
```

```
        continue

        // Test whether Security Models match or whether
        // vacmSecurityModel has been set to 'any'.

        if (sm == info.sm)
          smExactFlag <- true
        else if (info.sm == 'any')
          smExactFlag <- false
        else
          continue

        // Test whether vacmAccessSecurityLevel is
        // equal to or less than sl

        if (info.sl > sl)
          continue

        add {inst, info.context, contextExactFlag,
          smExactFlag, info.sl} to matches
    }

    // If no matches were found return an empty string.

    if (IsEmpty(matches))
        return ''

    // Find the matching row that is the best match
    // and use it to obtain either the read, write, or
    // notify MIB view

    inst <- GetBestMatch(matches)
    switch (op) {
        case 'r':
          getpdu <- {vacmAccessReadViewName.inst}

        case 'w':
          getpdu <- {vacmAccessWriteViewName.inst}

        case 'n':
          getpdu <- {vacmAccessNotifyViewName.inst}
    }

    viewpdu <- SnmpGet(getpdu)
    return GetVarBindValue(viewpdu, 1)
}
```

GetBestMatch is passed a collection of valid matches and whittles these matches down to the best possible match. During the whittling process, if a single match exists within the collection then the instance associated with the match is returned. GetBestMatch introduces several new routines which we will provide short descriptions for now.

SizeOf(*col*) returns the number of objects within a collection *col*.

GetFromCollection(*col*) returns the first object within *col*.

CountMatches(*col, pattern*) returns a count of the number of objects within *col* that match *pattern*.

DiscardAllRows(*col, pattern*) discards all objects from *col* that match *pattern*.

DiscardRow(*col, object*) discards *object* from *col*.

GetLongestContextLength(*matches*), given a collection of MatchElementStruct objects, returns the length of the longest context name within the collection.

FindHighestSecurityLevel(*matches*), given a collection of MatchElementStruct objects, returns the object with the highest securityLevel value.

```
procedure OBJECT IDENTFIER::GetBestMatch(matches)
{
    // Find the best match from all selected rows
    // from the vacmAccessTable.
    // Note. matches is a collection of elements, where each
    // element can be represented by the following C structure:
    //
    //    struct MatchElementStruct {
    //        OBJECT IDENTIFIER inst;
    //        SnmpAdminString context;
    //        Boolean contextExactFlag;
    //        Boolean smExactFlag;
    //        SecurityLevel sl;
    //    }

    // Test if only one match was found. If so, simply return
    // the instance associated with that match.

    if (SizeOf(matches) == 1)
```

```
{
   match <- GetFromCollection(matches)
   return match.inst
}

// If any rows match the SNMP message's securityModel,
// discard all other rows.

if (CountMatches(matches, {*, *, *, true, *}) >= 1)
   DiscardAllRows(matches, {*, *, *, false, *})

// Do we now only have one row left??

if (SizeOf(matches) == 1)
{
   match <- GetFromCollection(matches)
   return match.inst
}

// If any rows match the SNMP message's contextName
// exactly, discard all other rows.

if (CountMatches(matches, {*, *, true, *, *}) >= 1)
   DiscardAllRows(matches, {*, *, false, *, *})

// Do we now only have one row left??

if (SizeOf(matches) == 1)
{
   match <- GetFromCollection(matches)
   return match.inst
}

// Discard all entries with a context name shorter
// than the longest one remaining in the collection.

length <- GetLongestContextLength(matches)
foreach match in matches {
   if (LengthOf(match.context) < length)
     DiscardRow(matches, match)
}

// Do we now only have one row left??

if (SizeOf(matches) == 1)
{
   match <- GetFromCollection(matches)
   return match.inst
```

```
    }

    // Finally, pick the row with the highest securityLevel

    match <- FindHighestSecurityLevel(matches)
    return match.inst
}
```

To wrap up this section, we will provide the pseudocode for GetAccess. GetAccess is passed a MIB view and an OBJECT IDENTIFIER and will search through the vacm-ViewTreeFamilyTable to determine whether access should be allowed for the OBJECT IDENTI-FIER. It does this by finding all the possible matching rows within vacmViewTreeFamilyTable, and from this set finding the best matching row. Given this row, the vacmViewTreeFamilyType object is used to determine whether access should be granted or denied. Also, if no rows match, access will be denied.

```
    procedure Boolean::GetAccess(mibView, oid)
    {
        // Search vacmViewTreeFamilyTable for all entries
        // that match both the MIB view, mibView, and the
        // OBJECT IDENTIFIER, oid. If no entries exist, then
        // access is denied - return false.
        //
        // Select the best matching entry. If it's
        // vacmViewTreeFamilyType value is 'included', then
        // access is granted - return true. Otherwise, access
        // is denied - return false.

        flag <- true
        responsePDU <- {vacmViewTreeFamilyMask.mibView}
        origPDU <- responsePDU
        matches <- ''

        while (flag)
        {
            // Read all entries in the vacmViewTreeFamilyTable that
            // are indexed by the mibView. Build a list of
            // rows where oid falls under the row's subtree.

            pdu <- SnmpGetNext(responsePDU)
            responsePDU <- pdu
            flag <- CheckPDU(pdu, origPDU)

            if (flag == false)
              continue
```

```
        // Get the vacmViewTreeFamilySubtree value from
        // the instance.

        subtree <- GetVarBindInstance(
                    pdu,
                    1,
                    vacmViewTreeFamilyMask.mibView)
        mask <- GetVarBindValue(pdu, 1)
        if (IsUnderSubtree(subtree, mask, oid) == false)
           continue
        add {inst, subtree} to matches
    }

    // If no matches were found then deny access.

    if (SizeOf(matches) == 0)
        return false

    inst <- GetBestSubtreeMatch(matches)

    // Get the type value for the best matching row.
    // Use this to decide whether to grant or deny access.

    pdu <- {vacmViewTreeFamilyType.inst}
    respPDU <- SnmpGet(pdu)
    type <- GetVarBindValue(respPDU, 1)
    if (type == 'included')
        return true
    else
        return false
}
```

GetAccess introduces two new routines: IsUnderSubtree and GetBestSubtreeMatch. IsUnderSubtree is passed a subtree, a mask, and an OBJECT IDENTIFIER and will return true if the OBJECT IDENTIFIER falls under the subtree. GetBestSubtreeMatch is passed a collection of objects, where each object is an instance and a subtree. It will find the object whose subtree value has the most subidentifiers and return the associated instance. If two or more subtrees have this same number of subidentifiers, then it will pick the lexicographically largest one and return the associated instance.

The pseudocode for IsUnderSubtree is provided below.

```
    procedure Boolean::IsUnderSubtree(subtree, mask, oid)
    {
        // Return true if oid falls under subtree.
        //
```

```
// Get number of subidentifiers used in subtree.

n <- NumberSubIdentifiers(subtree)

// If subtree has more subidentifiers than oid
// then return false.

if (NumberSubIdentifiers(oid) < n)
    return false

bitpos <- n
for {i = 1; i <= n; i++}
{
    // Get the bit value within mask at postion bitpos.

    bitval <- GetBit(mask, bitpos)
    if (bitval == 0)
    {
      bitpos--
      continue
    }

    // Bit within mask is a 1, check if sub-identifiers
    // at corresponding position are equal.

    if (GetSubIdent(subtree, i) != GetSubIdent(oid, i))
      return false

    bitpos--
}
return true
}
```

7.8 Configuring the VACM MIB

There should be a good reason for creating complex MIB views. The more MIB views that are created — and the more subtrees that are added to each MIB view for excluding or including objects, the higher the overall management cost is going to be. This cost will include not only the time spent for the initial configuration, but the time spent trying to figure out why users/ applications can't access objects that they're expecting to access. Also, the more complex the configuration, the more difficult it will be to make changes (at least correct changes) later on. A similar analogy to this is software design — if you start off with a complex design (a high entropy level), the amount of effort needed to make even small changes can be immense. If you start off with a simple design (a low entropy level), changes can be made more easily. With each change that is made, though, the entropy level is most likely going to increase which is another reason we want to start off with as low an entropy level as possible. Finally, the more complex your configuration, the more likely it is you will need to check your configuration at a network-wide level for consistency.

Ideally, you should try to limit the number of MIB views to as small a number as possible. Possibly even keep it to two views — a monitor view and an administrative view. Also try to keep the number of group names as low as possible. If there are two MIB views defined, there should be no more than two group names defined.

So if we keep the MIB view configuration simple, everything should run smoothly, right? Well, that depends on whether vacmContextTable and vacmSecurityToGroupTable are being properly maintained. If contextNames are being used that haven't been added to vacmContext-Table, then access will end up being denied. Similarly, if securityNames can't be mapped to groupNames, then access will also end up being denied. So even in a simple configuration you will probably need to routinely check both vacmContextTable and vacmSecurityToGroupTable for each network device to verify that the contextNames that are being used have been config-ured and that all the securityNames that are being used are being mapped to groupNames.

In this section we will provide pseudocode to demonstrate

- Finding all vacmAccessTable entries that use a specified MIB view.
- Adding a MIB view.
- Removing a MIB view.
- Modifying subtree family inclusion/exclusion in an already existing MIB view.
- Modifying a vacmAccessTable row.

This first example simply searches through each entry within vacmAccessTable to see if vacmAccessReadViewName, vacmAccessWriteViewName, or vacmAccessNotifyViewName objects are set to a specific MIB view name. If any are, the instance for that row will be returned in a collection. This routine could be called before a MIB view is deleted so that any vacmAc-cessTable rows that reference the MIB view can be modified.

```
procedure Collection::SearchForMibView(mibView)
{
    // Return a collection of instance for each row
    // within vacmAccessTable which references mibView.

    flag <- true
    responsePDU <- {vacmAccessReadViewName,
```

```
                        vacmAccessWriteViewName,
                        vacmAccessNotifyViewName}
        origPDU <- responsePDU
        matches <- ''

        while (flag)
        {

            // Collect all the MIB views that are being
            // used in vacmAccessTable.

            pdu <- SnmpGetNext(responsePDU)
            responsePDU <- pdu
            flag <- CheckPDU(pdu, origPDU)

            if (flag == false)
              continue

            // Test whether any of the collected objects
            //are equal to mibView.

            readView <- GetVarBindValue(pdu, 1)
            writeView <- GetVarBindValue(pdu, 2)
            notifyView <- GetVarBindValue(pdu, 3)
            if ( (readView != mibView) &&
                 (writeView != mibView) &&
                 (notifyView != mibView))
              continue

            inst <- GetVarBindInstance(
                        pdu,
                        1,
                        vacmAccessReadViewName)

            add inst to matches
        }
        return matches
    }
```

In the next example, we want to pass a routine a new MIB view, a collection of subtree families to use for exclusion, and a collection of subtree families to use for inclusion. A subtree family will be represented as vacmViewTreeFamilySubtree and vacmViewTreeFamilyMask values. When creating new entries for vacmViewTreeFamilyTable, all exclusion entries need to be added first, followed by the inclusion entries. If we added the inclusion objects first, access could end up being granted to an object that we want excluded (but we haven't yet added the row that would explicitly exclude that object). When adding a new row to vacmViewTreeFamilyTable, vacmViewSpinLock will be used to protect against possible collisions.

```
procedure void::AddMibView(mibView, exCol, inCol)
{
    // For each subtree family within the exCol collection,
    // add a row in vacmViewTreeFamilySubtree to exclude
    // the subtree family for mibView.

    foreach object in exCol
    {
        subtree <- object.subtree
        mask <- object.mask
        inst <- mibView.subtree

        AddSubtreeFamily(mibView,
            inst, subtree, mask, 'excluded')
    }

    // For each subtree family within the inCol collection,
    // add a row in vacmViewTreeFamilySubtree to include
    // the subtree family for mibView.

    foreach object in inCol
    {
        subtree <- object.subtree
        mask <- object.mask
        inst <- mibView.subtree

        AddSubtreeFamily(mibView,
            inst, subtree, mask, 'included')
    }
}
```

A procedure AddSubtreeFamily is provided that does all the work in adding a new row to vacmViewFamilyTreeTable.

```
procedure void::AddSubtreeFamily(mibView, inst. subtree,
                    mask, type)
{
    // Add a new row to vacmViewFamilyTreeTable.
    // Where,
    //
    //    mibView, specifies the MIB view.
    //    inst, is the instance for the new row.
    //    subtree, is the MIB subtree.
```

```
//    mask, is the mask value to use. A combination
//         of subtree and mask will define a subtree
//         family.
//    type, 'included' or 'excluded'
//
// Note. This routine will raise an exception if
//         a row can not be added.

while (true)
{
   // If a row already exists for the MIB view and the
   // subtree, destroy it and re-add it below.

   if (TestObjectExists(vacmViewTreeFamilyStatus.inst))
     DestroyRow(vacmViewTreeFamilyStatus.inst)

   lockVal <- GetLockVal(vacmViewSpinLock.0)
   setpdu <-
     {vacmViewTreeFamilyStatus.inst <- 'createAndGo',
      vacmViewTreeFamilyMask.inst <- mask,
      vacmViewTreeFamilyType.inst <- type,
      vacmViewSpinLock.0 <- lockVal}
   pdu <- SnmpSet(setpdu)

   // Check whether a lock conflict was seen.
   // If so, try again after some random time.

   status <- GetErrorStatus(pdu)
   if (status == 'inconsistentValue')
   {
      // Since the row is guaranteed not to exist
      // before the SNMP Set operation, an
      // inconsistentValue will indicate a conflict
      // with the lock object. Wait some random
      // amount of time and try again.

      WaitRandomTime()
      continue
   }

   // If any other error was detected, raise
   // an exception

   if (status != 'noError')
     RaiseException(NewRowFailException)

   // Set operation succeeded - the new row has been added.
```

```
        return
    }
}
```

The pseudocode for TestObjectExists, DestroyRow, and GetLockVal is provided below:

```
procedure Boolean::TestObjectExists(oid)
{
    // Return true if oid exists, otherwise return false.

    respPDU <- SnmpGet(oid)
    return ObjectExists(respPDU, 1)
}

procedure void::DestroyRow(oid)
{
    // oid references an RowStatus object.
    // Simply perform an SnmpSet operation to destroy
    // the row referenced by oid.

    SnmpSet(oid <- 'destroy')
}

procedure int::GetLockVal(oid)
{
    // oid references a TestAndIncr object.
    // Simply return its value.

    respPDU <- SnmpGet(oid)
    return GetVarBindValue(respPDU, 1)
}
```

The next example demonstrates removing a MIB view from vacmViewFamilyTreeTable. The first step will be to read all the rows associated with the view and build two collections, one for rows which include a subtree family and one for rows which exclude a subtree family. When we delete the rows, we want to delete the "include" rows first, and then the "exlude" rows. The reason for this is if an SNMP operation arrives while we are in the process of the deletion, access to an object won't be improperly granted.

The pseudocode demonstrating the removal of a MIB view is provided below.

```
procedure void::RemoveMibView(mibView)
{
    // Remove all rows referenced by mibView from
    // vacmViewTreeFamilyTable. When removing rows,
    // remove all rows with vacmViewTreeFamilyType
```

```
// equal to 'include' first, and then the rows
// with the vacmViewTreeFamilyType equal to 'exclude'.
// This will prevent an SNMP operation from potentially
// accessing an object that it should not be allowed to.

flag <- true
responsePDU <- {vacmViewTreeFamilyType.mibView}
origPDU <- responsePDU
inCol <- ''
exCol <- ''

while (flag)
{
    // Read all entries in the vacmViewTreeFamilyTable that
    // are indexed by the mibView. Build inclusion and
    // exclusion collections.

    pdu <- SnmpGetNext(responsePDU)
    responsePDU <- pdu
    flag <- CheckPDU(pdu, origPDU)

    if (flag == false)
      continue

    // Get the instance value associated with the row.
    // Note. This will be the complete instance for the row
    // (mibView.subtree).

    inst <- GetVarBindInstance(
                pdu,
                1,
                vacmViewTreeFamilyTree)

    // Does this row include or exclude subtree families?

    type <- GetVarBindValue(pdu, 1)
    if (type == 'included')
      add inst to inCol
    else
      add inst to exCol
}

// First, remove all 'included' rows.

foreach inst in inCol
    DestroyRow(vacmViewTreeFamilyStatus.inst)

// Next, remove all 'excluded' rows.
```

```
    foreach inst in exCol
        DestroyRow(vacmViewTreeFamilyStatus.inst)
}
```

We can take advantage of AddMibView and RemoveMibView to configure a new set of inclusion and exclusion subtree families for an already existing MIB view. This is demonstrated by the following pseudocode:

```
procedure void::ModifyMibView(mibView, inCol, exCol)
{
    // Reconfigure vacmViewTreeFamilyTable to use a new
    // set of inclusion and exclusion rows for mibView.
    // This is done by simply calling RemoveMibView to
    // remove all previous rows, and the AddMibView to
    // add the new rows.

    RemoveMibView(mibView)
    AddMibView(mibView, exCol, inCol)
}
```

As our final example, we will demonstrate modifying the MIB views used within an existing vacmAccessTable row. Getting back to an earlier scenario, before removing a MIB view you want to find all the rows within vacmAccessTable which reference that MIB view (by using the SearchForMibView procedure that was shown earlier). Then for each row which references the soon to be obsoleted MIB view, replace the MIB view with a valid one. After this has been done, then go ahead and remove the MIB view.

ModifyAccessRow introduces two additional convenience routines, GetVarBindOID and AddToPDU.

- GetVarBindOID is passed a PDU and a position n, and returns the nth OBJECT IDENTIFIER within PDU's variable-bindings.

- AddToPDU is passed a PDU and a varbind. It simply adds the varbind to the PDU's variable-bindings.

```
procedure void::ModifyAccessRow(inst, obsoleteView, newView)
{
    // Modify a row within vacmAccessTable that is indexed by
    // inst by replacing any reference to obsoleteView with
    // newView.
```

```
pdu <- {vacmAccessReadViewName.inst,
        vacmAccessWriteViewName.inst,
        vacmAccessNotifyViewName.inst}

respPDU <- SnmpGet(pdu)
setpdu <- ''

// Check each view being used in row. If any
// equal obsoleteView, add a varbind to setpdu
// to set the view to newView.

for (i = 1; i <= 3; i++)
{
    view <- GetVarBindValue(respPDU, i)
    if (view != obsoleteView)
      continue

    oid <- GetVarBindOID(respPDU, i)

    // oid will equal either a fully instanced
    // vacmAccessReadViewName, vacmAccessWriteViewName,
    // or vacmAccessNotifyViewName object.

    AddToPDU(setpdu, {oid <- newView})
}

// If obsoleteView was not used then setPDU
// will be empty, so simply return without
// performing an SNMP Set.

if (SizeOf(setpdu) == 0)
    return

SnmpSet(setpdu)
}
```

7.9 Summary

This chapter described the View-based Access Control Model that is used to determine whether an SNMP protocol operation can access a MIB object. We provided pseudocode to show the logic used in determining whether access is allowed for a MIB object. We also provided pseudocode to demonstrate configuring the VACM MIB tables. Hopefully, this chapter also demonstrated the importance of keeping the VACM configuration simple.

Coexistence Issues

This chapter looks at coexistence issues when either a proxy needs to translate messages between different SNMP versions or when SNMPv1 (and SNMPv2c) are additionally supported by an SNMP engine.

8.1 Proxy Issues

As SNMPv3 devices are deployed, they will most likely be placed in heterogeneous environments where a large number of devices support only SNMPv1. Over time, if SNMPv3 proves itself in the marketplace, the SNMPv1 devices may or may not be upgraded to SNMPv3 depending on the cost involved.

One way of trying to keep the network management simple is to treat all devices as if they support the same version of SNMP. Assuming the version we want to deal with is SNMPv3, we need to set up SNMP entities throughout the network to act as proxies for the SNMPv1 devices. An SNMPv3 message will be sent to a proxy, which will translate it to a SNMPv1 message and forward it to the SNMPv1 device. When a response comes back, the proxy will translate it to an SNMPv3 message before forwarding it back to the network management station.

It is also possible that an environment has invested a large amount of money and time in network management software that supports only SNMPv1. This environment may be deploying SNMPv3 devices because it has no choice. In this case the environment may want to continue operating primarily using SNMPv1 but may need to set up proxies to translate SNMPv1 to SNMPv3 and vice versa.

The potential issues involved when translating between SNMPv1 and SNMPv3 messages are fairly straightforward:

- Translating notification messages.
- Handling Counter64 objects.
- Handling noSuchObject, noSuchInstance, and endOfMibView exceptions.
- Translating error statuses.

8.1.1   Translating Notification Messages

An SNMPv2-Trap or Inform may need to be translated to an SNMPv1 Trap (and vice versa) due to

a. A proxy needing to translate a notification to a different format before forwarding it.
b. A MIB instrumentation might generate a notification in a particular format but the entity's configuration requires it to be sent out in a different format.

The following table shows the notification parameters that make up an SNMPv1 Trap and both SNMPv2-Traps and Informs.

Table 8-1   Notification Parameters

SNMPv1 Trap	SNMPv2-Trap or Inform
enterprise value	sysUpTime (first variable-binding)
agent address	snmpTrapOID value (next variable binding)
generic-trap value	additional variable bindings
specific-trap value	
timestamp	
variable-bindings	

Translating an SNMPv1 Trap to an SNMPv2 notification:

- sysUpTime value is taken from SNMPv1 timestamp.
- snmpTrapOID will be either

a. if the SNMPv1 generic-trap value is `enterpriseSpecific` (6), then snmpTrapOID is formed by concatenating the SNMPv1 enterprise value with a '0' and the SNMPv1 specific-trap value.

b. if the SNMPv1 generic-trap value is not `enterpriseSpecific`, then the SNMPv1 generic-trap value will be mapped to one of the following snmpTrapOID values:

Table 8-2 Mapping SNMPv1 Generic-Trap Values to snmpTrapOID Values

Trap	Generic-Trap Value	snmpTrapOID.0
coldStart	0	1.3.6.1.6.3.1.1.5.1
warmStart	1	1.3.6.1.6.3.1.1.5.2
linkDown	2	1.3.6.1.6.3.1.1.5.3
linkUp	3	1.3.6.1.6.3.1.1.5.4
authenticatonFailure	4	1.3.6.1.6.3.1.1.5.5
egpNeighborLoss	5	1.3.6.1.6.3.1.1.5.6

• The SNMPv2 variable-bindings will be obtained from the SNMPv1 variable bindings. In addition, if the translation is being performed by a proxy in order to forward a received trap, three additional variable-bindings will be added to the end if they don't already exist within the SNMPv1 variable-bindings:

snmpTrapAddress.0, which will contain the SNMPv1 agent-address value.

snmpTrapCommunity.0, which will contain the value of the community-string field from the SNMPv1 message.

snmpTrapEnterprise.0, which will contain the SNMPv1 enterprise value.

As an example, let's look at converting an SNMPv1 topologyChange trap defined in the Bridge-MIB to an SNMPv2-Trap due to the MIB instrumentation:

SNMPv1 topologyChange Trap
_____

enterprise: 1.3.6.1.2.1.17
agent address: 158.101.1.121
generic trap: 6
specific trap: 2
time-ticks: 2019910

SNMPv2-Trap
_____

sysUptime: 2019910
snmpTrapOID.0: 1.3.6.1.2.1.17.0.2

If the translation was due to a proxy needing to forward a received trap, then snmpTrapAddress.0, snmpTrapCommunity.0, and snmpTrapEnterprise.0 would need to be added to the end of the SNMPv2-Trap's variable-bindings.

Translating an SNMPv2 notification to an SNMPv1 Trap:

• The first step is obtaining the SNMPv1 enterprise value. This is done based on whether the snmpTrapOID.0 value is one of the standard traps shown in Table 8-2. If it is, then the SNMPv1 enterprise value will be set to either

    a. the snmpTrapEnterprise.0 value if this object exists within the variable-bindings.
    b. otherwise, "snmpTraps" (1.3.6.1.6.3.1.1.5).

If the snmpTrapOID.0 value is not one of the standard traps, then the SNMPv1 enterprise value will be set to either

    a. snmpTrapOID.0 with the last two subidentifiers removed if the next-to-last subidentifier of snmpTrapOID.0 is zero.
    b. otherwise, snmpTrapOID.0 with the last subidentifier removed.

This can be described a little more succinctly by the following *if* statement:

```
if (snmpTrapOID.0 is one of the standard traps)
{
    if (snmpTrapEnterprise.0 is included in the varbinds)
        SNMPv1 enterprise <- snmpTrapEnterprise.0
    else
        SNMPv1 enterprise <- 'snmpTraps'
}
else
```

```
{
    n <- LengthOf(snmpTrapOID)

    // snmpTrapOID[1] will reference the first sub-identifier
    // snmpTrapOID[n] will reference the last sub-identifier

    if (snmpTrapOID[n-1] == 0)
        SNMPv1 enterprise <- snmpTrapOID[1 .. n - 2]
    else
        SNMPv1 enterprise <- snmpTrapOID[1 .. n - 1]
}
```

• The SNMPv1 agent-address value used is dependent on whether the notification is being translated due to a proxy or the MIB instrumentation.

If the translation is due to the MIB instrumentation:

    a. If the notification is going to be sent over UDP, then the SNMPv1 agent- address value will be set to the local IP address.

    b. If the notification is going to be sent over some other transport, the SNMPv1 agent-address value will be set to 0.0.0.0.

If the translation is due to a proxy forwarding a received notification:

    a. If the SNMPv2 variable-bindings contain the snmpTrapAddress.0 object, the SNMPv1 agent-address will be set to that value.

    b. Otherwise, if the original source of the notification was an IP address, SNMPv1 agent-address will be set to that value.

    c. Otherwise, SNMPv1 agent-address will be set to 0.0.0.0.

• The SNMPv1 generic-trap value will either be set to the corresponding value in Table 8-2 if a snmpTrapOID.0 is one of the standard traps, or 6.

• The SNMPv1 specific-trap value will either be set to zero if snmpTrapOID.0 is one of the standard traps, or the last subidentifier of the SNMPv2 snmpTrapOID value.

• The SNMPv1 timestamp value will be set to the SNMPv2 sysUpTime value.

• The SNMPv1 variable-bindings will be the same SNMPv2 variable-bindings. The only problem here is, what happens if a Counter64 variable is part of the variable-bindings? Since SNMPv1 doesn't support Counter64 objects, something has to happen and currently what's defined is to simply remove that object from the variable-bindings. There has been some discussion within the SNMPv3 mailing list about this, and there have been alternative proposals suggested — such as to encode a Counter64 object as an Opaque object. By the time this book comes out a different solution than simply throwing out potentially useful information might be agreed upon.

As an example, let's look at converting an SNMPv2 linkDown Trap to an SNMPv1 Trap due to the MIB instrumentation:

SNMPv2 linkDown Trap

sysUpTime: 71661143
sysTrapOID.0: 1.3.6.1.6.3.1.1.5.3
ifIndex.4: 4
ifAdminStatus.4: up
ifOperStatus.4: down

SNMPv1 Trap

enterprise:1.3.6.1.6.3.1.1.5
agent-address: local-address
generic: 2
specific: 0
time-stamp: 71661143
ifIndex.4: 4
ifAdminStatus.4: up
ifOperStatus.4: down

8.1.2   Handling Counter64 Objects

Since Counter64 objects are incompatible with SNMPv1, something has to be done when an SNMPv1 Request is made to retrieve or set a Counter64 object, or when an SNMPv3 message which contains a Counter64 object needs to be translated to an SNMPv1 message.

As far as handling an SNMPv1 Request to retrieve or set a Counter64 object, an SNMP entity will take the approach that Counter64 objects are excluded from view when processing an SNMPv1 message. Similarly, when translating an SNMPv3 message to an SNMPv1 message, Counter64 objects will be considered not in view. The following table both summarizes the potential issues between Counter64 objects and SNMPv1 and describes how the issues are handled

Table 8-3   Issues with Counter64 Objects and SNMPv1

Issue	Action
SNMPv1 Get Request accesses a Counter64 object.	A Response with an error-status of noSuchName and an error-index set to the position of the Counter64 object will be sent.
SNMPv1 Get-Next Request would access a Counter64 object.	Counter64 objects must be skipped, and the first non-Counter64 object following it will be fetched.
SNMPv1 Set Request accessing a Counter64 object.	This will cause an ASN.1 parse error, which will cause the snmpInASNParseErrs counter to be incremented. No response will be returned.
A proxy forwarder application must translate an SNMPv3 to an SNMPv1 message, and the PDU contains a Counter64 object.	An alternative response PDU will be generated, with an error-status of noSuchName and an error-index set to the position of the Counter64 object.
An SNMPv2 notification is translated to an SNMPv1 Trap.	Counter64 objects will be removed from the variable-bindings.

8.1.3   Mapping SNMPv2 Exceptions

As we saw in the SNMP basics chapter, SNMPv2 allows an SNMPv2 Response PDU to return as many MIB objects as it can for a Get, Get-Next, or Get-Bulk request. For a Get-Request, the Response PDU could possibly contain noSuchObject or noSuchInstance exceptions. For a Get-Next Request, the Response PDU could possibly contain endOfMib-View exceptions. Exceptions won't be returned for a Set Request. Since we don't have to worry about mapping a Get-Bulk Request to SNMPv1, we can skip looking at that.

So what happens if an SNMPv2 Response needs to be translated to an SNMPv1 Response, but it contains exceptions? An alternative Response PDU will be generated, setting error-status to noSuchName, error-index to the index of the variable binding where the exception occurred, and using the variable-binding from the original request. *Note*: If an SNMPv2 Response contains more than one exception, it is up to the implementation to choose which variable-binding to set the error-index to.

8.1.4   Translating Error-Statuses

When translating an SNMPv2 Response PDU to an SNMPv1 Response PDU, the following error-status mappings need to be done:

Table 8-4   Mapping SNMPv2 Error-Statuses to SNMPv1

SNMPv2 Error-Status	SNMPv1 Error-Status
noError	noError
tooBig	tooBig
genErr	genErr
wrongValue	badValue
wrongEncoding	badValue
wrongType	badValue
wrongLength	badValue
inconsistentValue	badValue
noAccess	noSuchName
notWritable	noSuchName
noCreation	noSuchName
inconsistentName	noSuchName
resourceUnavailable	genErr
commitFailed	genErr
undoFailed	genErr
authorizatonError	noSuchName

No error-status mapping needs to be done when translating an SNMPv1 Response PDU to an SNMPv2 Response PDU.

8.1.5   MiscellaneousTranslations

There are several additional translations that you should be aware of.

- If a proxy forwarder application needs to translate a Get-Bulk PDU to an SNMPv1 message, both the non-repeaters and max-repetitions fields will be set to 0, and the PDU type will be set to a Get-Next PDU.

- If an SNMPv1 Response PDU has an error-status of `tooBig`, and the message needs to be forwarded using either the SNMPv2c or SNMPv3 message version, the contents of the variable-bindings field will be removed before the Response is forwarded.

- If an Inform PDU is received, it can only be forwarded using the SNMPv2c or SNMPv3 message version. Any configuration information indicating that it should be forwarded as an SNMPv1 message will be ignored.

- A notification originator application will generate a Trap-PDU if the associated snmpTargetParamsMPModel value has been configured for SNMPv1, regardless of whether snmpNotifyType has been set to `inform`.

8.2 Supporting Multiple Message Processing Models

What we want to do is be able to adapt SNMPv1 (and SNMPv2c) into the SNMP architecture by somehow coming up with the necessary version-independent SNMP message parameters for an SNMPv1 (or SNMPv2c) message. The SNMP-COMMUNITY-MIB defines a table, snmpCommunityTable, which maps a community string into the following SNMP message parameters:

- securityName
- contextEngineID
- contextName

The snmpCommunityTable also allows you to validate the source of the message. We will show shortly how this is done.

We can further infer other SNMPv3 message parameters, such as a securityLevel value of `noAuthNoPriv`, a securityModel of 1 for an SNMPv1 message and 2 for an SNMPv2c message, and a messageProcessingModel value of 0 for an SNMPv1 message and 1 for an SNMPv2c message.

8.2.1   snmpCommunityTable

The snmpCommunityTable provides a mapping of a community string to a securityName, contextEngineID, and contextName. It futher allows the source address to be validated. An extension to the snmpTargetAddressTable will later be shown which will allow a source address to be compared against a range of addresses (for example, a subnet address).

By mapping an SNMPv1 (or SNMPv2c) community string to version-independent SNMP message parameters, SNMPv1 (and SNMPv2c) messages can be processed within the SNMP framework in the same manner as an SNMPv3 message.

Table 8-5   snmpCommunityTable, Indexed by snmpCommunityIndex

Object	Type	Access
snmpCommunityIndex	SnmpAdminString	not-accessible
snmpCommunityName	OCTET STRING	read-create
snmpCommunitySecurityName	SnmpAdminString	read-create
snmpCommunityContextEngineID	SnmpEngineID	read-create
snmpCommunityContextName	SnmpAdminString	read-create
snmpCommunityTransportTag	SnmpTagValue	read-create
snmpCommunityStorageType	StorageType	read-create
snmpCommunityStatus	RowStatus	read-create

snmpCommunityIndex: a unique identifier used to index this table. This value can be between 1 and 32 bytes long.

snmpCommunityName: community string that an SNMPv1 (or SNMPv2c) community name will be matched against. This can be an OCTET STRING between 1 and 64 bytes long.

snmpCommunitySecurityName: the corresponding securityName value.

snmpCommunityContextEngineID: the corresponding contextEngineID value. The default value will be the local snmpEngineID value. However, if this row is being set up to be used for proxy forwarding, then this value will be the snmpEngineID of the remote target.

snmpCommunityContextName: the corresponding context value. The default value for this is the empty string.

snmpCommunityTransportTag: a tag value which is used to validate the source address of this message. This is done by searching through the snmpTargetAddrTable for an snmpTargetAddrTagList object which contains this value. If an entry is found whose snmpTargetAddrTDomain object matches the messsage's transport domain and snmpTargetAddrTAddress matches the message's source address, then the message is properly authenticated. If the snmpCommunityTransportTag value is an empty string, then source address authentication is not attempted (and the row will match).

Note: If no matching entries are found within snmpCommunityTable (possibly because the source address could not be authenticated), processing the SNMPv1 (or SNMPv2c) message will fail because of an authentication failure.

The default value for this is the empty string.

snmpCommunityStorageType: specifies how a row in this table should be stored.

snmpCommunityStatus: a RowStatus object used for adding and removing rows to/from this table. A row cannot be made active until the snmpCommunityName and snmpCommunitySecurityName objects have been explicitly set.

The SNMP-COMMUNITY-MIB also defines the snmpTargetAddrMaskTable which augments the snmpTargetAddrTable. This table adds an snmpTargetAddrTMask object to a snmpTargetAddrTable row. The snmpTargetAddrTMask is defined as an OCTET STRING, between 0 and 255 bytes, and with read-create access. It is used so entries within snmpTargetAddrTable can match a range of addresses. The length of snmpTargetAddrTMask must either be the same as the corresponding snmpTargetAddrTAddress or 0 (an empty string). If snmpTargetAddrTMask is an empty string, then snmpTargetAddrTAddress must match an address exactly. Otherwise, each bit within snmpTargetAddrTAddress must match the identical bit within an address if the corresponding bit within snmpTargetAddrTMask is a one. For example, given an entry with an snmpTargetAddrTMask value of "FF FF FF 00 00 00" and a snmpTargetAddrTAddress value of "9E 65 79 11 00 A1" (158.101.121.17:161), then any address within the 158.101.121.0 Class C subnet will match this entry.

When an SNMPv1 (or SNMPv2c) Request is received, each row within snmpCommunityTable will be looked at until a matching row is found or all the rows have been exhausted. If no matching rows are found, then the request will result in an authorization failure and a Response will be sent with either an error-status of `noSuchName` (for an SNMPv1 Request) or `authorizationError` (for an SNMPv2c Request).

For a row to match, the snmpCommunityName must first match the community name within the Request message. If the corresponding snmpCommunityTransportTag value is an empty string, then the row matches! Otherwise, the snmpTargetAddrTable must be searched for a row that contains the snmpCommunityTransportTag value within its snmpTargetAddrTagList object, and whose snmpTargetAddrTAddress value matches the source address of the SNMP Request. This in effect allows you to provide source verification.

The following pseudocode demonstrates searching through an SNMP engine's snmpCommunityTable to see if a matching row exists for a given community string and source address:

```
procedure SnmpAdminString::FindMatchingRow(cstr, addr)
{
    // Search through snmpCommunityTable for
    // an entry whose snmpCommunityName value
    // matches cstr. If an entry is found, check
    // whether addr matches a corresponding row
    // within snmpTargetAddrTable. (This is done
    // using the snmpCommunityTransportTag value).
    // If a matching row is found, return the
    // corresponding snmpCommunityIndex value,
    // otherwise return null.

    flag <- true
    responsePDU <- {snmpCommunityName,
                    snmpCommunityTransportTag,
                    snmpCommunityStatus}
    origPDU <- responsePDU

    while (flag)
    {

        // Walk the snmpCommunityTable looking for a
        // matching row.

        pdu <- SnmpGetNext(responsePDU)
        responsePDU <- pdu
        flag <- CheckPDU(pdu, origPDU)

        if (flag == false)
          continue
```

```
cname <- GetVarBindValue(pdu, 1)
tag <- GetVarBindValue(pdu, 2)
status <- GetVarBindValue(pdu, 3)
if (status != 'active')
  continue

if (cstr != cname)
  continue

// Get the snmpCommunityIndex value
// for the row.

index <- GetVarBindInstance(
          pdu,
          1,
          snmpCommunityName)

// At this point we have found an active row
// whose snmpCommunityName value matches the
// the community string. If the tag value is
// an empty string, then we've found a matching
// row - return the corresponding snmpCommunityIndex.

if (tag == '')
  return index

// Does a row exist within snmpTargetAddrTable whose
// whose taglist contains tag, and whose target address
// matches addr?

if (FindMatchingAddress(tag, addr) != null)
  return index
}

// No matching rows found - return null.

return null
}
```

FindMatchingAddress is passed a tag value and an address and returns either an index for a matching row within snmpTargetAddrTable or null. A row matches if its taglist contains tag and its target address matches addr. *Note*: In determining whether addresses match, the snmpTargetAddrTMask value will be bitwise ANDED with both addresses (if the mask value is not an empty string).

```
procedure SnmpAdminString::FindMatchingAddress(tag, addr)
{
    // Search through snmpTargetAddrTable for an entry
    // which contains tag within its taglist, and whose
    // snmpTargetAddrTAddress value matches addr. If a
    // matching entry is found, return its index value,
    // otherwise return null. Note. This routine is assuming
    // only the UDP transport domain is being used.

    flag <- true
    responsePDU <- {snmpTargetAddrTAddress,
                    snmpTargetAddrTMask,
                    snmpTargetAddrTagList,
                    snmpTargetAddrRowStatus}
    origPDU <- responsePDU

    while (flag)
    {
        // Walk the snmpTargetAddrTable looking for an
        // whose taglist contains tag.

        pdu <- SnmpGetNext(responsePDU)
        responsePDU <- pdu
        flag <- CheckPDU(pdu, origPDU)

        if (flag == false)
          continue

        taddr <- GetVarBindValue(pdu, 1)
        mask <- GetVarBindValue(pdu, 2)
        taglist <- GetVarBindValue(pdu, 3)
        status <- GetVarBindValue(pdu, 4)

        if (status != 'active')
          continue

        if (tag not in taglist)
          continue

        // Get the snmpTargetAddrName value
        // for the row.

        index <- GetVarBindInstance(
                  pdu,
                  1,
                  snmpTargetAddrTAddress)
```

```
            // If mask is an empty string, then
            // check whether addr == taddr.
            // Otherwise check if addr && mask == taddr && mask.

            if (mask == '')
            {
              if (addr == taddr)
                return index
            }
            else
            {
              if ((addr & mask) == (taddr & mask))
                return index
            }
        }

        // A matching row has not been found. Return null.

        return null
    }
```

We'll wrap up this section (and chapter) by looking at how a Notification Originator application is supposed to use the snmpCommunityTable to generate an SNMPv1-Trap. The Coexistence between SNMP Versions document states that the parameters used for generating notifications will be obtained by examing the SNMP-TARGET-MIB and SNMP-NOTIFICATION-MIB, and that these will be used to locate an entry within snmpCommunityTable so we can obtain the community string to use in the outgoing notification. The document further states that an entry is found by matching securityName with the snmpCommunitySecurityName value, contextEngineID with the snmpCommunityContextEngineID value, and contextName with the snmpCommunityContextName value. We can obtain the securityName value to use from the associated snmpTargetParamsTable entry. The contextEngineID and contextName values will have to be determined in an implementation dependent manner, such as using the local value of snmpEngineID as the contextEngineID value. The contextName could possibly be provided through the MIB instrumentation.

CHAPTER   9

RMON2

While the RMON MIB lets you monitor traffic at the MAC layer, the RMON2 MIB lets you move up the protocol stack and see what's happening at the network and application layers. This allows you to gain insight into the specific protocol traffic occurring on your network. With RMON2 you can understand

- Protocol breakdown by segment.
- Protocol breakdown by network address.
- Protocol breakdown for traffic between different network addresses.
- Protocol breakdown by application layer for a network address.
- Application traffic breakdown for conversations between different network addresses.

You can also generate top N reports for the protocol and application layer conversations between different network addresses. RMON2 also allows you to translate between physical and network addresses. However, as we will be seeing later, this won't be all that useful if a router is attached to a segment that you are monitoring.

So how does this help you — other than maybe tracking what Websites your network users are visiting? A key to managing a network is understanding it. By periodically monitoring your protocol traffic usage, you can understand the normal protocol traffic loads and the times of the day that peaks occur for different application traffic (which can help you understand the times of the day when certain application response times may degrade). Over time this can also help you understand how your network and application traffic is growing. Also, by looking at the conversations occurring within your network, you can better arrange a switched network — possibly by placing a client that frequently accesses a specific server on the same segment, or at least attaching both client and server to the same switch.

RMON2 is made up of the following groups:

1. Protocol Directory Group
2. Protocol Distribution Group
3. Address Map Group
4. Network Layer Host Group
5. Network Layer Matrix Group
6. Application Layer Host Group
7. Application Layer Matrix Group
8. User History Collection Group
9. Probe Configuration Group
10. RMON Extensions

This chapter will first look at additional textual conventions that have been defined for RMON and RMON2 and then provide a quick overview of how RMON2 is configured. We will then look at the first eight groups listed above. As we'll be seeing, the Protocol Directory Group consists of a protocol directory table — which is really the key to configuring RMON2. The other groups that we'll be looking at are made up of control and data tables. The control tables are configured fairly consistently throughout RMON2, and the data tables are also accessed in a fairly consistent manner. We will spend a little time on the User History Collection Group, which is really a more generic form of the RMON history group. As a form of triage in trying to get this book written I will ignore the Probe Configuration Group and the RMON Extensions.

Just as network and application traffic monitoring provided the next logical step to the MAC layer monitoring that RMON provided, application response time monitoring is probably the next logical step to RMON2. The hotest area in network management today is the promise of end to end monitoring, namely understanding how applications are performing over a network and being able to validate through a service level agreement a level of performance. This has become today's Holy Grail for network management software. In some ways I think this is yet another example of running before learning how to walk. In any case, dozens of companies have popped up over the last couple of years to try to provide application response time and service level monitoring software. We will conclude this chapter by looking at several methods for measuring application response time.

9.1 Textual Conventions

The RMON and RMON2 MIBs have defined several textual conventions which we will describe here.

9.1.1 OwnerString

This resolves to a DisplayString and can be between 0 and 127 octets long. An Owner-String is used to identify the manager who configured a row within an RMON or RMON2 control table. It is suggested that an OwnerString object contain one or more of the following: IP address, management station name, network manager's name, location, or phone number. If a row is created by the agent, the OwnerString object should be set to start with the string "monitor".

The goal for associating OwnerString objects with RMON and RMON2 control table entries is to make it easier for different network managers to cooperate with each other.

9.1.2 ZeroBasedCounter32

This resolves to a Gauge32. You can think of this as being identical to a Counter32 object, except that it is guaranteed to be initialized to zero when an agent is restarted.

9.1.3 LastCreateTime

This resolves to a TimeTicks. A LastCreateTime object is used to identify when the row it is associated with was last created.

9.1.4 TimeFilter

This is probably the most interesting of the RMON2 textual conventions. A TimeFilter object resolves to a TimeTicks and is used to index rows within RMON2 data tables that have changed since a particular time. Let's walk through an example to make this a little clearer.

We'll define a table foo with three objects.

Table 9-1   TimeFilter Example, Table foo Indexed by fooTimeMark.fooIndex

Object	Type	Access
fooTimeMark	TimeFilter	not-accessible

Table 9-1   TimeFilter Example, Table foo Indexed by
fooTimeMark.fooIndex (Continued)

Object	Type	Access
fooIndex	Integer32	not-accessible
fooCounts	Counter32	read-only

Now let's show the table foo populated with several rows.

Table 9-2   TimeFilter Example, Table foo Populated
with Five rows

fooTimeMark	fooIndex	fooCounts
700	1	40
500	2	27
1000	3	199
200	4	31
500	5	22

What this table shows is that the row indexed by fooIndex 1 was last updated when sysUp-Time was equal to 700, the row indexed by fooIndex 2 was last updated when sysUpTime was equal to 500, etc.

If we perform a series of Get-Next operations to collect all fooCounts objects that have been updated since sysUpTime equaled 600, we would collect objects fooCounts.600.1 and foo-Counts.600.3.

The following pseudocode demonstrates this.

```
flag <- true
responsePDU <- {fooCounts.600}
origPDU <- responsePDU

while (flag)
{
   // Collect all fooCounts objects that have been updated
   // since sysUpTime was 600.

   pdu <- SnmpGetNext(responsePDU)
   responsePDU <- pdu
```

```
flag <- CheckPDU(pdu, origPDU)

if (flag == false)
  continue

index <- GetVarBindInstance(
            pdu,
            1,
            fooCounts.600)

val <- GetVarBindValue(pdu, 1)
print("Index " + index + "=" + val)
}
```

Which would produce as output

```
Index 1 = 40
Index 3 = 199
```

The RMON2 data tables can be huge. It is extremely powerful to be able to walk these tables and collect only the objects that have recently been modified. For example, the network layer host table which we'll be seeing later provides traffic information for each network address seen. If we're periodically polling this table every fifteen minutes to collect relevant data, we might first collect sysUpTime and then subtract fifteen minutes from it to create a TimeFilter value. Then by walking the table with a series of Get-Next operations, we can collect only the counter objects from rows that have been updated during the past fifteen minutes. A LastCreateTime object will be provided so we can tell whether the row was created during the current poll period. *Note*: If we were not able to use a TimeFilter object to index the table, we would have to walk the whole table and collect quite a bit of potentially stale information for every network address ever seen by the probe. This could end up producing significantly more Get-Next operations than our more efficient method using a TimeFilter value as an index.

9.1.5 DataSource

This resolves to an OBJECT IDENTIFIER and is used to identify a particular interface. The value of a DataSource object will be a fully instanced ifIndex object. For example, if we want to configure a control table to collect data on interface 3, we might set a correponding DataSource object to ifIndex.3 (1.3.6.1.2.1.2.2.1.1.3).

9.2 Quick Overview of RMON2 Configuration

There are two steps to configuring RMON2 for network and application layer monitoring:

1. Configure the network and application layer protocols to monitor. For each protocol specify the level of monitoring to perform.

2. Configure which interfaces to perform monitoring on.

The first step is accomplished through the configuration of the protocol directory table, which we'll be seeing soon. The second step is accomplished through the configuration of several control tables, which again we'll be seeing soon.

9.3 Protocol Directory Group

The Protocol Directory Group is made up of the protocolDirTable. This table is really the key to configuring RMON2. It defines the network and application layer protocols that are monitored, and the level of monitoring that is provided for each protocol. The protocols are defined by protocol identifiers. A protocol identifier is made up of one or more four-octet "layer identifiers." Currently five base "layer identifiers" have been defined:

Table 9-3   Base "Layer Identifiers"

Name	Identifier
ether2	0.0.0.1
llc	0.0.0.2
snap	0.0.0.3
vsnap	0.0.0.4
ianaAssigned	0.0.0.5

Additionally, a "wildcard-ether2" is defined by the identifier, 1.0.0.1. We will explain what this means a little later.

ether2

The "ether2" identifier will monitor all Ethernet-II frames. How do we build on this to specify IP packets running over Ethernet, or UDP packets running over IP and Ethernet, or SNMP packets running over UDP?

Protocol identfiers are encoded for children of "ether2" by appending an EtherType value to the "ether2" identifier. The EtherType value is encoded in the form of 0.0.a.b where 'a' and 'b' are the network byte order encodings of the MSB and LSB of this value.

As an example, the EtherType value for IP is 0x0800, so the protocol identifier for IP running over Ethernet-II would be 0.0.0.1.0.0.8.0. The EtherType value for IPX is 0x8137. Since 0x81 equals 129 and 0x37 equals 55, the protocol identifier for IPX running over Ethernet-II (or simply ether2.ipx) would be 0.0.0.1.0.0.129.55. The IANA Protocol Numbers and Assignment Services Website, http://www.iana.org/numbers.html, is a good source for locating, among other things, the EtherType assignments.

Now if we want to layer either TCP or UDP on top of IP running over Ethernet-II, we append the IP Protocol Number (in the form of 0.0.0.a, where a represents the IP Protocol Number) to the ether2.ip identifier. TCP has a protocol number of 6, so an identifier representing ether2.ip.tcp would be 0.0.0.1.0.0.8.0.0.0.0.6. UDP has a protocol number of 17, so an identifier representing ether2.ip.udp would be 0.0.0.1.0.0.8.0.0.0.0.17.

If we now want to build a protocol identifier for a TCP or UDP port number, we represent the port number as a 4-byte value and append it to either ether2.ip.tcp or ether2.ip.udp. For example, the protocol identifier for SNMP would be ether2.ip.udp.snmp or 0.0.0.1.0.0.8.0.0.0.0.17.0.0.0.161. If we had a proprietary application running over UDP port 2000, the protocol identifier 0.0.0.1.0.0.8.0.0.0.0.17.0.0.7.208 would be able to identify packets for that particular application.

The "wildcard-ether2" is used to represent any link layer. The identifier "wildcard-ether2.ip" (1.0.0.1.0.0.8.0) will identify all IP packets regardless of the underlying link layer. Similarly, "wildcard-ether2.ip.udp.snmp" will identify all SNMP packets running over UDP and IP regardless of the link layer.

llc

The "llc" identifier will monitor all llc (802.2) frames. Protocols layered on top of llc are identified by encoding the SAP value as a 4-byte value and appending it to the "llc" identifier. For example, IPX has a SAP value of 224, so the protocol identifier llc.ipx would be represented as 0.0.0.2.0.0.0.224.

snap

The Sub-Network Access Protocol (SNAP) is only present over LLC (802.2). For a SNAP frame, both the SSAP and DSAP values will be 0xaa. SNAP allows Ethernet-II protocols to be run over a media which is restricted to LLC. Protocol identifiers layered on top of "snap" are encoded identically to "ether2" (the EtherType value is encoded in the form 0.0.a.b and then appended to the "snap" identifier).

For example, the protocol identifier for snap.ip would be 0.0.0.3.0.0.8.0. The protocol identifier for snap.ip.udp would be 0.0.0.3.0.0.8.0.0.0.0.17, and the protocol identifier for snap.ip.udp.snmp would be 0.0.0.3.0.0.8.0.0.0.0.17.0.0.0.161.

vsnap

The "vsnap" identifier handles all SNAP packets which do not have a zero OUI. The EtherType value is encoded as an 8-byte value using the format 0.a.b.c.0.0.d.e where "a", "b" and "c" are the three octets of the OUI field in network byte order and "d" and "e" represent the MSB and LSB of the EtherType value. As an example, the protocol identifier vsnap.ip for an OUI value 00-10-4B (hex) would be 0.0.0.4.0.0.16.75.0.0.8.0.

ianaAssigned

The "ianaAssigned" identifier is used as kind of a catchall for protocols that don't map naturally under the other four link layer branches. An identifier for an IANA assigned protocol is formed by appending four octets (a.b.c.d) that represent a particular IANA protocol to the "ianaAssigned" identifier. For example, the IANA protocol number for ipxOverRaw8023 (IPX encapsulated directly in 802.3) is 1, so the protocol identifier for ianaAssigned.ipxOverRaw8023 would be 0.0.0.5.0.0.0.1.

The protocolDirTable is indexed by a combination of a protocol identifier and and a protocol parameters string. Each "layer" within a protocol identifier has a parameters "octet" associated with it. For example, ether2.ip.udp.snmp would have an associated four-octet parameters string, where the first octet would represent the parameters for ether2, the second octet would represent the parameters for ip, etc. Each octet is treated as a bitmask and indicates the special functions or capabilities that the agent provides for the corresponding protocol. The first two bits are reserved

Table 9-4   Reserved Parameters Bits

Bit	Name	Description
0	countsFragments	This bit specifies that higher layer protocols encapsulated within this protocol will be counted correctly even if this protocol fragments the higher layer protocol packets.
1	tracksSessions	This bit specifies that frames which are part of a remapped session are counted correctly. Some protocols, such as TFTP, will start sessions on a well-known port and then later transfer them to dynamically assigned ports.

The protocolDirTable is show below.

Table 9-5   protocolDirTable, Indexed by protocolDirID.protocolDirParameters

Object	Type	Access
protocolDirID	OCTET STRING	not-accessible
protocolDirParameters	OCTET STRING	not-accessible
protocolDirLocalIndex	Integer32	read-only
protocolDirDescr	DisplayString	read-create
protocolDirType	BITS	read-only
protocolDirAddressMapConfig	INTEGER	read-create
protocolDirHostConfig	INTEGER	read-create
protocolDirMatrixConfig	INTEGER	read-create
protocolDirOwner	OwnerString	read-create
protocolDirStatus	RowStatus	read-create

protocolDirID: a protocol identifier used to represent a network or application layer protocol. This is formed exactly as we saw earlier, except the first octet represents the number of octets that follow. For example, the protocol identifier for "ether2" would be represented as 4.0.0.0.1, the protocol identifier for "ether2.ip" would be represented as 8.0.0.0.1.0.0.8.0, etc.

This value, along with protocolDirParameters, is used to index this table.

protocolDirParameters: this represents a set of parameters for the associated protcol identifier. The protocol parameters string is formed as we had seen earlier, except the first octet represents the number of octets that follow. The protocol parameters value for protocol identifier "ether2.ip.udp.snmp' would be something like: 4.0.0.0.0.

protocolDirLocalIndex: a unique identifier associated with this protocolDirTable entry. The protocolDirTable uses this object to provide a mapping of a protocol identifier to an integer value. In order to understand the network or application layer protocol associated with an RMON2 data table entry, you must be able to match a protocolDirLocalIndex value to a row within the protocol directory table. Similarly, if you want to collect specific network or application layer protocol data from an RMON2 data table, you must use the protocol identifier to find a matching row within the protocolDirTable and then use this object as part of an index into the appropriate RMON2 data table.

Note: This value is meaningful only within a given SNMP entity. For each RMON2 device you want to collect data for, you will have to read the protocolDirTable to map protocol identifiers to local index values.

protocolDirDescr: a textual description of the network or application layer protocol (for example, "ether2.ip.udp.snmp").

protocolDirType: a bitmask used to define whether the entry is extensible (bit 0), meaning that an agent or manager may create entries that are children of this protocol; and whether the agent can recognize addresses for this protocol (bit 1).

protocolDirAddressMapConfig: this is used to configure whether network to physical address mapping is turned on for an associated protocol. This can have one of three values:

```
notSupported(1)
supportedOff(2)
```

supportedOn (3)

If a probe doesn't have the capability to perform address mapping for the associated protocol, then this object will be set to notSupported. Similarly, if the associated protocol is not a network layer protocol, this object will be set to notSupported. *Note*: If the value is notSupported, then it cannot be changed through a set operation.

If this object has been configured to supportedOff, then address mapping for the associated protocol will be turned off for all of the probe's interfaces. If this object has been configured to supportedOn, then the probe will attempt to perform address mapping for the associated protocol for all interfaces specified by the addressMapControlTable.

Note: Whenever this value changes from supportedOn to supportedOff, all related entries in the addressMapTable will be deleted.

protocolDirHostConfig: this is used to configure whether network and application layer monitoring is active for an associated protocol. This can have one of three values:

notSupported (1)

supportedOff (2)

supportedOn (3)

If a probe is unable to perform network or application layer monitoring for the associated protocol, then this object will be set to notSupported. *Note*: If the value is notSupported, then it cannot be changed through a set operation.

While this object can turn on network layer and application layer monitoring for the associated protocol, the interfaces that the monitoring occurs on is controlled by the hlHostControlTable.

Note: Whenever this value changes from supportedOn to supportedOff, all related entries in the RMON2 host and application data tables will be deleted.

protocolDirMatrixConfig: this is used to configure whether entries can be added to the network layer and application layer matrix data tables for an associated protocol. This can have one of three values:

```
notSupported (1)
supportedOff (2)
supportedOn (3)
```

If a probe is unable to track the matrix data tables for an associated protocol, then this object will be set to `notSupported`. *Note*: If the value is `notSupported`, then it cannot be changed through a set operation.

The interfaces that this monitoring will occur on is controlled by the hlMatrixControlTable.

Note: Whenever this value changes from `supportedOn` to `supportedOff`, all related entries in the network layer and application layer matrix data tables will be deleted.

protocolDirOwner: identifies the manager who configured this entry.

protocolDirStatus: a RowStatus object used for adding and removing rows to/from this table.

Any RMON2 application will first need to read the protocolDirTable for all RMON2 devices that it will access. This is both so it can understand the RMON2 device's configuration, but also so it can map a protocol to a local index (which it will need when accessing the RMON2 data tables). The following pseudocode demonstrates reading a protocol directory table.

```
procedure void::ReadProtDirTable(Col)
{
    // Read an RMON2 device's protocolDirTable. For each
    // row in the protocolDirTable add to the collection Col
    // an object containing the protocol name, protocol
    // parameters, local index, address map configuration,
    // host configuration, matrix configuration and owner.

    flag <- true
    responsePDU <- { protocolDirLocalIndex,
```

```
                    protcolDirDescr,
                    protcolDirAddressMapConfig,
                    protocolDirHostConfig,
                    protocolDirMatrixConfig.
                    protocolDirOwner,
                    protocolDirStatus}

    origPDU <- responsePDU

    while (flag)
    {
        // Collect all rows within protocolDirTable.

        pdu <- SnmpGetNext(responsePDU)
        responsePDU <- pdu
        flag <- CheckPDU(pdu, origPDU)

        if (flag == false)
          continue

        localIndex <- GetVarBindValue(pdu, 1)
        descr <- GetVarBindValue(pdu, 2)
        amc <- GetVarBindValue(pdu, 3)
        hc <- GetVarBindValue(pdu, 4)
        mc <- GetVarBindValue(pdu, 5)
        owner <- GetVarBindValue(pdu, 6)
        status <- GetVarBindValue(pdu, 7)

        // If row is not active,then skip.

        if (status != 'active')
          continue

        // Get the instance value. From this obtain
        // the protocol identifier and the parameters
        // string.

        inst <- GetVarBindInstance(
                    pdu,
                    1,
                    protocolDirLocalIndex)

        // The instance is the form n1.x.x.x...n2.x..x,
        // n1 specifies the length of the protocol identifier
        // and n2 specifies the length of the parameters string.
        // Set protocolID to the protocol identifier value
        // (including the length byte) and protocolParams to the
        // protocol parameters value (again, including the
```

```
// length byte. For example, if inst = '4.0.0.0.1.1.0'
// (ether2), protocolID will be set to '4.0.0.0.1' and
// protocolParams will be set to '1.0'.

n1 <- inst[0]
protocolID <- inst[0 .. n1]

n2 <- inst[n1 + 1]
protocolParams <- inst[n1 + 1 .. n1 + 1 + n2]

// Try to map the protocol identifier to a name.
// If we can't, use the protocolDirDescr value
// that was read as the protocol name.

protocolName <- MapProtocolIDtoName(protocolID)
if (protocolName == '')
  protocolName <- descr

// Add an object to collection Col that is made
// up the protocol name, protocol parameters
// string, local index, address map configuration
// host configuration, matrix configuration, and
// owner string.

add {protocolName, protocolParams,
  localIndex, amc, hc, mc, owner} to Col
    }
  }
```

ReadProtDirTable is passed an empty collection Col. It will cycle through a protocolDirTable, and for each entry add an object to Col that contains the protocol name, protocol parameters, local index, address map configuration, host configuration, matrix configuration, and owner string information for that entry. It calls a procedure MapProtocolIDtoName which attempts to map a protocol identifier to a protocol name (for example, '4.0.0.0.1' => 'ether2'). MapProtocolIDtoName could be written several ways — the simplest would simply be to define a C structure with two elements, protocolID and protocolName. Then define an array of this structure, filling it up with all the protocol identifiers and equivalent names that you care about. You can figure out all the protocol identifiers and names algorithmically, or you can take a simpler approach and read the protocolDirDescr values from an RMON2 probe. You can use the values that were read as a base, and add in what's missing (such as any proprietary UDP or TCP ports that your network applications use). If for some reason MapProtocolIDtoName is unable to map a protocol identifier, the protocolDirDescr value will be used as the protocol name.

It makes life simpler to deal with network and application layer protocols by names instead of the more cumbersome protocol identifiers. Let's define routines GetProtLocalIndex and GetProtName which map a protocol name to a local index, and vice versa:

```
procedure int::GetProtLocalIndex(Col, protocolName)
{
    // Col was built previously by ReadProtDirTable.
    // Search through Col for an object with a
    // protocol name equal to protocolName. If one
    // is found return the corresponding localIndex,
    // otherwise return -1.

    foreach object in Col
    {
       if (object.protocolName == protocolName)
          return object.localIndex
    }

    return -1
}

procedure String::GetProtName(Col, localIndex)
    {
        // Col was built previously by ReadProtDirTable.
        // Search through Col for an object with a
        // local index equal to localIndex. If one
        // is found return the corresponding protocolName,
        // otherwise return an empty string.

        foreach object in Col
        {
           if (object.localIndex == localIndex)
              return object.protocolName
        }

        return ''
    }
```

9.4 Protocol Distribution Group

The Protocol Distribution Group is made up of one control and one data table. The control table, protocolDistControlTable, is used to specify the interfaces you want to monitor protocol distribution information on. The data table, protocolDistStatsTable, contains packet and octet counts and is indexed indirectly by an interface number and a network or application layer protocol.

Table 9-6   protocolDistControlTable, Indexed by protocolDistControlIndex

Object	Type	Access
protocolDistControlIndex	Integer32	not-accessible
protocolDistControlDataSource	DataSource	read-create
protocolDistControlDroppedFrames	Counter32	read-only
protocolDistControlCreateTime	LastCreateTime	read-only
protocolDistControlOwner	OwnerString	read-create
protocolDistControlStatus	RowStatus	read-create

protocolDistControlIndex: a unique identifier between 1 and 65,535 used to index this table.

protocolDistControlDataSource: specifies an interface (a fully instanced ifIndex object) to peform protocol distribution monitoring on.

protocolDistControlDroppedFrames: the number of valid frames which were not analyzed (dropped) by the probe. A probe may not have the resources to analyze every frame. This is obviously dependent on the capabilities of the device and on how many interfaces are being monitored. Some switches, which could conceivably be monitoring quite a few interfaces at one time, implement a sampling algorithm where the switch will only attempt to monitor for RMON2 a fixed percentage of overall frames.

protoclDistControlCreateTime: the value of sysUpTime when this row was last made active.

protocolDistControlOwner: identifies the manager who configured this entry.

protocolDistControlStatus: a RowStatus object used for adding and removing rows to/from this table. If the value of this object is changed from `active` to `notInService` (or `destroy`), all associated entries within the protocolDistStat-sTable will be deleted.

The following pseudocode demonstrates turning on protocol distribution monitoring for a particular interface:

```
// Configure Interface n for protocol distribution monitoring.

index <- GetUniqueInstance(protocolDistControlStatus)
pdu <- { protocolDistControlDataSource.index <- ifIndex.n,
         protocolDistControlOwner.index <- 'monitor',
         protocolDistControlStatus.index <- 'active'}
SnmpSet(pdu)
```

The protocolDistStatsTable provides packet and octet counts for the different network and application layer traffic seen on a segment. This table is indexed by protocolDistControlIndex (which indirectly identifies the interface) and protocolDirLocalIndex (which identifies the network or application layer protocol).

Table 9-7 protocolDistStatsTable, Indexed by protocolDistControlIndex.protocolDirLocalIndex

Object	Type	Access
protocolDistStatsPkts	ZeroBasedCounter32	read-only
protocolDistStatsOctets	ZeroBasedCounter32	read-only

protocolDistStatsPkts: number of packets received without error for a particular protocol. This is actually the number of link-layer packets that were seen, so if a single network-layer packet has been fragemented into several link-layer packets, this will include each of the fragmented link-layer packets.

protocolDistStatsOctets: number of octets in packets received for a particular protocol.

In order to access or make sense of the entries within the protocolDistStatsTable, we need to be able to map an interface number to a protocolDistControlIndex value and a protocol name to a protocolDirLocalIndex value. We will provide pseudocode for a routine GetControlIndex which is passed an OBJECT IDENTIFIER representing a DataSource object, an OBJECT IDENTIFIER representing a corresponding RowStatus object, and an interface number. It will return either a corresponding control index value or -1 if the interface hasn't been added to the control table.

```
procedure int::GetControlIndex(ds, rowstatus, n)
{
    // ds is an OBJECT IDENTIFIER for a DataSource
    // object (such as, protocolDistControlDataSource),
    // rowstatus is an OBJECT IDENTIFIER for a corresponding
    // RowStatus object (such as, protocolDistControlStatus).
    // n is an interface number. Return either a corresponding
    // control index value or -1.

    flag <- true
    responsePDU <- { ds,rowstatus }
    origPDU <- responsePDU

    while (flag)
    {
        // Collect rows within RMON2 Control Table until a
        // DataSource object is found which matches n.
        // If a row is found, return the index otherwise
        // return -1.

        pdu <- SnmpGetNext(responsePDU)
        responsePDU <- pdu
        flag <- CheckPDU(pdu, origPDU)

        if (flag == false)
          continue

        oid <- GetVarBindValue(pdu, 1)
        status <- GetVarBindValue(pdu, 2)

        // If row is not active,then skip.

        if (status != 'active')
          continue

        // oid has been set to a DataSource value,
        // which is in the form ifIndex.i
        //(1.3.6.1.2.1.2.2.1.1.i. The interface number
        // is obtained by oid[11] (where oid[1] accesses
        // the first byte of the OBJECT IDENTIFIER).

        if (n != oid[11]}
          continue

        // A matching row has been found - return the
        // index value.
```

```
            index <- GetVarBindInstance(
                        pdu,
                        1,
                        ds)
        return index
    }
    return -1
}
```

We will now write pseudocode for a routine ShowDistStats which is passed a collection that had previously been built by ReadProtDirTable, an interface number, and a protocol name. ShowDistStats will map the interface number into a control index value by using the GetControlIndex routine that we have just looked at. This isn't the most efficient way of doing things since every time we want to collect protocol distribution statistics we would have to read the protocolDistControlTable. What would be better would be to map the interface numbers to control indexes once, save the values in an array or collection, and access that structure whenever we need to get a control index value for an interface. ShowDistStats also uses the GetProtLocalIndex routine that had been shown earlier to map a protocol name into a local index value. *Note*: If either the interface number cannot be mapped to a control index or the protocol name cannot be mapped to a local index, null will be returned. Otherwise, a Response PDU to an SNMP Get operation will be returned.

```
procedure PDU::ShowDistStats(Col, n, protocolName)
{
    // Return a PDU containing the packet and octet
    // counts seen for protocolName on interface n.
    // If either the interface hasn't been configured
    // within the protocolDistControlTable or the
    // protocolName within the protocolDirTable, then
    // return null.
    //
    // Note. Col is a collection that has been built
    // previous by ReadProtDirTable.

    controlIndex <-
        GetControlIndex(protocolDistControlDataSource,
            protocolDistControlStatus, n)

    if (controlIndex == -1)
    {
        print("Interface " + n + " not configured")
        return null
    }
```

```
localIndex <- GetProtLocalIndex(Col, protocolName)

if (localIndex == -1)
{
    print(protocolName + " has not been configured.")
    return null
}

pdu <- {  protocolDistStatsPkts.controlIndex.localIndex,
          protocolDistStatsOctets.controlIndex.localIndex }
return (SnmpGet(pdu))
}
```

9.5 Address Map Group

The Address Map Group is made up of three objects, a control table, and a data table. The control table, addressMapControlTable, is used to specify the interfaces you want to build a collection of network to physical address mappings for. The data table, addressMapTable, contains rows mapping a network address to a physical address. This table is indexed by a TimeFilter, a network protocol, a network address, and an interface or port number.

The three additional objects for the Address Map Group are

addressMapInserts: this is a Counter32 object with read-only access. It provides the number of times entries have been added into the addressMapTable.

addressMapDeletes: this is a Counter32 object with read-only access. It provides the number of times entries have been deleted from the addressMapTable.

addressMapMaxDesiredEntries: this is an Integer32 value between -1 and 2,147,483,647, and with read-create access. This is used to set the maximum size of the addressMapTable. If this is set to -1, then the probe may create any number of entries that it has resources for. *Note*: If this value is set to a smaller number than the current number of rows within the addressMapTable, then rows will be deleted in an implementation dependent manner until the number of rows within the table matches this value.

Note: The RMON2 MIB states that the size of the addressMapTable can be determined by

$$\text{addressMapInserts} - \text{addressMapDeletes} \qquad (9.1)$$

This will be true most of the time, but if the device stays up long enough, then it is possible that the addressMapInserts counter could wrap (if the addressMapDeletes counter later wraps, then the two counters will be back in sync!)

Table 9-8   addressMapControlTable, Indexed by addressMapControlIndex

Object	Type	Access
addressMapControlIndex	Integer32	not-accessible
addressMapControlDataSource	DataSource	read-create
addressMapControlDroppedFrames	Counter32	read-only
addressMapControlOwner	OwnerString	read-create
addressMapControlStatus	RowStatus	read-create

addressMapControlIndex: a unique identifier between 1 and 65,535 used to index this table.

addressMapControlDataSource: specifies an interface (a fully instanced ifIndex object) to perform monitoring on.

addressMapControlDroppedFrames: the number of valid frames which were not analyzed (dropped) by the probe.

addressMapControlOwner: identifies the manager who configured this entry.

addressMapControlStatus: a RowStatus object used for adding and removing rows to/from this table. If the value of this object is changed from `active` to `notInService` (or `destroy`), all associated entries within the addressMapTable will be deleted.

The following pseudocode demonstrates turning on address mapping for a particular interface:

```
// Configure Interface n for address mapping.

index <- GetUniqueInstance(addressMapControlStatus)
pdu <- { addressMapControlDataSource.index <- ifIndex.n,
         addressMapControlOwner.index <- 'monitor',
         addressMapControlStatus.index <- 'active'}
SnmpSet(pdu)
```

The addressMapTable provides mapping between a network and physical address. It is indexed by a TimeFilter, a protocol, a network address, and either an interface or port number. Address mapping will only occur for the protocols within the protocolDirTable whose corresponding protocolDirAddressMapConfig object has been set to supportedOn.

Table 9-9   addressMapTable, Indexed by

addressMapTimeMark.protocolDirLocalIndex.addressMapNetworkAddress.addressMapSource

Object	Type	Access
addressMapTimeMark	TimeFilter	not-accessible
addressMapNetworkAddress	OCTET STRING	not-accessible
addressMapSource	OBJECT IDENTIFIER	not-accessible
addressMapPhysicalAddress	OCTET STRING	read-only
addressMapLastChange	TimeStamp	read-only

addressMapTimeMark: a TimeFilter object used to index this table.

addressMapNetworkAddress: an OCTET STRING representing a network address. For IP, the first byte would be 4 (the length of the IP address) and the next 4 bytes represent the IP address in network byte order.

addressMapSource: the interface or port on which the address was seen.

If the address was discovered on an interface, then the first byte would be ll (representing the length of the rest of the value) and the rest of the value would be the OBJECT IDENTIFIER for ifIndex.n (where n is the interface number). For example, if this was address was seen on interface 7, then this value would be 11.1.3.6.1.2.1.2.2.1.1.7.

If this address was discovered on a repeater port, then the first byte would be 14 (representing the length of the rest of the value) and the rest of the value would be the OBJECT IDENTIFIER for rptrPortIndex.$g.p$ (where g is the group index which contains the port and p is the port number). For example, if the address was seen on port 3 within repeater group 1, then this value would be 14.1.3.6.1.2.1.22.1.3.1.1.2.1.3.

If a DataSource is specified as an ifIndex object within the addressMapControlTable, how can a repeater port be discovered as a source within this data table? This can happen if the DataSource object references an interface which is a locally attached repeater and the agent has additional information about the port which was the source of the traffic seen on that repeater.

addressMapPhysicalAddress: the physical address associated with the network address for this entry.

addressMapLastChange: the value of sysUpTime when this entry was either created or last updated.

One obvious thing that you would want to be able to do with the addressMapTable is to try to locate a specific IP address to get its MAC address. So ideally you would form a fully instanced addressMapPhysicalAddress object using a TimeFilter of 0, a protocolDirLocalIndex value representing ether2.ip, the network address you want to search for, and an interface that is being monitored — and then use it within a Get operation. In an ideal world this would work. Unfortunately, I have seen RMON2 probes which only seem to work properly if they are passed a fully instanced addressMapPhysicalAddress object within a Get-Next operation. For example, with some probes if I specify a fully instanced addressMapPhysicalAddress object within a Get operation, I would be returned a noSuchName error. With these same probes, if I try a partially instanced OID number within a Get-Next operation, I would always retrieve the first accessible object within the addressMapTable that matches the TimeFilter value that was used. This means that if I want to see if one of these probes is able to map the network address 158.101.121.7 to a physical address, I would have to form a fully instanced addressMapPhysicalAddress object using a network address of 158.101.121.6 as part of the instance:

addressMapPhysicalAddress.0.*ipLocalIndex*.4.158.101.121.6.11.1.3.6.1.2.1.2.2.1.1.*n*

(where *ipLocalIndex* is the local index value for ether2.ip and *n* is the interface being monitored)

I would then add this object to a variable-binding used by a Get-Next operation.

Another thing that you might want to do is periodically walk the addressMapTable for new entries. The following pseudocode will walk the addressMapTable and find all network addresses and their corresponding physical addresses that had been discovered by a probe during the past hour:

```
// Form a TimeFilter by collecting sysUpTime and
// subtracting 1 hour from it.

pdu <- SnmpGet(sysUpTime.0)
n <- GetVarBindValue(pdu, 1)
n <- (n - 360000)
if (n < 0)
   n <- 0

// Use n as a TimeFilter. Walk the addressMapTable
// to find all entries that have been added during
// the past hour. For each entry, add the physical address,
// network address, local index, and interface number
// to an AddressMap collection.

flag <- true
responsePDU <- {addressMapPhysicalAddress.n }
origPDU <- responsePDU

while (flag)
{
   pdu <- SnmpGetNext(responsePDU)
   responsePDU <- pdu
   flag <- CheckPDU(pdu, origPDU)

   if (flag == false)
      continue

   // Get the physical address that was returned.

   physaddr <- GetVarBindValue(pdu, 1)

   // Get the Network address, protocol name, and
   // interface number from the instance.

   inst <- GetVarBindInstance(
                   pdu,
                   1,
                   addressMapPhysicalAddress.n)

   // First byte in the instance is the protocolDirLocalIndex
```

```
        // value.

        localIndex <- inst[1]

        // Next, get the network address.

        n1 <- inst[2]
        netAddress <- inst[3 .. 2 + n1]

        // Finally, get the interface or port number.

        n2 <- inst[3 + n1]
        i <- inst[3 + n1 + n2]

        add {phsyaddr, netAddress, localIndex, i} to
            AddressCollection
    }
```

Using the addressMapTable within a routed environment does not work very well. IP packets reaching their destination subnet will be encapsulated within an Ethernet frame using the MAC address associated with the router's interface. The source address within the IP packet will be the original source IP address. If an RMON2 probe is attached to the same segment, it could end up seeing thousands of different network addresses associated with the same MAC address — and adding thousands of these "bogus" entries into the addressMapTable. The following diagram illustrates this:

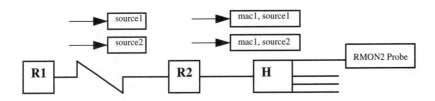

This diagram shows packets being routed across a network. When the packets reach router R2, they are encapsulated within Ethernet frames and forwarded to their destination addresses. Each Ethernet frame will use the MAC address assigned to the router's interface and the encapsulated IP packet will contain the original source IP address. As the frames are forwarded to hub H, the RMON2 probe will see each frame and build entries in the addressMapTable for {network address = source1, physical address = mac1} and {network address = source2, physical address = mac1}.

9.6 Network Layer Host Group

The Network Layer Host Group is made up of one control table and one data table. The control table, hlHostControlTable (higher layer host control table), is used to configure which interfaces to provide traffic monitoring on. The level of monitoring provided is both the amount of network-layer traffic sent to and received by each network address, and the amount of application-layer traffic sent to and received by each network address. The network-layer traffic statistics will be maintained within the nlHostTable (network-layer host table) and will be indexed by a control table index (which indirectly references an interface), a TimeFilter, a protocol, and a network address. The application-layer traffic statistics will be maintained within the alHostTable (application-layer host table) which is defined within the Application Layer Host Group. This table has the same index as a nlHostTable index, with an additional protocolDirLocalIndex value added to reference the application-layer protocol.

Table 9-10 hlHostControlTable, Indexed by hlHostControlIndex

Object	Type	Access
hlHostControlIndex	Integer32	not-accessible
hlHostControlDataSource	DataSource	read-create
hlHostControlNlDroppedFrames	Counter32	read-only
hlHostControlNlInserts	Counter32	read-only
hlHostControlNlDeletes	Counter32	read-only
hlHostControlNlMaxDesiredEntries	Integer32	read-create
hlHostControlAlDroppedFrames	Counter32	read-only
hlHostControlAlInserts	Counter32	read-only
hlHostControlAlDeletes	Counter32	read-only
hlHostControlAlMaxDesiredEntries	Integer32	read-write
hlHostControlOwner	OwnerString	read-create
hlHostControlStatus	RowStatus	read-create

hlHostControlIndex: a unique identifier between 1 and 65,535 used to index this table.

hlHostControlDataSource: specifies an interface (a fully instanced ifIndex object) to peform network and application-layer traffic monitoring on.

hlHostControlNlDroppedFrames: the number of valid frames which were not analyzed (dropped) by the probe for network-layer traffic statistics. *Note*: If the nlHostTable is inactive because no protocols have been enabled within the protocol directory table, this value will be zero.

hlHostControlNlInserts: number of times an entry has been inserted into the nlHostTable.

hlHostControlNlDeletes: number of times an entry has been deleted from the nlHostTable.

hlHostControlNlMaxDesiredEntries: an Integer32 value between -1 and 2,147,483,647. This is used to set the maximum size of the nlHostTable. If this is set to -1, then the probe may create any number of entries that it has resources for. *Note*: If this value is set to a smaller number than the current number of rows within the nlHostTable, then rows will be deleted in an implementation-dependent manner until the number of rows within the table matches this value.

hlHostControlAlDroppedFrames: the number of valid frames which were not analyzed (dropped) by the probe for application-layer traffic statistics. *Note*: If the alHostTable is inactive because no protocols have been enabled within the protocol directory table, this value will be zero.

hlHostControlAlInserts: number of times an entry has been inserted into the alHostTable.

hlHostControlAlDeletes: number of times an entry has been deleted from the alHostTable.

hlHostControlAlMaxDesiredEntries: an Integer32 value between -1 and 2,147,483,647. This is used to set the maximum size of the alHostTable. If this is set to -1, then the probe may create any number of entries that it has resources for. *Note*: If this value is set to a smaller number than the current number of rows within the alHostTable, then rows will be deleted in an implementation-dependent manner until the number of rows within the table matches this value.

hlHostControlOwner: identifies the manager who configured this entry.

hlHostControlStatus: a RowStatus object used for adding and removing rows to/ from this table. If the value of this object is changed from `active` to `notInService` (or `destroy`), all associated entries within the nlHostTable and alHostTable will be deleted.

The following pseudocode demonstrates turning on network and application layer monitoring for a particular interface.

```
// Configure Interface n for network and application traffic
// monitoring. Allow up to 5,000 entries to be added to
// either nlHostTable or alHostTable.

index <- GetUniqueInstance(hlHostControlStatus)
pdu <- { hlHostControlDataSource.index <- ifIndex.n,
         hlHostControlNlMaxDesiredEntries.index <- 5000,
         hlHostControlAlMaxDesiredEntries.index <- 5000,
         hlHostControlOwner.index <- 'monitor',
         hlHostControlStatus.index <- 'active'}
SnmpSet(pdu)
```

The nlHostTable provides statistics for particular network layer addresses seen on an interface. Packets that are sent to or from a network address are examined, and both packet and octet counts are maintained. Network traffic monitoring will only occur for the protocols within the protocolDirTable whose corresponding protocolDirHostConfig object has been set to `supportedOn`.

Table 9-11   nlHostTable, indexed by hlHostControlIndex.nlHostTimeMark. protocolDirLocalIndex.nlHostAddress

Object	Type	Access
nlHostTimeMark	TimeFilter	not-accessible
nlHostAddress	OCTET STRING	not-accessible
nlHostInPkts	ZeroBasedCounter32	read-only
nlHostOutPkts	ZeroBasedCounter32	read-only
nlHostInOctets	ZeroBasedCounter32	read-only

Table 9-11   nlHostTable, indexed by hlHostControlIndex.nlHostTimeMark.
protocolDirLocalIndex.nlHostAddress (Continued)

Object	Type	Access
nlHostOutOctets	ZeroBasedCounter32	read-only
nlHostOutMacNonUnicastPkts	ZeroBasedCounter32	read-only
nlHostCreateTime	LastCreateTime	read-only

nlHostTimeMark: a TimeFilter object used to index this table.

nlHostAddress: an OCTET STRING representing a network address. For IP, the
first byte would be 4 (the length of the IP address) and the next four bytes represent
the IP address in network byte order.

nlHostInPkts: number of packets without errors received by the corresponding network address. This counts the number of link-layer packets so if a single network-
layer packet is fragmented into several link-layer frames, each fragment will be
counted.

nlHostOutPkts: number of packets without errors sent by the corresponding network address. This counts the number of link-layer packets so if a single network-
layer packet is fragmented into several link-layer frames, each fragment will be
counted.

nlHostInOctets: number of octets received by the corresponding network address.
This will exclude any octets in packets that contained errors. *Note*: It will count all
of the octets in the packet which encapsulated the network layer frame.

nlHostOutOctets: number of octets sent by the corresponding network address.
This will exclude any octets in packets that contained errors. *Note*: It will count all
of the octets in the packet which encapsulated the network layer frame.

nlHostOutMacNonUnicastPkts: number of packets without errors sent from the
corresponding network address to any MAC broadcast or multicast addresses. This
counts the number of link-layer packets so if a single network-layer packet is fragmented into several link-layer frames, each fragment will be counted.

nlHostCreateTime: value of sysUpTime when this entry was created. This can be used by network management software to guarantee that the entry was not deleted and re-created between polls.

By periodically reading the nlHostTable you can build reports showing the host traffic for each network protocol. The following pseudocode demonstrates walking the entries within the nlHostTable that have been updated during the past fifteen minutes.

```
procedure void::ReadHostTable(n, Col)
{
    // Read all entries discovered on interface n that
    // have been updated during the past 15 minutes.
    // For each entry, add {protocolDirLocalIndex,
    // host address, in pkts, in octets, out pkts,
    // out octets} to Col.
    //
    // Note. If a row has been created during the
    // past 15 minutes, ignore it (we'll catch up with
    // it next poll cycle).

    ci <- GetControlIndex(hlHostControlDataSource,
             hlHostControlStatus, n)

    // Form a TimeFilter by collecting sysUpTime and
    // subtracting fifteen minutes from it.

    pdu <- SnmpGet(sysUpTime.0)
    uptime <- GetVarBindValue(pdu, 1)

    // If agent has been running less than
    // 15 minutes, return.

    if (uptime < 90000)
       return

    t <- (uptime - 90000)

    // Use t as a TimeFilter. Walk the nlHostTable
    // to find all entries that have been added during
    // the past fifteen. For each entry, add the interface,
    // local index, host address, in pkts, in octets,
    // out pkts, and out octets to HostStats collection.

    flag <- true
    responsePDU <- { nlHostInPkts.ci.t,
                     nlHostOutPkts.ci.t,
```

```
                        nlHostInOctets.ci.t,
                        nlHostOutOctets.ci.t,
                        nlHostCreateTime.ci.t}

      origPDU <- responsePDU

      while (flag)
      {
         pdu <- SnmpGetNext(responsePDU)
         responsePDU <- pdu
         flag <- CheckPDU(pdu, origPDU)
         if (flag == false)
           continue

         inpkts <- GetVarBindValue(pdu, 1)
         outpkts <- GetVarBindValue(pdu, 2)
         inoctets <- GetVarBindValue(pdu, 3)
         outoctets <- GetVarBindValue(pdu, 4)
         createtime <- GetVarBindValue(pdu, 5)

         // If the row was created within the past 15 minutes
         // then ignore it.

         if (createtime > t)
           continue

         // Get the protocol number and network address from
         // the instance.

         inst <- GetVarBindInstance(
                     pdu,
                     1,
                     nlHostInPkts.ci.t)

         // The first byte in the instance is the
         // protocolDirLocalIndex value.

         localIndex <- inst[1]

         // Next, get the network address.

         n1 <- inst[2]
         hostAddress <- inst[3 .. 2 + n1]

         add { n, localIndex, hostAddress, inpkts, inoctets,
               outpkts, outoctets} to Col
      }
   }
```

9.7 Network Layer Matrix Group

The Network Layer Matrix Group is made up of several control and data tables. This group allows conversations between pairs of network addresses to be monitored. The group also contains a top N data table (nlMatrixTopNTable) so you can see which conversations are generating the most traffic. By utilizing this information, you can better arrange a switched network. For example, if you can see that a client is frequently talking to a specific server, you can move the client so it's attached to the same switch as the server — or at least move it so the traffic isn't being routed.

Monitoring will only occur for the protocols within the protocolDirTable whose corresponding protocolDirMatrixConfig object has been set to `supportedOn`.

The hlMatrixControlTable is used to configure the interfaces to monitor both network and application-layer conversations on. Statistics for the network layer conversations will be added to the nlMatrixSDTable and the nlMatrixDSTable. Statistics for the application-layer conversations will be added to the alMatrixSDTable and the alMatrixDSTable.

Table 9-12 hlMatrixControlTable,
Indexed by hlMatrixControlIndex

Object	Type	Access
hlMatrixControlIndex	Integer32	not-accessible
hlMatrixControlDataSource	DataSource	read-create
hlMatrixControlNlDroppedFrames	Counter32	read-only
hlMatrixControlNlInserts	Counter32	read-only
hlMatrixControlNlDeletes	Counter32	read-only
hlMatrixControlNlMaxDesiredEntries	Integer32	read-create
hlMatrixControlAlDroppedFrames	Counter32	read-only
hlMatrixControlAlInserts	Counter32	read-only
hlMatrixControlAlDeletes	Counter32	read-only
hlMatrixControlAlMaxDesiredEntries	Integer32	read-write

Table 9-12 hlMatrixControlTable,
Indexed by hlMatrixControlIndex (Continued)

Object	Type	Access
hlMatrixControlOwner	OwnerString	read-create
hlMatrixControlStatus	RowStatus	read-create

hlMatrixControlIndex: a unique identifier between 1 and 65,535 used to index this table.

hlMatrixControlDataSource: specifies an interface (a fully instanced ifIndex object) to peform network and application-layer conversation monitoring on.

hlMatrixControlNlDroppedFrames: the number of valid frames which were not analyzed (dropped) by the probe for network-layer conversation statistics. *Note*: If the nlMatrixTables are inactive because no protocols have been enabled within the protocol directory table, this value will be zero.

hlMatrixControlNlInserts: number of times an entry has been inserted into the nlMatrixTables.

hlMatrixControlNlDeletes: number of times an entry has been deleted from the nlMatrixTables.

hlMatrixControlNlMaxDesiredEntries: an Integer32 value between -1 and 2,147,483,647. This is used to set the maximum size of either of the nlMatrixTables. If this is set to -1, then the probe may create any number of entries that it has resources for. *Note*: If this value is set to a smaller number than the current number of rows within the nlMatrixTables, then rows will be deleted in an implementation-dependent manner until the number of rows within the two tables matches this value.

hlMatrixControlAlDroppedFrames: the number of valid frames which were not analyzed (dropped) by the probe for application-layer conversation statistics. *Note*: If the alMatrixTables are inactive because no protocols have been enabled within the protocol directory table, this value will be zero.

hlMatrixControlAlInserts: number of times an entry has been inserted into the

hlMatrixControlAlDeletes: number of times an entry has been deleted from the alMatrixTables.

hlMatrixControlAlMaxDesiredEntries: an Integer32 value between -1 and 2,147,483,647. This is used to set the maximum size of either of the alMatrixTables. If this is set to -1, then the probe may create any number of entries that it has resources for. *Note*: If this value is set to a smaller number than the current number of rows within the alMatrixTables, then rows will be deleted in an implementation-dependent manner until the number of rows within the two tables matches this value.

hlMatrixControlOwner: identifies the manager who configured this entry.

hlMatrixControlStatus: a RowStatus object used for adding and removing rows to/from this table. If the value of this object is changed from `active` to `notInService` (or `destroy`), all associated entries within the nlMatrixSDTable, nlMatrixDSTable, alMatrixSDTable, and alMatrixDSTable will be deleted.

The following pseudocode demonstrates turning on network and application-layer conversations monitoring for a particular interface:

```
// Configure Interface n for network and application
// conversation monitoring. Allow up to 5,000 entries to be
// added to the nlMatrixTables and alMatrixTables.

index <- GetUniqueInstance(hlHostControlStatus)
pdu <- { hlMatrixControlDataSource.index <- ifIndex.n,
         hlMatrixControlNlMaxDesiredEntries.index <- 5000,
         hlMatrixControlAlMaxDesiredEntries.index <- 5000,
         hlMatrixControlOwner.index <- 'monitor',
         hlMatrixControlStatus.index <- 'active'}
SnmpSet(pdu)
```

The nlMatrixSDTable provides statistics for conversations between different network layer addresses. Entries within the table are indexed by a control table index (which indirectly references the interface the packet was seen on), a TimeFilter object, a protocol, a network-layer source address, and a network layer destination address. An entry provides packet and octet counts for packets which were sent from the source address to the destination address. *Note*: Only packets with no MAC errors will be looked at.

Network conversation monitoring will only occur for the network-layer protocols within the protocolDirTable whose corresponding protocolDirMatrixConfig object has been set to `supportedOn`.

Table 9-13 nlMatrixSDTable, Indexed by
hlMatrixControlIndex.nlMatrixSDTimeMark.protocolDirLocalIndex.
nlMatrixSDSourceAddress.nlMatrixSDDestAddress

Object	Type	Access
nlMatrixSDTimeMark	TimeFilter	not-accessible
nlMatrixSDSourceAddress	OCTET STRING	not-accessible
nlMatrixSDDestAddress	OCTET STRING	not-accessible
nlMatrixSDPkts	ZeroBasedCounter32	read-only
nlMatrixSDOctets	ZeroBasedCounter32	read-only
nlMatrixSDCreateTime	LastCreateTime	read-only

nlMatrixSDTimeMark: a TimeFilter object used to index this table.

nlMatrixSDSourceAddress: an OCTET STRING representing the network source address for this entry. For IP, the first byte would be 4 (the length of the IP address) and the next four bytes represent the IP address in network byte order.

nlMatrixSDDestAddress: an OCTET STRING representing the network destination address for this entry. For IP, the first byte would be 4 (the length of the IP address) and the next four bytes represent the IP address in network byte order.

nlMatrixSDPkts: number of packets without errors transmitted from the source address to the destination address. This counts the number of link-layer packets so if a single network-layer packet is fragmented into several link-layer frames, each fragment will be counted.

nlMatrixSDOctets: number of octets in packets transmitted from the source address to the destination address. This will exclude any octets in packets that contained errors. *Note*: It will count all of the octets in the packet which encapsulated the network layer frame.

nlMatrixSDCreateTime: value of sysUpTime when this entry was created. This can be used by network management software to guarantee that the entry was not deleted and re-created between polls.

One thing we might want to do is understand which clients are frequently communicating with a particular server, and how much traffic is being generated from the server to each client. We could use this information to move certain clients either to the same switch as a server or at least to the same subnet.

The following pseudocode demonstrates collecting statistics for the IP traffic that has been sent from a server address to each of its clients. Only the entries that have been updated during the past fifteen minutes will be looked at.

```
void procedure::CollectServerStats(server, n,Col, ProtCol)
{
    // Collect statistics for conversations between
    // a source address, server, and any destination
    // address. The interface which the statistics were
    // collected on is n. Col references a collection used to
    // add collected statistics to. ProtCol references
    // a collection that had been previously built
    // by ReadProtDirTable.

    ci <- GetControlIndex(hlMatrixControlDataSource,
            hlMatrixControlStatus, n)

    li <- GetProtLocalIndex(ProtCol, 'wildcard-ether2.ip')

    // Form a TimeFilter by collecting sysUpTime and
    // subtracting fifteen minutes from it.

    pdu <- SnmpGet(sysUpTime.0)
    uptime <- GetVarBindValue(pdu, 1)

    // If agent has been running less than
    // 15 minutes, return.

    if (uptime < 90000)
        return

    t <- (uptime - 90000)

    // Walk the nlMatrixSDTable and find all entries for
    // interface n, source address server, which
    // have been updated during the past 15 minutes.
```

```
//
// For each entry found, add the interface,
// local index, source address, destination address,
// packet count, and octet count to Col.

flag <- true
responsePDU <- { nlMatrixSDPkts.ci.t.li.4.server,
                 nlMatrixSDOctets.ci.t.li.4.server,
                 nlMatrixSDCreateTime.ci.t.li.4.server}

origPDU <- responsePDU

while (flag)
{
    pdu <- SnmpGetNext(responsePDU)
    responsePDU <- pdu
    flag <- CheckPDU(pdu, origPDU)

    if (flag == false)
      continue

    pkts <- GetVarBindValue(pdu, 1)
    octets <- GetVarBindValue(pdu, 2)
    createtime <- GetVarBindValue(pdu, 3)

    // If the row was created within the past 15 minutes
    // then ignore it.

    if (createtime > t)
      continue

    // Get the destination address from the instance.

    inst <- GetVarBindInstance(
              pdu,
              1,
              nlMatrixSDPkts.ci.t.li.4.server)

    // The first byte in the instance will be 4
    // (the length of the destination IP address).
    // Bytes 2 - 5 are the destination address.

    destAddr <- inst[2 .. 5]

    add { n, localIndex, server, destAddr, pkts, octets}
         to Col
}
}
```

The nlMatrixDSTable is the companion to nlMatrixSDTable. It provides the same packet and octet statistics as the nlMatrixSDTable, but it is indexed by destination and then source address. This table makes it easy to locate the source addresses for any destination address. For example, you could search this table to find all the clients which are sending packets to a server. Any entry that is in the nlMatrixSDTable will have a corresponding entry within this table.

Table 9-14   nlMatrixDSTable, Indexed by hlMatrixControlIndex.nlMatrixDSTimeMark.protocolDirLocalIndex. nlMatrixDSDestAddress.nlMatrixDSSourceAddress

Object	Type	Access
nlMatrixDSTimeMark	TimeFilter	not-accessible
nlMatrixDSSourceAddress	OCTET STRING	not-accessible
nlMatrixDSDestAddress	OCTET STRING	not-accessible
nlMatrixDSPkts	ZeroBasedCounter32	read-only
nlMatrixDSOctets	ZeroBasedCounter32	read-only
nlMatrixDSCreateTime	LastCreateTime	read-only

nlMatrixDSTimeMark: a TimeFilter object used to index this table.

nlMatrixDSSourceAddress: an OCTET STRING representing the network source address for this entry. For IP, the first byte would be 4 (the length of the IP address) and the next four bytes represent the IP address in network byte order.

nlMatrixDSDestAddress: an OCTET STRING representing the network destination address for this entry. For IP, the first byte would be 4 (the length of the IP address) and the next four bytes represent the IP address in network byte order.

nlMatrixDSPkts: number of packets without errors received by the destination address from the source address. This counts the number of link-layer packets so if a single network-layer packet is fragmented into several link-layer frames, each fragment will be counted.

nlMatrixDSOctets: number of octets in packets received by the destination address from the source address. This will exclude any octets in packets that contained errors. *Note*: It will count all of the octets in the packet which encapsulated the network layer frame.

nlMatrixDSCreateTime: value of sysUpTime when this entry was created. This can be used by network management software to guarantee that the entry was not deleted and re-created between polls.

An example of the indexing of this table is

nlMatrixDSPkts.1.0.32768.4.158.101.121.1.4.158.101.121.63

where the hlMatrixControlIndex would be 1, the TimeFilter would be 0, the protoclDirLocalIndex would be 32768, the destination address would be 158.101.121.1, and the source address would be 158.101.121.63.

You can generate top N reports for the network-layer conversations. This is done by adding entries to the nlMatrixTopNControlTable. For each entry you need to specify

• a control index
• whether you want the report to be based on packets or octets
• how often you want the report to be generated
• the maximum number of entries for the report

The nlMatrixTopNControlTable is presented below.

Table 9-15   nlMatrixTopNControlTable,
Indexed by nlMatrixTopNControlIndex

Object	Type	Access
nlMatrixTopNControlIndex	Integer32	not-accessible
nlMatrixTopNControlMatrixIndex	Integer32	read-create
nlMatrixTopNControlRateBase	INTEGER	read-create
nlMatrixTopNControlTimeRemaining	Integer32	read-create
nlMatrixTopNControlGeneratedReports	Counter32	read-only
nlMatrixTopNControlDuration	Integer32	read-only

Table 9-15   nlMatrixTopNControlTable,
Indexed by nlMatrixTopNControlIndex (Continued)

Object	Type	Access
nlMatrixTopNControlRequestedSize	Integer32	read-create
nlMatrixTopNControlGrantedSize	Integer32	read-only
nlMatrixTopNControlStartTime	TimeStamp	read-only
nlMatrixTopNControlOwner	OwnerString	read-create
nlMatrixTopNControlStatus	RowStatus	read-create

nlMatrixTopNControlIndex: a unique index for this table. This value can be between 1 and 65535 and is used to identify entries within the nlMatrixTopNTable that make up the top N report that is generated by this entry.

nlMatrixTopNControlMatrixIndex: an index that uniquely identifies an entry in the hlMatrixControlTable. This indirectly references the interface that the monitoring is performed on.

nlMatrixTopNControlRateBase: specifies whether the top N report is sorted by the packet or octet counts. This can be set to either `nlMatrixTopNPkts` (1) or `nlMatrixTopNOctets` (2).

nlMatrixTopNControlTimeRemaining: this object is initially set to how often you want to generate a top N report (in seconds). It will be decremented every second, and when it reaches zero a new report will be made accessible in the nlMatrixTop-NTable, overwriting any previous report that is associated with this entry. After this object is decremented to zero and a new report is generated, the object will be reset to the last value that was written into the object. For example, if this object is set to 300, a new report will be generated every five minutes.

Note: If this object is modified through a Set operation, then the currently running report will be aborted and a new collection is started. This object has a default value of 1800 (30 minutes).

nlMatrixTopNControlGeneratedReports: the number of reports that have been generated by this entry.

nlMatrixTopNControlDuration: this object keeps track of the last value that was written into nlMatrixTopNControlTimeRemaining. This value is used as the sampling interval for generating reports.

nlMatrixTopNControlRequestedSize: the requested number of entries for the top N report. This has a default value of 150.

nlMatrixTopNControlGrantedSize: the actual number of entries for the top N report. This can be less than nlMatrixTopNControlRequestedSize if there are not enough available resources.

nlMatrixTopNControlStartTime: the value of sysUpTime when this top N report was last started.

nlMatrixTopNControlOwner: identifies the manager who configured this entry.

nlMatrixTopNControlStatus: a RowStatus object used for adding and removing rows to/from this table. If the value of this object is changed from `active` to `notInService` (or `destroy`), all associated entries within the nlMatrixTopNTable will be deleted.

The following pseudocode will add an entry in the nlMatrixTopNControlTable which will generate top N reports every hour. The reports will have at most 20 entries and will be sorted by the network conversations with the highest packet counts.

```
// Get the control table index for interface n.

ci <- GetControlIndex(hlMatrixControlDataSource,
             hlMatrixControlStatus, n)

// Generate a unique index. Note. This will be used
// to index the nlMatrixTopNTable

i <- GetUniqueInstance(nlMatrixTopNControlStatus)

pdu <- { nlMatrixTopNControlMatrixIndex.i <- ci,
       nlMatrixTopNControlRateBase.i <- 'nlMatrixTopNPkts',
       nlMatrixTopNControlTimeRemaining.i <- 3600,
       nlMatrixTopNControlRequestSize.i <- 20,
       nlMatrixTopNControlOwner.i <- 'monitor',
       nlMatrixTopNControlStatus.i <- 'active'}
```

```
SnmpSet(pdu)
```

The nlMatrixTopNTable contains the reports generated by the entries added to the nlMatrixTopMControlTable. The table is indexed by a control index and an integer identifying an entry's location within a report. For example, if a report associated with control index *i* is generated so that it is sorted by packet rate then the instance *i*.1 would reference the entry with the highest packet rate, *i*.2 would reference the entry with the next highest packet rate, etc.

Table 9-16   nlMatrixTopNTable, Indexed by
nlMatrixTopNControlIndex.nlMatrixTopNIndex

Object	Type	Access
nlMatrixTopNIndex	Integer32	not-accessible
nlMatrixTopNProtocolDirLocalIndex	Integer32	read-only
nlMatrixTopNSourceAddress	OCTET STRING	read-only
nlMatrixTopNDestAddress	OCTET STRING	read-only
nlMatrixTopNPktRate	Gauge32	read-only
nlMatrixTopNReversePktRate	Gauge32	read-only
nlMatrixTopNOctetRate	Gauge32	read-only
nlMatrixTopNReverseOctetRate	Gauge32	read-only

nlMatrixTopNIndex: identifies the position within the top N report. The value of this will be between 1 and N, where N is the number of entries making up the top N report.

nlMatrixTopNProtocolDirLocalIndex: identifies the network-layer protocol that was used.

nlMatrixTopNSourceAddress: an OCTET STRING representing the network source address for this entry. For IP, the first byte would be 4 (the length of the IP address) and the next four bytes represent the IP address in network byte order.

nlMatrixTopNDestAddress: an OCTET STRING representing the network destination address for this entry. For IP, the first byte would be 4 (the length of the IP address) and the next four bytes represent the IP address in network byte order.

nlMatrixTopNPktRate: number of packets seen from the source address to the destination address during this sampling interval. If the value of the associated nlMatrixTopNControlRateBase object is `nlMatrixTopNPkts`, then this object is used to sort the report.

nlMatrixTopNReversePktRate: number of packets seen from the destination address to the source address.

nlMatrixTopNOctetRate: number of octets seen from the source address to the destination address during this sampling interval. If the value of the associated nlMatrixTopNControlRateBase object is `nlMatrixTopNOctets`, then this object is used to sort the report.

nlMatrixTopNReverseOctetRate: number of packets seen from the destination address to the source address.

We earlier showed how to create an entry in the nlMatrixTopNControlTable to create a top N report every hour that will show the top 20 conversations by packet rates. The next logical step would be to periodically read the top N report and perform some processing with it (such as writing the data to a database, or generating an hourly html report). The following pseudocode demonstrates reading information from the nlMatrixTopNControlTable to know when the next report will be generated for an associated control index, and then collecting the report when it is ready. The pseudocode will stay in a loop, periodically reading and processing a top N report until the associated entry within the nlMatrixTopNControlTable is taken out of the `active` state.

```
procedure void::LoopTopNReport(ci)
{
    // This procedure will periodically read and process
    // the top N report associated with the control index ci.
    // Note. This procedure will stay in a loop until the
    // associated entry within the nlMatrixTopNControlTable is
    // either placed in the 'notInService' state or destroyed.

    pdu <- {nlMatrixTopNControlTimeRemaining.ci,
            nlMatrixTopNControlStartTime.ci,
            nlMatrixTopNControlStatus.ci}

    firstTimeFlag <- true
```

```
while (true)
{
// See how much time is remaining until the next is
// generated, when the last report was generated, and
// the status of the corresponding nlMatrixTopNControlTable
// row.

    responsePDU <- SnmpGet(pdu)

    seconds <- GetVarBindValue(responsePDU, 1)
    startTime <- GetVarBindValue(responsePDU, 2)
    state <- GetVarBindValue(responsePDU, 3)

    if (state != 'active')
      return

    if (firstTimeFlag == true)
    {
      // If first time in the loop then save
      // the value of nlMatrixTopNControlStartTime in
      // last.

      last <- startTime
      firstTimeFlag <- false
    }

    if (last == startTime)
      sleep(seconds + 15)
    else
    {
      // A new report has been generated. Read and process
      // it.

      ClearCollection(Col)
      ReadTopNReport(ci, Col)
      ProcessTopNReport(ci, Col)
      last <- startTime
    }
  }
}
```

LoopTopNReport will enter a while loop and read the time remaining, start time, and status objects for an entry within the nlMatrixTopNControlTable. If at any time the status object is not active, LoopTopNReport will return. The first time through the while loop, the variable *last* will be set to the start time that was read. If *last* equals the start time value, then the procedure will sleep for the number of seconds remaining to generate the next report, plus fifteen additional seconds to make sure the report will be ready. If *last* doesn't equal the start time value, then a new report has been generated. In this case we will call ClearCollection to clear a collection, ReadTopNReport to read the new report, and ProcessTopNReport to perform some processing on the new report.

The pseudocode for ReadTopNReport is presented below.

```
procedure void::ReadTopNReport(ci, Col)
{
    // Read all entries from the nlMatrixTopNTable associated
    // with control index ci. Add {position, local index,
    // source address,destination address, packet rate,
    // reverse packet rate, octet rate, reverse octet rate} to
    // Col for each entry read.

    flag <- true
    responsePDU <- { nlMatrixTopNProtocolDirLocalIndex.ci,
                     nlMatrixTopNSourceAddress.ci,
                     nlMatrixTopNDestAddress.ci,
                     nlMatrixTopNPktRate.ci,
                     nlMatrixTopNReversePktRate.ci,
                     nlMatrixTopNOctetRate.ci,
                     nlMatrixTopNReverseOctetRate.ci }

    origPDU <- responsePDU

    while (flag)
    {
        pdu <- SnmpGetNext(responsePDU)
        responsePDU <- pdu
        flag <- CheckPDU(pdu, origPDU)

        if (flag == false)
          continue

        localIndex <- GetVarBindValue(pdu, 1)
        sourceAddr <- GetVarBindValue(pdu, 2)
        destAddr <- GetVarBindValue(pdu, 3)
        pktRate <- GetVarBindValue(pdu, 4)
        rvpktRate <- GetVarBindValue(pdu, 5)
        octetRate <- GetVarBindValue(pdu, 6)
        rvoctetRate <- GetVarBindValue(pdu, 7)

        // Get the nlMatrixTopNIndex value from the instance.

        n <- GetVarBindInstance(
                 pdu,
                 1,
```

```
                    nlMatrixTopNProtocolDirLocalIndex.ci)

        // Add to collection Col.

        add {  n, localIndex, sourceAddr, destAddr, pktRate,
                rvpktRate, octetRate, rvoctetRate } to Col
    }
}
```

9.8 Application Layer Host Group

The Application Layer Host Group contains the alHostTable. The alHostTable provides information about the amount of application-layer traffic sent to and received by each network address. This table is indexed similarly to the nlHostTable, with an additional protocolDirLocal-Index value added to reference the application-layer protocol. As we have already discussed, the hlHostControlTable is used to configure which interfaces to provide both network and application-tion-layer traffic monitoring on.

Packets will be examined for the alHostTable if they contain no MAC errors. Also the associated entries within the protocolDirTable for the network and application-layer protocols must have their protocolDirHostConfig objects equal to `supportedOn`.

The alHostTable is presented below.

Table 9-17   alHostTable, Indexed by
hlHostControlIndex.alHostTimeMark.protocolDirLocalIndex.nlHostAddress.
protocolDirLocalIndex

Object	Type	Access
alHostTimeMark	TimeFilter	not-accessible
alHostInPkts	ZeroBasedCounter32	read-only
alHostOutPkts	ZeroBasedCounter32	read-only
alHostInOctets	ZeroBasedCounter32	read-only
alHostOutOctets	ZeroBasedCounter32	read-only
alHostCreateTime	LastCreateTime	read-only

alHostTimeMark: a TimeFilter object used to index this table.

alHostInPkts: number of packets of this application type received by the corresponding network address. This counts the number of link-layer packets so if a single network-layer packet is fragmented into several link-layer frames, each fragment will be counted.

alHostOutPkts: number of packets of this application type sent by the corresponding network address. This counts the number of link-layer packets so if a single network-layer packet is fragmented into several link-layer frames, each fragment will be counted.

alHostInOctets: number of octets within packets of this application type which have been received by the corresponding network address. This will exclude any octets in packets that contained errors. *Note*: It will count all of the octets in the packet which encapsulated the protocol frame.

alHostOutOctets: number of octets within packets of this application type which have been sent by the corresponding network address. This will exclude any octets in packets that contained errors. *Note*: It will count all of the octets in the packet which encapsulated the protocol frame.

alHostCreateTime: value of sysUpTime when this entry was created. This can be used by network management software to guarantee that the entry was not deleted and re-created between polls.

By periodically reading the alHostTable, you can understand the application-layer protocol traffic seen at each host address. The procedure we showed earlier to demonstrate reading the nlHostTable, ReadHostTable, can be extended easily to handle the alHostTable. This can be done by simply changing how the instance is parsed and adding the application-layer local index to the collection that is built.

The instance of an alHostTable object would look something like this:

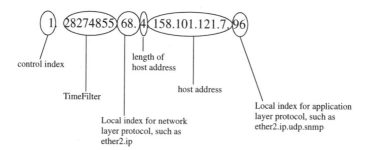

control index

TimeFilter

length of
host address

host address

Local index for network
layer protocol, such as
ether2.ip

Local index for application
layer protocol, such as
ether2.ip.udp.snmp

   If the alHostTable is walked by using a partial instance made up of the control index and
TimeFilter, then the following pseudocode will parse the remaining instance to obtain the protocolDirLocalIndex value for the network protocol, the host address, and the protocolDirLocalIndex value for the application-layer protocol.

```
// The first byte in the remainder of the
// instance is the protocolDirLocalIndex value
// for the network protocol.

networkLocalIndex <- inst[1]

// Next, get the network address.

n1 <- inst[2]
hostAddress <- inst[3 .. 2 + n1]

// Next, get the protocolDirLocalIndex value for the
// application-layer protocol

applicationLocalIndex <- inst[3 + n1]
```

9.9 Application Layer Matrix Group

   The Application Layer Matrix Group provides a finer level of detail than the Network
Layer Matrix Group, allowing you to collect statistics about application-layer conversations
between different network addresses. This group has an alMatrixSDTable and an alMatrixD-
STable, both similar to the nlMatrixSDTable and nlMatrixDSTable except that they are indexed
by an additional protocolDirLocalIndex value which represents the application-layer protocol.
This group also has an alMatrixTopNControlTable and an alMatrixTopNTable which work the
same as their network layer counterparts, except that they provide top N reports for the application-layer conversations between different network addresses.

The alMatrixSDTable and alMatrixDSTable are presented below. They provide statistics for application-layer traffic between different network addresses. For the most part these two tables work identically to their network layer counterparts. Packets with MAC errors will be ignored. Also, for a packet to be examined by this matrix group the protocolDirMatrixConfig value for the associated application-layer protocol must be equal to `supportedOn`. The one difference is that the indexes for these tables contain an additional component for the application-layer protocolDirLocalIndex value.

Table 9-18   alMatrixSDTable, Indexed by
hlMatrixControlIndex.alMatrixSDTimeMark.protocolDirLocalIndex.
nlMatrixSDSourceAddress.nlMatrixSDDestAddress.protocolDirLocalIndex

Object	Type	Access
alMatrixSDTimeMark	TimeFilter	not-accessible
alMatrixSDPkts	ZeroBasedCounter32	read-only
alMatrixSDOctets	ZeroBasedCounter32	read-only
alMatrixSDCreateTime	LastCreateTime	read-only

alMatrixSDTimeMark: a TimeFilter object used to index this table.

alMatrixSDPkts: number of packets of this protocol type which have been transmitted from the source address to the destination address. This counts the number of link-layer packets so if a single network-layer packet is fragmented into several link-layer frames, each fragment will be counted.

alMatrixSDOctets: number of octets in packets of this protocol type which have been transmitted from the source address to the destination address. This will exclude any octets in packets that contained errors. *Note*: It will count all of the octets in the packet which encapsulated the protocol frame.

alMatrixSDCreateTime: value of sysUpTime when this entry was created. This can be used by network management software to guarantee that the entry was not deleted and recreated between polls.

Table 9-19   alMatrixDSTable, Indexed by
hlMatrixControlIndex.alMatrixDSTimeMark.protocolDirLocalIndex.
nlMatrixDSDestAddress.nlMatrixDSSourceAddress.protocolDirLocalIndex

Object	Type	Access
alMatrixDSTimeMark	TimeFilter	not-accessible
alMatrixDSPkts	ZeroBasedCounter32	read-only
alMatrixDSOctets	ZeroBasedCounter32	read-only
alMatrixDSCreateTime	LastCreateTime	read-only

alMatrixDSTimeMark: a TimeFilter object used to index this table.

alMatrixDSPkts: number of packets of this protocol type which have been transmitted from the source address to the destination address. This counts the number of link-layer packets so if a single network-layer packet is fragmented into several link-layer frames, each fragment will be counted.

alMatrixDSOctets: number of octets in packets of this protocol type which have been transmitted from the source address to the destination address. This will exclude any octets in packets that contained errors. *Note*: It will count all of the octets in the packet which encapsulated the protocol frame.

alMatrixDSCreateTime: value of sysUpTime when this entry was created. This can be used by network management software to guarantee that the entry was not deleted and re-created between polls.

The following pseudocode demonstrates parsing the instance returned by a Get-Next operation on alMatrixDSPkts.*ci*.*tf*, where *ci* is a control index and *tf* is a TimeFilter.

```
pdu <- SnmpGetNext(alMatrixDSPkts.ci.tf)
if (CheckPDU(pdu, alMatrixDSPkts.ci.tf) == false)
    return
inst <- GetVarBindInstance(
            pdu,
            1,
            alMatrixDSPkts.ci.tf)
```

```
// Assuming that the network layer addresses are IP,
// inst will be something like:
// 56.4.158.101.121.16.4.158.101.121.17.9871, where
// 56 would be the protocolDirLocalIndex value for the
// network layer protocol, 158.101.121.16 would be the
// destination address, 158.101.121.17 would be the
// source address, and 9871 would be the protocolDirLocalIndex
// value for the application-layer protocol.

netProt <- inst[1]
n1 <- inst[2]
destAddr <- inst[3 .. 2 + n1]
i <- 3 + n1
n2 <- inst[i]
sourceAddr <- inst[i + 1 .. i + n2]
applProt <- inst[i + n2 + 1]
```

The alMatrixTopNTable is used to generate topN reports. As with the nlMatrixTopNControlTable, an entry within the alMatrixTopNControlTable specifies how often a report should be generated, the size of the report, how the report should be sorted, and (indirectly) the interface that is monitored.

Table 9-20 alMatrixTopNControlTable, Indexed by alMatrixTopNControlIndex

Object	Type	Access
alMatrixTopNControlIndex	Integer32	not-accessible
alMatrixTopNControlMatrixIndex	Integer32	read-create
alMatrixTopNControlRateBase	INTEGER	read-create
alMatrixTopNControlTimeRemaining	Integer32	read-create
alMatrixTopNControlGeneratedReports	Counter32	read-only
alMatrixTopNControlDuration	Integer32	read-only
alMatrixTopNControlRequestedSize	Integer32	read-create
alMatrixTopNControlGrantedSize	Integer32	read-only
alMatrixTopNControlStartTime	TimeStamp	read-only

Table 9-20   alMatrixTopNControlTable,
Indexed by alMatrixTopNControlIndex (Continued)

Object	Type	Access
alMatrixTopNControlOwner	OwnerString	read-create
alMatrixTopNControlStatus	RowStatus	read-create

The only difference between the alMatrixTopNControlTable objects and their equivalent nlMatrixTopNControlTable objects is the way alMatrixTopNControlRateBase is defined. The nlMatrixTopNControlRateBase object is used only for sorting a top N report. The alMatrixTop-NControlRateBase object is used not only for sorting the associated top N report, but also for selecting the protocol traffic that can be included within the top N report. This object can have the following values:

```
alMatrixTopNTerminalsPkts (1)

alMatrixTopNTerminalsOctets (2)

alMatrixTopNAllPkts (3)

alMatrixTopNAllOctets (4)
```

The `alMatrixTopNTerminalPkts` and `alMatrixTopNTerminalsOctets` values cause collection only from protocols that have no child protocols that are counted. The `alMatrixTopNAllPkts` and `alMatrixTopNAllOctets` values will cause collection from all alMatrix entries. Whether the entries are sorted by packet or octet counts depends on whether a *Pkts or *Octets value is used.

The top N reports that are generated are placed in the alMatrixTopNTable. As with the nlMatrixTopNTable, this table is indexed by a control index and a number indicating the order of the entry within the top N report.

Table 9-21   alMatrixTopNTable, Indexed by
alMatrixTopNControlIndex.alMatrixTopNIndex

Object	Type	Access
alMatrixTopNIndex	Integer32	not-accessible
alMatrixTopNProtocolDirLocalIndex	Integer32	read-only
alMatrixTopNSourceAddress	OCTET STRING	read-only
alMatrixTopNDestAddress	OCTET STRING	read-only

Table 9-21   alMatrixTopNTable, Indexed by
alMatrixTopNControlIndex.alMatrixTopNIndex (Continued)

Object	Type	Access
alMatrixTopNAppProtocolDirLocalIndex	Integer32	read-only
alMatrixTopNPktRate	Gauge32	read-only
alMatrixTopNReversePktRate	Gauge32	read-only
alMatrixTopNOctetRate	Gauge32	read-only
alMatrixTopNReverseOctetRate	Gauge32	read-only

The objects within the alMatrixTopNTable are equivalent to their nlMatrixTopNTable counterparts. The only difference is a new object, alMatrixTopNAppProtocolDirLocalIndex, has been added to the alMatrixTopNTable. This new object, as its name suggests, is the protocolDirLocalIndex value for the application-layer protocol that this entry identifies. The LoopTopN-Report pseudocode which we have seen earlier could be modified slightly to periodically collect a top N report from the alMatrixTopNTable.

9.10 User History Collection Group

The User History Collection Group (usrHistory) is made up of two control tables (usrHistoryControlTable and usrHistoryObjectTable) and one data table (usrHistoryTable). This group allows you to periodically collect and log data. The data collected can be either the value of a MIB object or how much the MIB object has changed during the sample interval. The data that is collected is logged into the usrHistoryTable and can be read later by a network management application. While the RMON 1 history group allows etherHistoryTable objects to be collected and logged, the usrHistory group allows any INTEGER based objects (Integer32, Counter, Gauge, or TimeTicks) to be collected and logged. The two control tables specify the objects to be collected, the sampling interval, and the number of samples that can be logged. Objects are collected in something called "bucket-groups," with the intent that all objects in the same bucket-group are collected as atomically as possible by the RMON2 probe.

The usrHistoryControlTable defines how many objects are collected in a bucket-group, how often the collection is done (the sampling interval), and how many buckets can be loggged to the usrHistoryTable.

The usrHistoryControlTable is shown below.

Table 9-22   usrHistoryControlTable, Indexed by usrHistoryControlIndex

Object	Type	Access
usrHistoryControlIndex	Integer32	not-accessible
usrHistoryControlObjects	Integer32	read-create
userHistoryControlBucketsRequested	Integer32	read-create
usrHistoryControlBucketsGranted	Integer32	read-only
usrHistoryControlInterval	Integer32	read-create
usrHistoryControlOwner	OwnerString	read-create
usrHistoryControlStatus	RowStatus	read-create

usrHistoryControlIndex: a unique identifier between 1 and 65535 that is used to index this table, the usrHistoryObjectTable, and the usrHistoryTable.

usrHistoryControlObjects: number of MIB objects for this "bucket-group."

userHistoryControlBucketsRequested: requested number of samples to log to the usrHistoryTable. This has a default value of 50.

usrHistoryControlBucketsGranted: number of samples that can be logged to the usrHistoryTable. The probe should set this value to as close to usrHistoryControl-BucketsRequested as possible, depending on its implementation and available resources.

As samples are collected, the number of buckets that have been logged to the usrHistoryTable will reach this value. When this happens and the next sample needs to be logged, the oldest bucket associated with this entry will first be deleted. You can think of this as being implemented as a circular queue.

Note: This value can shrink or grow if usrHistoryControlBucketsRequested is modified.

usrHistoryControlInterval: defines the sampling interval in seconds. This has a default value of 1800 (30 minutes).

Note: If you are collecting counter objects you should be aware of how quickly these counters objects can wrap, and set the usrHistoryControlInterval to a smaller number.

usrHistoryControlOwner: identifies the manager who configured this entry.

usrHistoryControlStatus: a RowStatus object used for adding and removing rows to/from this table. If the value of this object is changed from `active` to `notIn-Service` (or `destroy`), all associated entries within the usrHistoryTable will be deleted.

The usrHistoryObjectTable is used to specify the MIB objects that are collected within a bucket-group and whether the data that is logged is the value of a MIB object or the delta value of a MIB object (how much the object has changed during the sampling interval). This table is tied to the usrHistoryControlTable through the usrHistoryControlIndex.

The usrHistoryObjectTable is shown below.

Table 9-23 usrHistoryObjectTable, Indexed by usrHistoryControlIndex.usrHistoryObjectIndex

Object	Type	Access
usrHistoryObjectIndex	Integer32	not-accessible
usrHistoryObjectVariable	OBJECT IDENTIFIER	read-create
usrHistoryObjectSampleType	INTEGER	read-create

usrHistoryObjectIndex: used with usrHistoryControlIndex to uniquely identify an entry. This can have a value between 1 and 65535.

usrHistoryObjectVariable: the MIB object to be sampled.

usrHistoryObjectSampleType: defines whether the value of an object or the delta value is logged. This can be either

```
absoluteValue(1)
deltaValue(2)
```

If the value is `absoluteValue` then the value of the associated MIB is logged. If the value is `deltaValue`, then the current value minus the last sample value will be logged.

As an example, if we want to log every fifteen minutes the delta values of ifInOctets.1, ifOutOctets.1, ifInErrors.1, and ifOutErrors.1, and we want to be able to maintain 60 samples within the usrHistoryTable, we would set up the following usrHistoryControl entry:

Table 9-24   usrHistoryControlTable Example

usrHistoryControlIndex.1	1
usrHistoryControlObjects.1	4
userHistoryControlBucketsRequested.1	60
usrHistoryControlBucketsGranted.1	60
usrHistoryControlInterval.1	900
usrHistoryControlOwner	"monitor"
usrHistoryControlStatus	active

We would also set up the following usrHistoryObjectTable entries:

Table 9-25

	1.1	1.2	1.3	1.4
usrHistoryObjectIndex	1	2	3	4
usrHistoryObjectVariable	ifInOctets.1	ifOutOctets.1	ifInErrors.1	ifOutErrors.1
usrHistoryObjectSampleType	deltaValue	deltaValue	deltaValue	deltaValue

Once these entries have been configured, every 15 minutes a "bucket" will be added to the usrHistoryTable. The bucket will contain the delta values for the four corresponding MIB objects (ifInOctets.1, ifOutOctets.1, ifInErrors.1, and ifOutErrors.1). Once 60 buckets have been added, the oldest bucket for this "bucket-group" must be deleted before a new bucket can be added.

The usrHistoryTable is shown below.

Table 9-26   usrHistoryTable, Indexed by
usrHistoryControlIndex.usrHistorySampleIndex.usrHistoryObjectIndex

Object	Type	Access
usrHistorySampleIndex	Integer32	not-accessible
usrHistoryIntervalStart	TimeStamp	read-only
usrHistoryIntervalEnd	TimeStamp	read-only
usrHistoryAbsValue	Gauge32	read-only
usrHistoryValStatus	INTEGER	read-only

usrHistorySampleIndex: an index that uniquely identifies a sample. The sample index will start at one and increase as each new sample is added.

usrHistoryIntervalStart: value of sysUpTime when the interval was started. *Note*: If a probe keeps track of the time of day, it should start the first sample at the start of the next hour. For example, if entries have been added to the usrHistoryControlTable and usrHistoryObjectTable at 1:09, the first sample collected for those entries should start at 2:00.

usrHistoryIntervalEnd: value of sysUpTime when the interval ended.

usrHistoryAbsValue: absolute value (unsigned) logged for the corresponding MIB object (specified by the usrHistoryObjectTable). Whether this object represents a positive or negative value is determined by the usrHistoryValStatus object. If for some reason the MIB object could not be accessed during this sampling interval, this object will be set to zero and the associated usrHistoryValStatus object will be set to `valueNotAvailable`.

usrHistoryValStatus: this can have one of three values:

> `valueNotAvailable` (1)
>
> `valuePositive` (2)
>
> `valueNegative` (3)

Continuing the example that we started, the delta values within the first sample would be accessed as follows:

Table 9-27   Accessing the First Sample

MIB Object	Accessed by
ifInOctets.1	usrHistoryAbsValue.1.1.1
ifOutOctets.1	usrHistoryAbsValue.1.1.2
ifInErrors.1	usrHistoryAbsValue.1.1.3
ifOutErrors.1	usrHistoryAbsValue.1.1.4

The delta values logged by the second sample would be accessed as follows:

Table 9-28   Accessing the Second Sample

MIB Object	Accessed by
ifInOctets.1	usrHistoryAbsValue.1.2.1
ifOutOctets.1	usrHistoryAbsValue.1.2.2
ifInErrors.1	usrHistoryAbsValue.1.2.3
ifOutErrors.1	usrHistoryAbsValue.1.2.4

9.11 Ideas on Measuring Application Response Time

A major shift has been occurring in network management over the last several years. The focus has been moving away from the underlying network infrastructure and toward end-to-end monitoring. Network administrators are now spending more of their time trying to understand how their network applications are performing. Because of this, one of the hot areas in network management today is application response time monitoring. A response time monitoring system typically provides information about what the average and peak application response times are at different times of the day, and will track these values over time so you can understand if the response times are degrading. Poor application response time can be caused by a number of reasons; including a server being overwhelmed, applications being poorly designed to run over a network, and network problems (such as congestion or high error rates due to a bad card or cable). By correlating the measured application response times with the collected statisitics on the underlying network infrastructure, you can have a better idea of whether a problem is due to the network or the application. If you can also determine how many requests a server is receiving, you can better understand if a server is being overwhelmed. This section will look briefly at several possible methods for trying to measure application response time.

One way to try to measure application response time is to periodically send application requests and measure how long it takes to get a response back. This might be sending SQL commands to perform some set of operations on an Oracle database, or it might be sending a DNS packet to a DNS host, or any number of application-specific tests. By periodically sending the same application request from the same workstation, you can get a feel for what the normal response times are at different times of the day. Of course, you don't want your testing to impact either the network or an application's performance. Realistically, sending application requests every 5 to 15 minutes should have little to no impact on either the network or the application's performance (this depends on how intensive the requests are - routinely sending an Oracle database a set of complex SQL queries could obviously have some impact on the Oracle database server).

How good a measurement does this provide? Well, you're only looking at small discrete samples. If you are performing tests every 5 minutes and the test lasts less than 10 seconds, then your discrete sample only reflects what was going on for about 3 percent of that 5-minute period. At different times during the 5-minute period the response time could have been significantly different. If you take enough samples over a long enough period of time, you can probably get a good feel for what's normal and what isn't. And remember, since the response times are going to be different at different times of the day, you not only need a large number of samples but you also need a large number of samples taken at the same time of the day before you can attempt to characterize how an application is performing.

Another method that can be used to try to understand application response time is to extend the RMON2 application monitoring to recognize request and response identifiers for certain applications. If a probe can recognize application request and response pairs, it can effectively measure the response times for the application.

Albin Warth and Jim McQuaid from NetScout Systems, Inc., have proposed an Applications Response Time MIB as a draft IETF document. Currently this MIB has been implemented within NetScout probes. It uses the RMON2 protocol directory table to identify protocols which the probe can match request and response pairs for. It further extends the protocol directory table by adding an object for turning on or off application response time support for the different protocols within the table. It also adds a control table and data table that are similar in concept to the RMON2 matrix top N tables. The control table specifies the data source (interface), the ranges for grouping response time results, a reporting interval, and the number of entries that can be added to the data table. The data table provides response time statistics for protocol conversations between different hosts. The statisitics are calculated for the sampling interval and provide information such as the average, minimum, and maximum response times, the number of responses measured (number of requests that were successfully paired with responses), a request retry count, number of times the probe timed out while waiting for a response to a client request, response time distributions, and some 64-bit counters for traffic octet counts. The response time distribution information depends on how the control table entry was configured but provides information such as how many response times were measured between 0 and 25 milliseconds, between 25 and 50 milliseconds, between 50 and 100 milliseconds, etc. The MIB provides an additional data table that summarizes source-destination (client-server) information into destination information. This allows you to easily index the table to get the response time measurements for a particular server.

How does this approach compare to the first? First of all this approach adds no overhead to any server machines, and very little overhead to the network. Data still needs to be collected from the probes, but this should be fairly insignificant. Second, instead of providing small, discrete measurements as the first method did, this is far more comprehensive. One disadvantage this approach has, though, is it can't tell the difference in weights between different requests. With the previous approach we're measuring apples to apples. With this approach we could be measuring apples to oranges. A complex SQL query will be looked at the same as a simpler SQL query. If a server is seeing a set of complex requests during a certain time period, then this could skew the response time measurements during a sampling interval. Overall, though, this approach deserves quite a bit of merit and provides a good indication of how busy a server is and how much time applications are spending processing requests. Using this method along with performing network delay measurements, you can isolate whether poor application response time is due to the application, the server, or the network infrastructure. Also by using two probes you can determine both the application response time and the network delay. This is done by having one probe monitor the segment the server is on, and the other probe monitor the segment the client is on. The following diagram illustrates this.

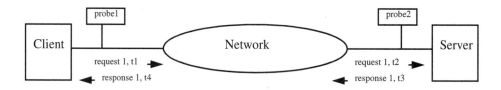

As the diagram illustrates, probe 2 will see request 1 at about the same time the server does ($t2$). It will also see the corresponding response at about the same time the server sends it ($t3$). Probe 2 would calculate the application response time as $t3 - t2$.

Probe 1, which monitors the segment the client is on, will see the request when it was originally transmitted by the client ($t1$). It will also see the response at about the same time as the client does ($t4$). Probe 1 would then calculate the application responsse time as $t4 - t1$. This measurement in effect includes both the network delay and the application delay. By monitoring both probes, the network delay component can be calculated by subtracting the application response time measured by probe 2 from the response time measure by probe 1.

A final method that we will very briefly discuss is adding MIB instrumentation to applications. If an application can provide MIB objects that indicate how busy it is (similar to the CPU utilization provided by quite a few network devices), how many requests per minute it has been handling during the last sampling interval, the peak requests per minute it had to handle, and the average and peak response times during the sampling interval, then a network management application can periodically poll the applications to understand how busy they are and how they are performing. This is probably the ideal method to use to understand application performance, but it is obviously the most intrusive since it requires additional code and overhead to be added to applications.

Using Cisco Private MIBs

Network hardware vendors implement private MIBs to add value over what is provided by standard MIBs. Private MIBs may provide additional resource information (such as how busy a device is), chassis information (what boards are installed), topology information, additional network statistics, or any number of other classes of information. They may also be used to configure nonstandard features, such as assigning protocol filters to interfaces. They can also be used to perform tests or operations, such as sending an ICMP ping to a remote address to measure network delay, performing a traceroute to a remote system, transfering a collection of statistics to a network management station, or any number of other possible operations. By extending the standard MIBs vendors can differentiate their devices and allow network managers to get a better handle over what is going on within the network.

This chapter will take a look at a sample of Cisco private MIBs and see how they can be utilized by a network manager. It is not intended for this chapter to provide an exhaustive study of Cisco private MIBs, nor will it even provide an exhaustive look at the Cisco private MIBs that this chapter focuses on. The goal for this chapter is suggest ways in which private MIBs can be utilized to gain insight into a network.

The functionality provided by these MIBs is not necessarily unique to Cisco. Other vendors have implemented similar types of MIBs. I chose to show Cisco private MIBs over other vendors for several reasons. First, the majority of networks in the industry have Cisco devices within their backbones. Second, Cisco has done a good job of standardizing their private MIBs across a wide range of devices. And finally, Cisco has done an excellent job a making their private MIBs available through their Website. Cisco private MIBs can be found at:

http://www.cisco.com/public/sw-center/netmgmt/cmtk/mibs.shtml

Not only can you access the Cisco private MIBs from this site, but you can also get a list of the MIBs supported by each device, including the MIB support that was added at each software version.

10.1 Cisco Ping MIB

Quite a few vendors have implemented Ping MIBs. A Ping MIB allows you to direct a device to send a number of ICMP Echo Requests to a remote device and measure the delay in receiving responses. By doing this you can in effect measure subnet to subnet delay as opposed to measuring the network delay from a workstation to a list of remote addresses. One useful application could be something that builds a matrix of the different subnets within your network and shows the subnet to subnet delays that have been measured. This matrix can be built as long as a device exists within each subnet that can perform a ping test.

Table 10-1   Example Output of a Subnet-Subnet Delay Matrix

	Subnet A	Subnet B	Subnet C
Subnet A	*********	400 msecs	550 msecs
Subnet B	370 msecs	*********	720 msecs
Subnet C	560 msecs	740 msecs	*********

The Cisco Ping MIB allows you to specify a request which includes

• network protocol to use
• remote address to send ICMP Echo Requests to
• number of pings to send
• size of each ping packet
• timeout value to use
• time to wait after getting a response from one ping before sending out the next ping
• whether to send a notification when the sequence of ping tests are complete

When the test is completed, you can read from the MIB the number of requests which were sent, the number of responses that were received, and the minimum, average, and maximum round-trip times that were measured.

The following steps are taken to use the Cisco Ping MIB to measure network delay.

1. Use a RowStatus object to create an entry within the ciscoPingTable.

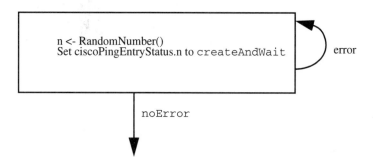

2. Set the network protocol, the remote address to test, the number of packets to send, the size of the packets to send, and the delay between sending packets. For this example we will use IP as the network protocol. The test will send 10 packets, with each packet being 128 bytes, and a delay of 1 second between receiving a response and sending the next ping. The default 2-second timeout will be used. *Note*: The Cisco Textual Conventions (Cisco-TC) MIB defines the network protocol enumerations that ciscoPingProtocol uses.

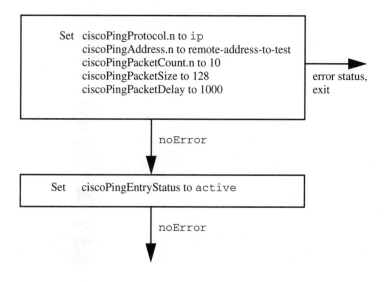

3. Periodically read ciscoPingCompleted.n to see if the test has finished.

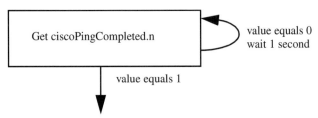

4. Collect the results. *Note*: If no Echo Responses were received then ciscoPingMinRtt.n, ciscoPingAvgRtt.n, and ciscoPingMaxRTT.n are not created.

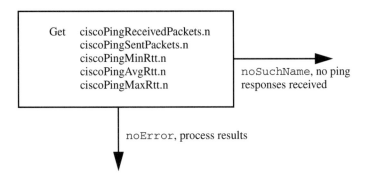

5. After test has been completed, remove entry. *Note*: Old entries will eventually be aged out.

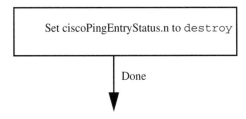

10.2 Cisco Syslog Message MIB

The Cisco IOS generates messages that can be logged to a "syslog" file. These same messages can also be stored in a MIB table (clogHistoryTable) and read later by a network management application. The table is treated as a circular queue — when the table reaches its maximum size, the oldest message will be removed before a new message is added.

When configuring the MIB a user will define

- whether to send a notification when a syslog message is added
- severity level at which messages will be logged
- maximum number of entries that the table can contain

Each entry within the clogHistoryTable contains a display string representing a facility, a severity value, a message name, a message text, and a timestamp representing the value of sysUpTime when the message was generated. Each entry also contains an integer that is used as an index. This index will start at 1 and will be increased after each new message is logged. When it reaches its maximum value, the agent will flush all entries from the clogHistoryTable and set the index value back to 1.

An example of a syslog message indicating that the DHCP process could not allocate the memory that it needs is shown below.

Table 10-2   clogHistoryTable Entry Indicating a DHCP Memory
Allocation Error

MIB Object	Value
clogHistIndex.20	20
clogHistFacility.20	DHCPD
clogHistSeverity.20	critical (2)
clogHistMsgName.20	MALLOC_ERROR
clogHistMsgText.20	There is inadequate memory for DHCP services
clogHistTimestamp.20	646023

The CiscoSyslog Message MIB also provides information about the

- number of messages that were ignored by the clogHistoryTable because the severity value was greater than clogMaxSeverity. *Note*: A severity value of 1 indicates an emergency, 2 an alert, etc. The lower the value the more severe the problem.

• number of clogMessageGenerated notifications that have been sent. This value can be used by a network management station to determine if notifications that were sent are missing. If they are, the syslog information can be polled from the clogHistoryTable.

• number of syslog messages which could not be processed due to a lack of system resources.

• number of entries that have been removed from the clogHistoryTable to make room for new entries.

Using this table you could build an application which periodically collects (either through notifications or by polling) all syslog messages that indicate a critical or worse problem. The application could perform some analysis of the syslog message, post it so the information is available through a Web server, and perform some action such as dialing a network manager's beeper or generating an SNMP notification. By proactively looking at the syslog messages as they are generated — as opposed to periodically reading and parsing a syslog file — problems can be caught before they have a severe impact on a network.

10.3 Cisco Queue MIB

The Cisco Queue MIB allows you to understand the interface queuing being used and the resource limitations associated with interfaces. If you see a high discard rate on an interface, then this additional information might help you reconfigure the interface to provide it with the necessary resources.

This MIB contains three tables. The first table, cQIfTable, provides information about the type of queuing algorithm used on an interface, the maximum number of messages that can be placed into the hardware transmission queue, and the number of subqueues used. The diagram below shows subqueues feeding an interface's hardware transmission queue.

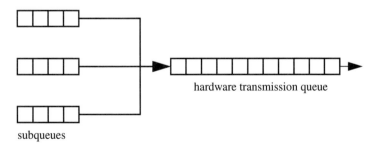

subqueues   hardware transmission queue

The queuing algorithms that can be used to empty the subqueues into the hardware transmission queue are

- First In First Out (FIFO), messages are transmitted in the order they are received.

- Priority Queuing, messages are sorted by the use of access lists. Messages in a higher priority queue are sent before messages in lower priority queues.

- Custom Queuing, messages are sorted by the use of access lists. Subqueues are selected in round-robin order until a subqueue is emptied or a given number of octets is moved from the subqueue to the transmission queue.

- Weighted Fair Queuing, messages are sorted by "conversations" (source-destination network addresses and socket or port numbers). Using this method each conversation is given a proportion of the available bandwidth.

The cQStatsTable provides statistics about each subqueue for an interface. This includes the number of messages in a sub-queue, the maximum number of messages allowed in a subqueue, and the number of messages discarded from a subqueue since the agent was restarted.

A final table, cQRotationTable, provides the number of octets which may be transmitted from a queue that is using Custom Queuing, before it must yield to another queue.

10.4 Cisco Discovery Protocol MIB

If spanning tree is running within a switched environment, then you can build a spanning tree map, and from that understand how devices are physically connected. If spanning tree is not running, then you need to use a proprietary method to understand how devices are connected within a switched network. Cisco has implemented a proprietary protocol called the Cisco Discovery Protocol (CDP) which is used for discovering devices on a network. Each CDP-compatible device will send periodic messages to a well-known multicast address. Devices discover each other by listening at that address. Information about each CDP message that is received on an interface can be read from the CDP MIB.

The following diagram shows a Catalyst 1900 cascaded off a Catalyst 5000. By reading the Catalyst 1900's CDP MIB, a network management application can determine that the Catatlyst 1900 is connected to the Catalyst 5000, and both the local and remote interfaces that are used for the connection.

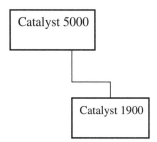

The CDP MIB has a table for enabling or disabling CDP on an interface. It also has a table for reading the CDP messages that are received by an interface. This table provides the following information:

- network address of the device which sent the CDP message.
- CDP version.
- Device identifier.
- Port identifier, usually just the ifName object of the interface that the message was sent out over.
- Device platform.
- Device's functional capabilities.

This table is indexed by the local ifIndex value and by a device index. A device index is needed since there can be several levels of devices cascaded off each other. Using our previous example, lets now connect a repeater that supports CDP to the Catalyst 1900. The interface for the Catalyst 5000 that is connected to the Catalyst 1900 would now receive CDP messages from both the Catalyst 1900 and the repeater.

10.5 Cisco Bulk File MIB and Cisco FTP Client MIB

The Cisco Bulk File MIB can be used to create a file of SNMP data. The Cisco FTP Client MIB can then be used to transfer that file using FTP.

The following steps demonstrate creating a bulk file that contains the ifTable and sysDescr.0.

1. Create an entry in the cbfDefineFileTable. This entry defines the bulk file name, the type of file storage to use, and the file format to use.

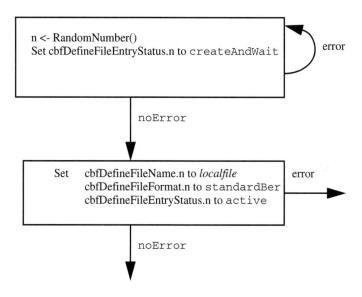

2. Add an entry in the cbfDefineObjectTable for each MIB object or MIB table to add to the bulk file.

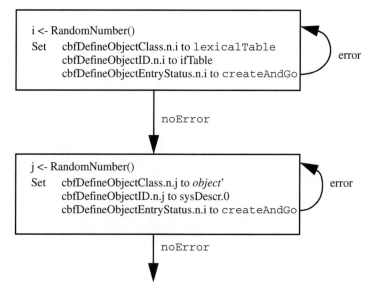

3. Set the corresponding cbfDefineFileNow object to `create`.

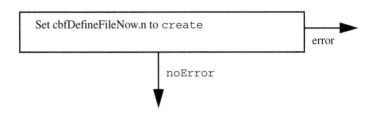

4. Monitor the state of the file creation by periodically monitoring the cbfStatusFileTable. *Note*: After the file has been read, we will destroy the entry so that there is only one entry in the table indexed by $n.*$, where n is the cbfDefineFileIndex value. By doing this we can simply perform a Get-Next operation on cbfStatusFileState.n as opposed to performing a series of Get-Next operations to find the appropriate cbfStatusFileState.$n.*$ object.

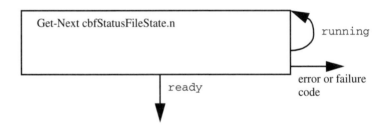

You can stop the creation of a bulk file by setting the corresponding cbfStatusFileEntryStatus object to `destroy`.

Note: Files can be stored in one of three ways; `ephemeral` which will create a file that can be read once, `volatile` which will store a file in volatile memory, and `permanent` which will store a file in non-volatile memory. There are also three file formats that can be used: `standardBER` which is identical to an SNMP variable bindings, `bulkBinary` which uses a tag-data format, and `bulkASCII` which is identical to `bulkBinary` except that it has been translated to ASCII.

Once a file has been created, it can be transferred to a network management station by using the Cisco FTP Client MIB.

Perform the following steps to transfer a file:

1. Use a RowStatus object to create an entry within the cfcRequestTable.

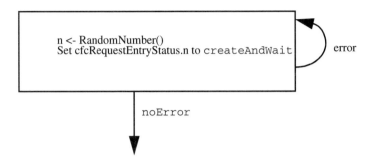

2. Set the following objects within the new entry. *localfile* is the name of the file to transfer, *filename* is the name of the file to create, *target-address* is the address of workstation to transfer the file to, *username* is the user name to use for the FTP login, and *password* is the password to use for the FTP login.

Set   cfcRequestOperation.n to `putBinary`
        cfcRequestLocalFile.n to *localfile*
        cfcRequestRemoteFile.n to *filename*
        cfcRequestServer.n to *target-address*
        cfcRequestUser.n to *username*
        cfcRequestPassword.n to *password*
        cfcRequestEntryStatus.n to `active`

10.6 Cisco System MIB

The Cisco System MIB contains, among other things, information about the buffer resources of a device and its CPU utilization. By periodically monitoring these MIB objects, a network manager can understand how busy a device is and whether a device has enough buffer resources. A short list of useful MIB objects to monitor are provided below.

avgBusy1   1-minute exponentially decayed moving average of the CPU

                        utilization.

bufferFail	Buffer allocation failures.
bufferNoMem	Buffer create failures due to no free memory.
bufferElMiss	Buffer element misses.
bufferSmMiss	Number of small buffers that were requested that could not be allocated due to resource limitations.
bufferMdMiss	Number of medium buffers that were requested that could not be allocated due to resource limitations.
bufferBgMiss	Number of big buffers that were requested that could not be allocated due to resource limitations.
bufferLgMiss	Number of large buffers that were requested that could not be allocated due to resource limitations.
bufferHgMiss	Number of huge buffers that were requested that could not be allocated due to resource limitations.

10.7 Cisco Interfaces MIB

The Cisco Interfaces MIB can be thought of as augmenting the ifTable. It is indexed by ifIndex and, among other things, provides additional error and packet information for data seen over an interface. This MIB allows you to closely look at an interface that is showing either high errors or congestion so that you can better understand what is going on. If you are seeing a high receive error rate on an interface, this MIB can help identify whether the errors are caused by

- runts
- giants
- crc errors
- frame allignment errors
- overrun errors

It will also give you counts for

- input packets that are ignored by an interface
- input packets that have been aborted
- packets that have been dropped because an input queue is full
- number of times an interface has been reset
- number of times an interface has been restarted
- number of times an interface saw the carrier signal change
- collisions
- output packets that have been dropped because the output queue is full

The Cisco Interface MIB also provides packet and octet counts for different protocols. Specifically, you can tell how much ip, decnet, XNS, CLNS, appletalk, IPX, apollo, vines, SRB, chaos, PUP, MOP, LanMan, and STUN protocol traffic is received and transmitted over an interface. The Cisco Interface MIB also provides counts for ARP and Spanning Tree packets, along with information about whether packets are being routed with fast or slow switching. It will also give you a five-minute exponentially decayed moving average for

- bits received over an interface
- packets received over an interface
- bits transmitted over an interface
- packets transmitted over an interface

10.8 Cisco Frame Relay MIB

One of the things that network managers need to know to manage a frame relay network are the DLCI and interface numbers at both ends of a frame relay circuit. While the Frame Relay MIB allows you to understand the traffic going over a frame relay circuit, it doesn't help you to map a local DLCI number to its remote counterpart. The Cisco Frame Relay MIB extends the Frame Relay DTE MIB (RFC 2115) so that, among other things, you can figure out the remote address, DLCI number, and interface number that matches a local frame relay circuit. While the Cisco Frame Relay MIB provides other information, such as LMI statistics associated with a frame relay circuit and whether packets are being dropped, the ability to map a local DLCI to a remote DLCI is probably the most useful part of this MIB.

Given a local interface *i* and DLCI *dlci,* you can get the remote interface and DLCI values by reading cfrExtCircuitRoutedIf.*i.dlci* and cfrExtCircuitRoutedDlci.*i.dlci*. The remote address can be determined by performing a Get-Next operation on cfrMapAddress.*i.dlci*. *Note*: For a point-to-point DLCI, this value will be the string "point-to-point." In this case you can try to obtain the remote address by searching the ipRouteTable.

10.9 Cisco Response Time Monitor MIB (RTTMON)

While a standard traceroute tool can trace an IP path from a workstation to a destination address, what is often more useful is to be able to trace a path from a router to a destination. The Cisco Response Time Monitor MIB provides several testing capabilities, including measuring network response time using different protocols, tracing a path to a destination address and measuring the response time for each hop along the path, measuring how long it takes to write and read a file to a preconfigured file server, and measuring how long it takes to execute a preconfigured script. This section will demonstrate using the Cisco RTTMON MIB to trace a path to a destination address.

1. Create an entry in the rttMonCtrlAdminTable. *Note*: Use the default threshold, frequency , and timeout values.

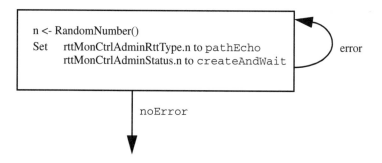

2. Specify the protocol and destination address within the rttMonEchoAdminTable.

3. Schedule the path trace to occur after the rttMonCtrlAdminTable entry is made active.

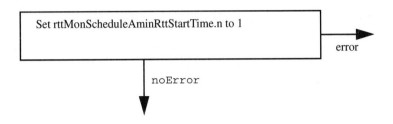

4. Set rttMonCtrlAdminStatus to `active`. This will start the path trace.

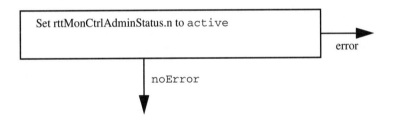

5. Wait until test has completed, then read the rttMonStatsCollectTable to get the path information.

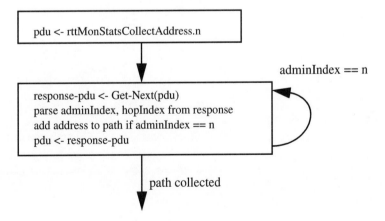

6. Delete the rttMonEchoAdminTable entry.

> Set rttMonCtrlAdminStatus.n to `destroy`

10.10 Summary

This chapter briefly looked at several Cisco Private MIBs and showed how they can be utilized to provide useful information about a network. This includes additional physical topology information, statistics to help troubleshoot potential problems, network delay measurements, and path trace results. While there are quite a few other Cisco Private MIBs (and countless other vendors' Private MIBs) that we did not look at, this chapter hopefully gives some ideas of how private MIBs can be taken advantage of.

Bibliography

References

1. Rose, M. and McCloghrie, K., "Structure and Identification of Management Information for TCP/IP-based internets", STD 16, RFC 1155, May 1990.
2. Case, J., Fedor, M., Schoffstall, M., and Davin, J., "The Simple Network Management Protocol", STD 15, RFC 1157, University of Tennessee at Knoxville, Performance Systems s International, Performance International, and the MIT Laboratory for Computer Science, May 1990.
3. The SNMPv2 Working Group, Case, J., McCloghrie, K., Rose, M., and Waldbusser, S., "Introduction to Community-based SNMPv2", RFC 1901, January 1996.
4. The SNMPv2 Working Group, Case, J., McCloghrie, K., Rose, M. and Waldbusser, S., "Structure of Management Information for Version 2 of the Simple Network Management Protocol (SNMPv2)", RFC 1902, January 1996.
5. The SNMPv2 Working Group, Case, J., McCloghrie, K., Rose, M., and Waldbusser, S., "Textual Conventions for Version 2 of the Simple Network Management Protocol (SNMPv2)", RFC 1903, January 1996.
6. The SNMPv2 Working Group, Case, J., McCloghrie, K., Rose, M., and Waldbusser, S., "Conformance Statements for Version 2 of the Simple Network Management Protocol (SNMPv2)", RFC 1904, January 1996.
7. The SNMPv2 Working Group, Case, J., McCloghrie, K., Rose, M. and Waldbusser, S., "Protocol Operations for Version 2 of the Simple Network Management Protocol (SNMPv2)", RFC 1905, January 1996.
8. The SNMPv2 Working Group, Case, J., McCloghrie, K., Rose, M. and Waldbusser, S., "Transport Mappings for Version 2 of the Simple Network Management Protocol (SNMPv2)", RFC 1906, January 1996.
9. The SNMPv2 Working Group, Case, J., McCloghrie, K., Rose, M. and Waldbusser, S., "Management Information Base for Version 2 of the Simple Network Management Protocol (SNMPv2)", RFC 1907, January 1996.
10. The SNMPv2 Working Group, Case, J., McCloghrie, K., Rose, M. and Waldbusser, S., "Coexistence between Version 1 and Version 2 of the SNMP-standard Network Management Framework", RFC 1908, January 1996.
11. Case, J., Harrington, D., Presuhn, R., and Wijnen, B., "Message Processing and Dispatching for the Simple Network Management Protocol (SNMP)", <draft-ietf-snmpv3-mpc-02.txt>, November 1998.
12. Blumenthal, U., and Wijnen, B., "The User-Based Security Model for Version 3 of the Simple Network Management Protocol (SNMPv3)", <draft-ietf-snmpv3-usm-v2-03.txt>, November 1998.
13. Wijnen, B., Presuhn, R., and McCloghrie, K., "View-based Access Control Model for the Simple Network Man-

agement Protocol (SNMP)", <draft-ietf-snmpv3-vacm-02.txt>, November 1998.

14.   Levi, D. B., Meyer, P., and Stewart, B., "SNMPv3 Applications", <draft-ietf-snmpv3-appl-v2-01.txt>, September 1998.

15.   Harrington, D., Presuhn, R., and Wijnen, B., "An Architecture for Describing SNMP Management Frameworks", <draft-ietf-snmpv3-arch-02.txt>, November 1998.

16.   Frye, R., Levi, D., Routhier, S., and Wijnen, B., " Coexistence between Version 1, Version 2, and Version 3 of the Internet-standard Network Management Framework", <draft-ietf-snmpv3-coex-02.txt>, November 1998.

17.   Warth, A., McQuaid, J., "Applications Response Time MIB (ART MIB)", <draft-ietf-rmonmib-rmon2-artmib-00.txt>, NetScout Systems, Inc. July 1998

18.   IETF RMON MIB Working Group, Waldbusser, S., and Bierman, A., "Remote Network Monitoring MIB", RFC 2021, May 1996.

19.   "CISCO-PING-MIB", Cisco Systems, Inc., November 1994.

20.   Sastry, A., "CISCO-CDP-MIB", Cisco Systems, Inc., October 1994.

21.   Stewart, B., "CISCO-BULK-FILE-MIB", Cisco Systems, Inc., August 1997.

22.   Metzger, L., "CISCO-RTTMON-MIB", Cisco Systems, Inc., March 1996

23.   Mordock, S., "CISCO-SYSLOG-MIB", Cisco Systems, Inc., August 1995.

24.   Baker, F., "CISCO-QUEUE-MIB", Cisco Systems, Inc., May 1995.

25.   Stewart, B., "CISCO-FTP-CLIENT-MIB", Cisco Systems, Inc., July 1997.

26.   Johnson, J., "Cisco System MIB file", Cisco Systems, Inc., July 1994.

27.   Johnson, J., "Cisco Interfaces MIB file", Cisco Systems, Inc., May 1994.

28.   Cheng, C., "CISCO-FRAME-RELAY-MIB", Cisco Systems, Inc., January 1996.

29.   Rose, M. and McCloghrie, K., "Concise MIB Definitions", STD 16, RFC 1212, March 1991.

30.   McCloghrie, K., and Rose, M., Editors, "Management Information Base for Network Management of TCP/IP-based internets: MIB-II", STD 17, RFC 1213, Hughes LAN Systems, Performance Systems International, March 1991.

31.   Rivest, R., "The MD5 Message-Digest Algorithm", RFC 1321, MIT Laboratory for Computer Science and RSA Data Security, Inc. April 1992.

32.   McCloghrie, K., and Kastenholz, F., "The Interfaces Group MIB using SMIv2", RFC 2233, November 1997.

33.   Baker, F., "IP Forwarding Table MIB", RFC 2096, Cisco Systems, Inc., January 1997.

34.   McCloghrie, K., and Kastenholz, F., "Evolution of the Interfaces Group of MIB-II", RFC 1573, January 1994.

Index

Prentice Hall: Professional Technical Reference

Back | Forward | Home | Reload | Images | Open | Print | Find | Stop

http://www.phptr.com/

What's New? | What's Cool? | Destinations | Net Search | People | Software

PRENTICE HALL

Professional Technical Reference

Tomorrow's Solutions for Today's Professionals.

Keep Up-to-Date with
PH PTR Online!

We strive to stay on the cutting-edge of what's happening in professional computer science and engineering. Here's a bit of what you'll find when you stop by **www.phptr.com**:

@ Special interest areas offering our latest books, book series, software, features of the month, related links and other useful information to help you get the job done.

Deals, deals, deals! Come to our promotions section for the latest bargains offered to you exclusively from our retailers.

$ Need to find a bookstore? Chances are, there's a bookseller near you that carries a broad selection of PTR titles. Locate a Magnet bookstore near you at www.phptr.com.

! What's New at PH PTR? We don't just publish books for the professional community, we're a part of it. Check out our convention schedule, join an author chat, get the latest reviews and press releases on topics of interest to you.

✉ Subscribe Today! Join PH PTR's monthly email newsletter!

Want to be kept up-to-date on your area of interest? Choose a targeted category on our website, and we'll keep you informed of the latest PH PTR products, author events, reviews and conferences in your interest area.

Visit our mailroom to subscribe today! **http://www.phptr.com/mail_lists**